ENGAGING OUR DIVERSITY

ENGAGING OUR DIVERSITY

Interculturality and Consecrated Life Today

Edited by
Maria Cimperman, RSCJ
Roger P. Schroeder, SVD

ORBIS BOOKS
Maryknoll, New York 10545

Founded in 1970, Orbis Books endeavors to publish works that enlighten the mind, nourish the spirit, and challenge the conscience. The publishing arm of the Maryknoll Fathers and Brothers, Orbis seeks to explore the global dimensions of the Christian faith and mission, to invite dialogue with diverse cultures and religious traditions, and to serve the cause of reconciliation and peace. The books published reflect the views of their authors and do not represent the official position of the Maryknoll Society. To learn more about Orbis Books, please visit our website at www.orbisbooks.com.

Manufactured in the United States of America
Manuscript editing and typesetting by Joan Weber Laflamme

Library of Congress Cataloging-in-Publication Data

Names: Cimperman, Maria, editor. | Schroeder, Roger, 1951– , editor.
Title: Engaging our diversity : interculturality and consecrated life today / Maria Cimperman, RSCJ, and Roger P. Schroeder, SVD, editors.
Description: Maryknoll, NY : Orbis Books, 2020. | Includes bibliographical references and index. | Summary: Leading practitioners, theologians, and psychologists from across the globe engage the essential topic of interculturality in consecrated life today
Identifiers: LCCN 2019042400 (print) | LCCN 2019042401 (ebook) | ISBN 9781626983748 (paperback) | ISBN 9781608338382 (ebook)
Subjects: LCSH: Monastic and religious life.
Classification: LCC BX2435. E54 2020 (print) | LCC BX2435 (ebook) | DDC 248.4—dc23
LC record available at https://lccn.loc.gov/2019042400
LC ebook record available at https://lccn.loc.gov/2019042401

Contents

Introduction

North America, along with every other part of the world, is growing in terms of its diversity of cultures, races, nationalities, and religions. We know that this brings both opportunities and challenges. At a minimum we can hope for civil tolerance in the midst of differences. This would already be a gift in many areas. However, Christians—particularly those in consecrated life—hope for much more. Going beyond surface-level coexistence, we strive for living and working interculturally, that is, *building and maintaining mutually enriching and challenging relationships among all peoples*. Why? For the sake of acknowledging and participating in the already-and-not-yet essential component of the reign of God—all people gathered around and sharing at the one table of plenty in the spirit of love, mercy, respect, and justice. Such a commitment to intercultural living and ministry is a prophetic voice today.

In response to this vision the Center for the Study of Consecrated Life (CSCL) at Catholic Theological Union (CTU) in Chicago sponsored a three-year program (2017–20) in which twenty core teams of men's and women's congregations/institutes served as catalysts and resources for fostering and developing intercultural projects for their own religious communities and others. The entire process for the congregational core teams included developing case studies, using sociological tools and questionnaires; developing action plans and submitting progress reports; attending three programs at CTU; and interacting with members of other teams. In November 2017 and 2018 the CSCL sponsored interculturality conferences with plenary input, break-out workshops, small-group processing, participant exercises, intercultural prayer/liturgies, and core team work sessions.

This book is being published in order to share the rich resources of the plenary and break-out presentations by the multicultural and international group of experts with the congregations who participated in the CSCL multi-year program and with the broader circle of women and men religious and others who are interested in and dedicated to intercultural living and ministry. In terms of diversity the seven 2017 conference presenters were born in seven different countries, three of the chapters were co-written by men and women of different cultural/racial backgrounds, and the multiculturality of North America well represented.

The book is divided into three sections. The opening four chapters of Part One provide the context and landscape for the opportunities and challenges of interculturality within religious congregations. Slovenian American Maria Cimperman, RSCJ, poses the critical questions for addressing this absolutely urgent issue. Anthony Gittins, CSSp, Teresa Maya, CCVI, and Tony Pernia, SVD—from their British, Mexican, and Filipino perspectives, respectively, and their expansive multicultural experiences—lay out the blueprint for engaging this issue. To continue with this architectural imagery, Part Two, the next four chapters, lays the necessary foundations. Adriana Milmanda, SSpS, of Argentina and Korean-born Sophia Park, SNJM, provide a nuanced biblical basis for understanding the intercultural journeys of Jesus and the early church in relation to our situation today. US-born Robert Schreiter, CPPS, provides a theoretical framework for reconciliation and interculturality. And Sia Temu, MM, develops the practical implications and applications on this theme from her experience in East Africa.

The eight chapters in Part Three focus on some particular and practical aspects of interculturality and consecrated life—concrete building blocks. Tim Norton, SVD, of Australia describes twelve skills for building intercultural competency. Vietnamese-born Maria Nguyen, OSB, and German American Roger Schroeder, SVD, offer a joint presentation on socio-centric and individual-centric societies and include three case studies. African American LaReine-Marie Mosely, SND, explores the important issue of race and gender from an intercultural perspective. Another joint chapter on the topic of personality and culture was written by two licensed psychologists—Kevin McClone and Crystal Taylor-Dietz—coming from different racial intercultural backgrounds. Chapters 13–15 treat three key areas within consecrated life itself that need to be addressed through the lens of interculturality. Tony Pernia, SVD, and Judette Gallares, RC—both from the Philippines—discuss leadership and formation, respectively. German-born Birgit Oberhofer of the lay Focolare movement of consecrated life provides some concrete suggestions for spirituality and intercultural living. The final chapter, written jointly by Lebanese-born Michel Andraos and Japanese American Joanne Doi, MM, addresses the intercultural topics of decoloniality and pilgrimage.

We would like to thank a number of people for their help with this volume. First of all, the multi-year CSCL interculturality program itself and the publication of this volume would not have been possible without the generous financial support and other assistance from the Conrad N. Hilton Foundation. The Catholic Sisters Initiative has been a wonderful partner, supporting our efforts and assisting us as we developed tools for evaluation and learning. We hope our joint efforts continue to build opportunities for women religious to thrive and serve the entire people of God, locally and globally. Second, we want to thank our editor, Jill Brennan O'Brien, Editor-in-Chief Robert Ellsberg, and other Orbis Books staff for their interest, support, and varied levels of assistance in making this book a reality. Third, we wish to thank the authors, who committed their time and expertise to offering their presentations in person for the two CSCL conferences in Chicago and prepared their talks for publication. We want to acknowledge the contributions of Maria Nguyen, OSB, and Joanne Doi, MM, who joined the two of us on the organizing team for this CTU program. We are immensely grateful to our colleagues on the staff, administration, and faculty at CTU for their support and assistance in a myriad of ways during the three-year interculturality program. A special thank you to Peter Cunningham for his invaluable services behind the scenes as the CSCL administrative assistant and assistant program coordinator. Last, but not least, we are exceedingly grateful to the participants of this Engaging Our Diversity program for their openness, commitment, and creativity.

On a personal level, I (Maria) want to say that the importance of building intercultural communities has never felt more crucial in religious life, in the church, and in the world. Every area of consecrated life is influenced by our openness toward becoming and being transformed into intercultural communities. This work is transforming me, and for this I am deeply grateful. For me (Roger), living and working for fuller mutual interculturality have become a passion driving my being and doing. The publication of this volume reflects both the rich possibilities and the realistic means and spiritual motivation for overcoming the parallel challenges.

Our work together over the past three years has been a wonderful opportunity for intercultural collaboration across congregations, disciplines, genders, generations, and personal styles. We ourselves and the program itself have benefited and been enriched by our work together.

May the vision and practice of interculturality continue to harvest the fruit of God's reign!

PART ONE

MAPPING THE OPPORTUNITIES AND CHALLENGES

1

·

What Is at Stake?

Maria Cimperman, RSCJ

The call to interculturality is God's gift to us in this time. It is present and obvious, not hidden. In order to live and grow and be transformed into intercultural communities, we must trust in God's abundant love. We ask for the grace of transformation and do our necessary growth work personally, communally, congregationally.

What's at stake in this? Everything. Anthony J. Gittins, CSSp, among other scholars, asserts that "the future of international religious life depends significantly on the ability of each community (local and institutional) to live interculturally; those that fail to do so will fragment or die."[1] I assert that with the rise of extreme nationalism and decreasing acceptance of the "other," one we perceive to be not like "us," our way of being a human community is in peril. When we see the earth simply as an object for our use rather than as God's creation requiring dignity, care, and respect, many in the human community, particularly the most vulnerable, will struggle and perish. The call to interculturality is a call to life for all, including generations yet to be born. This is a life issue!

Where will the impact of our efforts toward becoming intercultural communities be felt? Everywhere. Consecrated life. Church.

---

[1] Anthony J. Gittins, *Living Mission Interculturally: Faith, Culture, and the Renewal of Praxis* (Collegeville, MN: Liturgical Press, 2015), 30.

Society. No area will be untouched, from the personal and local to the communal and global. What is possible? Much! This is part of our participation in the reign of God. What will it cost? Much! Ways of relating that are not life generating must be let go and die; new intercultural ways of relating are emerging that can bring new life and bear much fruit for consecrated life and the world. This is a Paschal time.

These are admittedly bold statements. Yet this is how much is at stake. We often ask, "What are the new, emerging aspects of religious life today?" The call to interculturality is clearly one of these aspects. While we may acknowledge this in general, it is helpful to look at some particular areas of consecrated life to note what is possible as we deepen our living of interculturality.

I offer here some broad strokes, in three parts. First, I offer twelve areas that are interlinked in consecrated life today and that are calls and invitations toward interculturality, that is, building and maintaining mutually enriching and challenging relationships among all peoples. Second, I offer some brief thoughts on what it will take to live into this call of our time. Third, I offer some initial thoughts on what is possible as we live into this call and what we will receive from the Spirit as we journey. Now, the Spirit is far more creative and generous than my own imagination, so these are simply opening ideas, but they will, I hope, help us begin to imagine and to envision possibilities.

TWELVE CALLS
OF INTERCULTURALITY

Interculturality Writ Large

First, interculturality is to be a visible sign of the reign of God in our *church* today. The global diversity of our church is calling forth new conversations in our parishes, schools, and ministries. What does it mean to belong to one another? How shall we together call forth a fuller vision of church? This is part of the "new" the Spirit is continually creating among us, asking us to find better ways to love, care for, and call forth one another. God the Creator delights in all of creation. Jesus's life among us was one of radical inclusion, and we must walk toward this as well. A culture of encounter beckons.

Second, interculturality is a call to our *world* today, asking us to see the diversity of cultures, nationalities, genders, generations, races, religious traditions, and nations as a gift and to ensure that the dignity and rights of each are respected and promoted so all can thrive. Interculturality is in direct opposition to xenophobia, religious extremism, and all "isms" plaguing our world. Interculturality invites us to see the immense possibilities of gifts available in the diversity of humankind.

Each nation must listen to its calls. Interculturality is a call to the *United States of America* today, for one example, asking us to see that the diversity of cultures, ethnicities, indigenous peoples, generations, and genders build up and strengthen this nation. This call reminds us that the United States is a land first inhabited by Native American peoples, and then by immigrants. The United States was built on a desire for religious and political freedom. While proclaiming opportunity for all, this nation has in its history the sins of slavery and unjust and cruel treatment of peoples (Native Americans, for example) as well as care and advocacy for the oppressed and vulnerable. All are part of this nation. The call to interculturality asks us to continue to see the gifts and possibilities of all persons. This is the direct opposite of racism, sexism, and any and all forms of exclusion.

Third, interculturality is evident as we see in the diversity of *creation* a glimpse of God's incredible imagination. In the evolutionary nature of creation we see God's continual involvement with all life. The call to recognize the gifts of God's diverse creation moves us to cherish, care for, and change our relationship with creation. No longer is it possible simply to "use" nature; now we must "see" differently and learn how we are all intricately linked. Trees are not simply a source of paper but part of the ecosystem that helps humans breathe. A different ebb and flow longs to emerge with all creation as we humans see ourselves as part of creation.

Interculturality and Consecrated Life

Fourth, interculturality asks to be lived through our *charisms*— part of the deepening and widening the Spirit longs to offer us.

Each member in consecrated life comes with a baptismal call as well as a set of cultures to be lived through the charism of the congregation or institute. As such, religious life naturally has the elements of diversity and commonality that can build not only a multicultural and/or international community, but also one that is intercultural. The possibilities are endless.

Charism, a gift of the Spirit to each congregation for the sake of the church and the world, manifests itself in particular ways to particular persons. Each new member brings both commonality (charism) and particularity (uniqueness of each) to the diversity of a congregation. Charism is dynamic, continually evolving in the midst of the signs and the times. Therefore, with each new member of a congregation, the charism also evolves. We experience the words of Isaiah:

> I am about to do a new thing;
>   now it springs forth, do you not
>   perceive it? (Isa 43:19)

In addition, as consecrated life understands the wider charism of family (associates, colleagues in mission, and all who share this charism in their life call) as ever more integrally connected with consecrated life, the opportunities for building intercultural relationships grow exponentially.

Fifth, the transformative call of interculturality affects all areas of vowed life. Intercultural living of the vow of *celibate chastity* asks us to widen our responses to the questions of whom we shall love and how we shall love. Our relationship with God will open us to depths, breadth, and diversity we cannot yet imagine, and our response in love will quite naturally flow outward. Not only will no one be excluded, but our intercultural hearts will be as wide as the world.

Sixth, interculturality calls us, through the vow of *poverty*, to claim a world of plenty. We come to know our emptiness without the other, whose living presence can show us a face of God and who is a gift of the God of all creation. Living interculturally helps us recognize the gifts of and in one another and allows our gifts to be named and called forth. In so doing we praise and proclaim the good news of a God who so loved the world—a God who, linked to our humanity in the form of Jesus of Nazareth, loved extravagantly, even unto death (John 3:16). Love abounded, persisted, and resurrected.

God's vision is one of abundance. Through our vowed poverty our lived witness to the good news is to see the gifts of each person and all creation and to follow Jesus's example in loving, nurturing, and protecting the diversity of all.

Seventh, the call to interculturality invites us to new ways of living the vow of *obedience*. Our choice of whom to listen and respond to has transformative implications for us and for our congregations. The more I am willing to hear Wisdom from persons whose backgrounds are distinct from mine, the more I may hear new insights that widen the horizon of my perspective and peripheries and create the new longing to emerge. In addition, interculturality can help us hear with more depth, as we seek to link the calls and cries around us with God's cries to us. The Spirit has no limits in communicating; interculturality assists us in hearing and responding to the Spirit's leads.

The implications for communal discernment follow in the same way. So much is possible when we listen to the Spirit of God among and in us—personally and together. When we listen together and hear from the diversity around us, inside and outside our congregations, we are better able to distinguish the good and bad spirits[2] and find the creative responses that flow from our discernment.

Eighth, interculturality transforms our *prayer*. God has many ways of speaking to us. Prayer is a language without limit, and as we experience different ways of prayer, such as supplication, praise, and hearing God call us "beloved" (*amado, wapenzi, hajang salangahen, gajang salanghaneun, bien amie,* or in American Sign Language, the right hand under the left hand over the heart), there is a movement in us that is beyond words, feelings, and senses. We find that the God of all, beyond all understanding, present in even the smallest particle of all created matter, abides in all, in us—and here a Oneness with God and all creation emerges.

Ninth, interculturality can transform the way we live and build *community*, opening doorways and taking us on journeys with companions who can point us to new horizons of relationship.

---

[2] I refer here to the Ignatian lens of good and bad spirits. Part of discernment requires knowing which responses are of the Spirit and which are confusions, distractions, and so forth.

We will be called out of our ruts (shallow graves) to new routes to building the reign of God. Our efforts to build community among us, with its manifold gifts and challenges, offer a prophetic witness of God's desires for unity amid diversity.

From this shall come prophetic ways of living and ministry, denouncing injustice of all kinds and proclaiming new ways of relationship that are trinitarian, as we begin to see infinite possibilities across cultures, generations, genders, and more.

Tenth, any efforts toward intercultural community will affect *ministry*. How we pray and live flows into both internal and external ministries.[3] In ministry, collaboration for mission will have the impact of seeing what more is possible when we do build relationships that call upon one another's diversity to build the reign of God everywhere and with everyone. Even disagreements will offer witness to new ways of working through challenges in a manner that can build skills and strengthen community. This will greatly influence ministry relationships and also flow outward even further. Outreach will have as a focus welcoming the other who offers so much. Our needs and wounds will be seen within the wide love of God, who longs for us to heal, thrive, and build unity among all people and all creation.

Eleventh, the call to interculturality entails looking again at our styles and ways of *leadership*, opening ourselves to see new responses to present and emerging needs. We see the gifts that each person's culture, experiences, hopes, and dreams offer to the whole. We find ways to listen, hear, speak, write, and move for the sake of the reign of God. We allow ourselves to be vulnerable with one another and share from this vulnerability, knowing that the strength of our love for one another grows as we find the way together. We will see new ways together to incarnate the new calling to us as individuals and to our congregations. This, beyond words, will speak volumes to the communities we are blessed to serve.

Twelfth, *initial and ongoing formation* must be influenced by the work toward interculturality. New members, who will naturally see both the commonality and diversity in the congregation

---

[3] Internal ministries are those within the congregation, such as leadership, finances, and formation. External ministries are those external to the inner workings of the congregation. They include but are not limited to teaching, healthcare, social work, and law.

each joins, will see the intentionality with which the formative journey into a congregation (sometimes called the process of incorporation into a congregation/institute) values the many dimensions of culture—including their own. Ongoing, lifelong formation efforts will be essential for building intercultural communities. It is impossible to ask new members to build what few others in the congregation are working toward. It is only together that we can participate in the new life the Spirit is creating among us.

WHAT WILL IT TAKE TO MOVE TOWARD INTERCULTURALITY IN CONSECRATED LIFE?

I offer four starting points. First, religious life must be willing to take some risks, to go beyond what we have done to what is calling us now. This will take us beyond our comfort zones and into our growth zones. Second, for interculturality to take root in our congregations (and world) there must be a realization that all are needed for the reign of God. Something is created when the various gifts and persons encounter one another and work together to build a world of peace, love, and mercy. Third, ongoing learning is essential. Interculturality requires skill building as well as opening ourselves to the spiritual dimensions of cultural encounters. Fourth, while intercultural transformation requires our willingness, this is ultimately a conversion point, and as such, is a grace. This conversion will entail a letting go of ways that no longer serve us and that limit the possibilities we have together. This dying will lead to new life, seeing a new way of relating, understanding, and being in the world and consecrated life today. The process asks everything of us—and gives us all in return.

WHAT IS POSSIBLE?

God longs to create new life through us and for the world. I offer three possibilities and some gifts that will find us along the way. First, interculturality opens in us possibilities for forgiveness and reconciliation. We can acknowledge what we have done and what we have failed to do so that a new relationship can commence. This moves us into peacebuilding, our call in the world.

Second, interculturality will build our religious imagination. Scripture passages as well as narratives from our communities will evoke the "dangerous memories"[4] of what happens when love of God and love of neighbor are conjoined. All cultures can lead us to the call to build the "beloved community."[5] If the human, Jewish, male Jesus of Nazareth could be converted to greater inclusion by the Syro-Phoenician/Canaanite woman,[6] conversion is possible for all of us.

Third, the journey of interculturality is the journey of missionary disciples. The followers of Jesus were willing to go to the ends of the earth to preach his good news. Their "ministry" required that they go beyond their own vision of who belongs. As missionary disciples our ministry of preaching the good news will lead us to the peripheries and areas of great need where we will see the other as a great gift. We will be able to see, with the risen Christ, how everyone participates in God's vision.

CONCLUSION

What's at stake? Everything. What is possible? Everything. Isaiah's promise—"I am about to do a new thing; . . . Do you not perceive it?"—remains true today. Our call as consecrated persons is to the depths of God, and the depths of God lead us to the depths of humanity and God's creation. As we seek to love with depth and breadth, and as we intentionally and persistently practice this way of loving, we will slowly and surely become intercultural communities. This will most certainly serve consecrated life, yet this is not simply for us but for the life seeking to thrive all around us.

What will this cost us? Everything. What will this offer us? Everything. The reign of God here and now.

---

[4] See Johann-Baptist Metz, *Faith in History and Society: Toward a Practical Fundamental Theology,* trans J. Matthew Ashley (New York: Herder and Herder, 2007).

[5] This phrase was often used during the US civil rights movement, after being used in Martin Luther King Jr.'s "I Have a Dream" speech.

[6] This is developed herein in Chapter 5, "The Intercultural Journey of Jesus," by Adriana Carla Milmanda, SSpS.

2

Beyond International and Multicultural

Mission and Intercultural Community Living Today

ANTHONY J. GITTINS, CSSP

STATING THE THESIS

From Albuquerque to Accra, Boston to Buenos Aires, and Chicago to Shanghai, understandings and experiences of personal identity and community have changed significantly in a century, and geographical and social mobility have local and international relations. With this in mind, I would like to bring into relief both a general and a specific reality. I first identify the broader features and purposes of interculturality; I then tighten the focus and consider how it poses a challenge and becomes a stimulus specifically to international religious institutes, whose mission statements declare their commitment to forging organic moral communities from the raw materials of their diverse ethnicities, cultures, experiences, and religious perspectives.

The words *international* and *multicultural* are now common currency, but *intercultural* is less familiar. I argue that de facto *international* religious communities must become increasingly and intentionally *intercultural,* and that in an increasingly pluralistic world, parochialism must be countered and xenophobia or discrimination roundly repudiated. Without a virtual tectonic shift from *international* to *intercultural* community living, there will simply be no viable future for international religious faith communities. To establish and defend this thesis in four steps, I explore some contested terminology, identify theological implications, clarify the challenge, and finally evaluate the prospects for achieving such a shift.

FROM MONOCULTURAL TO INTERCULTURAL: THE TERMINOLOGY

True communication depends on a high degree of mutual intelligibility. Precision of language and a common vocabulary are prerequisites. But every discipline creates its own jargon, which is often misunderstood across the disciplines. Consequently, I try to clarify some important terminology that is being used increasingly by theologians and missiologists but that was originally part of the vocabulary of the social sciences and is now therefore a frequent source of confusion across the disciplines.

Monocultural and Bicultural

Historically, most non-nomadic peoples lived and died within a primary area of less than ten miles' radius and in a community with a common language and culture. Relatively speaking therefore, few human beings have been truly bicultural. Exceptionally, climate or hunger dictates a move, but usually a monocultural group is involved. Beyond the familiar "people like us" are "people not like us"—pejoratively, "them."

However, children who are socialized within a stable domestic arena, where each parent speaks a different native language, can become bicultural quite naturally. Raised as bilingual, perhaps benefiting from moving physically between the primary cultures of the parents, a child will find it perfectly natural to switch languages and cross geographical territories. But those raised in one cultural milieu, who encounter another culture and language only as adults,

1. **Monocultural Living**

2. **Cross-Cultural Living**

3. **Multicultural Living**

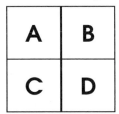

4. **Intercultural Living**

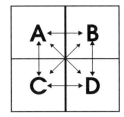

Figure 2–1. Mono-Cross-Multi-
Intercultural Living

may become bicultural only by formally learning each culture and language sufficiently to move easily between two worlds. True biculturality thus characterizes someone living *simultaneously* in two distinguishable cultural and linguistic worlds, as do many bilingual Mexican Americans, Korean Americans, and so on. But when a person intentionally leaves home as a more or less permanent commitment, the appropriate term would be *cross-cultural.*

Cross-Cultural

People growing up in what we can call Culture A, who move later and reside for years elsewhere (Culture B), may—with appropriate industry and dedication—gradually become cross-cultural. Members of the host community (Culture B) are, of course, and significantly, at home, living in their own Culture A, but the interlopers are out of place, not at home, outsiders or strangers[1] who, being now in their Culture B, must learn this new culture and its language. Learning another culture is every bit as challenging as learning another language. To assume that a culture can be informally "picked up" is naive and dangerous, at times even arrogant and condescending.

Cross-cultural persons remain outsiders and cannot, nor need be, fully assimilated culturally. But there are different kinds of outsiders—typically *participating* and *non-participating* outsiders.[2] Participating, contributing, and relevant outsiders can be of great value to the insiders.[3] Nonparticipating outsiders are at best culturally or morally irrelevant (like ungracious tourists), and at worst destructive (like invaders, some colonials, or doctrinaire missionaries). Unsurprisingly, the host population will take its time, carefully scrutinizing newcomers before fully accepting them. This is necessary self-protection for communities that often carry bad memories of previous graceless and dangerous strangers. During this transitional time—which may last years—the incoming resident is expected to be learning the cultural rules, responsibilities, and sanctions that govern day-to-day living. From the stranger's perspective, this is neither simple nor painless; it is a process of liminality or "betwixt and between-ness" as one

---

[1] There is a significant body of literature on the sociology and theology of the stranger. See Anthony J. Gittins, *A Presence That Disturbs: A Call to Radical Discipleship* (Liguori, MO: Liguori, 2002), 143–62; and idem, *Ministry at the Margins: Spirituality and Strategy for Mission* (Maryknoll, NY: Orbis Books, 2002), 121–60.

[2] Gittins, *A Presence That Disturbs*, 96–107.

[3] Gittins, *Ministry at the Margins*, 135–41. "To participate means to discover one's place on the agenda, to contribute to the felt needs of the community, to be a servant, yet to be able to challenge and support, to be spiritually and culturally life-transmitting and life-propagating. These are challenges for every missionary stranger" (ibid., 141).

moves from one social status to another. Becoming cross-cultural, therefore, depends as much on the response of the local people as on one's own bona fides.[4] But if intercultural communities are to form, all members must already be, or intentionally becoming, cross-cultural—choosing to live outside their comfort zone, and willing to cope with ambiguity and uncertainty as an act of faith in the process of building God's realm.

Multicultural

Any culturally mixed group is de facto *multi*cultural, but that says nothing about how individuals actually relate, which is a measure of *inter*culturality. Human responses in a multicultural context range from simple avoidance to rank hostility or from conventional courtesy to deep friendship, and differences may be eliminated (by measures ranging from assimilation to genocide), tolerated (by attitudes from indifference to unconcern), or managed. Separate development or mutual apathy would be negative management, leaving everyone in a state of enduring (pathological) *liminality*. More positively, differences can be managed by mutual cooperation and the encouragement of diversity, as one might create an orchestra or chorus. Often, though, multicultural communities can be appropriately characterized as people living together, separately. This is as dangerous as it is unacceptable for communities of faith, and yet it is far from an uncommon experience for many.

Intercultural

Beginning in the 1950s, as multinational companies and global commerce expanded, the study of *cross-cultural* contact was in vogue, as employment moved people away from home. Vocabulary was still unstable, and the words *multicultural* and *intercultural* were often used synonymously. The language itself, and the underlying theory, derived largely from the social sciences of cultural anthropology, sociology, and psychology. Corporations

---

[4] Ibid., 121–60.

were hiring people to travel and reside internationally, but they were also trying to provide needed skills for communicating with a variety of culturally and linguistically diverse business partners. Consequently, and for decades now, such skills have been identified, widely taught, and acquired across the business world.

Christian missionaries, of course, had been exposed for centuries to cross-cultural living and had accumulated much informal knowledge and experience, not to say real expertise. But as missions have increasingly operated as a two-way street and the reality of global Christianity has become clearer, the challenges posed by de facto multicultural faith communities have become acute. Missiologists became increasingly aware of the cultural dynamics at work in mission situations, including "reverse mission" from Africa and Asia to Europe and America, that is, two-way, cross-cultural living that changed the shape and dynamics of myriad local communities within and beyond the Americas.

Social science is generally not concerned with religious faith, but the subject of theology is, of course, God. So, when theology *adopts* sociological language, it also *adapts* it, so that theologian and sociologist no longer speak quite the same language. Sociology used *multicultural* and *intercultural* as effectively synonymous—or else *intercultural* focused on the social dynamics of international relations, while *multicultural* simply identified a social fact within neighborhoods or voluntary associations. But *theologically*—and very significantly—the word *intercultural* relates explicitly to God and/or to interpersonal relationships shaped and motivated by a common faith commitment. *Theologically speaking, intercultural communities consist of members drawn from diverse cultural backgrounds but sharing a single charism and an intentional commitment to fellowship, motivated not simply by pragmatic considerations but by a shared religious conviction and commitment to a common mission.*

Many communities have experienced the challenges posed by the diversity and cultural differences among their members. The standard assimilation model of recruitment to religious orders—"Come join us, and we will teach you to do things our way"—has been shown to be obsolete, as the demands of true intercultural living and ministry have become increasingly clear. But many community members remain unaware of, or struggle with, or even resist the challenge (which is quickly becoming a real imperative), while failing to profit from hard-won gains from the social sciences and the rich resources to be found in the diversity of their own membership. Such resistance may amount to thinly disguised racism masquerading as pious traditionalism. Intercultural living, then, is a faith-based and lifelong process of conversion, emerging as a requirement for members of intentional, international religious communities.[5] But healthy intercultural living depends on the level of commitment and support generated by the wider membership. Individuals vary in adaptability and learning levels, but everyone generates positive or negative energy. A small, resistant group can produce enough negative energy to thwart the whole undertaking.

Before identifying the dynamics of intercultural living, however, it is important to acknowledge the challenge of culture itself, since culture is the context for lived faith. Culture is not innate: nobody is born with culture. It is learned through the process of socialization or *enculturation*. There is no person without culture, and faith can only be lived culturally. We do not live our faith in a vacuum or outside a specific cultural context. But *inter*cultural living is *multi*cultural rather than *mono*cultural, and nobody can be expected to live his or her faith in and through an entirely alien culture or through the dominant culture of the majority.

CULTURE

Most people too readily assume they understand culture, which is actually a subtle, elusive, and shape-changing reality. Recognizable under many forms, culture is constitutive of every human person raised in a social world. In different circumstances, anyone might have been raised—enculturated—differently. A baby born and raised in Beijing by Chinese parents becomes culturally Chinese; the same baby, if adopted by Euro-American parents in Chicago, will become a person of their culture. Environment and

---

[5] Intercultural living constitutes a challenge and opportunity for many other people working and ministering among people of several or many languages and cultures. Though by no means all of these people can or will learn the skills and virtues mentioned here, dedicated ministers will resonate with many aspects of intercultural living and may find much insight into how to respond to the challenges they face.

socialization are critically important, and everyone learns and assumes a particular culture or constellation of cultural traits.

Faith can only be expressed culturally, so an intercultural community should value every person's cultural identity as gift. Each one's lived faith constitutes an alternative (and in principle, legitimate) way of being. Yet different perspectives, habits, and propensities pose challenges to harmonious community living. The ability to live *with* and not simply *despite* cultural differences is a hallmark of an intercultural community. Diversity is good, since God made it intrinsic to creation. Consider the following five descriptive definitions of culture and their implications for intercultural diversity.[6]

First, *culture is the humanly created part of the environment,* what social groups do to the worlds they inhabit. Universally, culture is *material* (artifacts, buildings); *institutional* (law and order, kinship and economic systems, and religion); *symbolic* (speech, maybe writing, and words-objects-gestures that "say the unsayable"); and *moral* (values and virtues, and their opposites, vices). These are the social glue of every human society.

Second, *culture is the form of social life,* the way a particular social group normally behaves, including rule-breaking behaviors and their sanctioned consequences. Standardized behavior must be interpreted through the underlying belief-system and thought-system and cannot be judged merely by opinionated outsiders. And yet there is always a discrepancy between what people *say* they believe and the way they actually live. But insiders (and appropriately informed outsiders) can identify and judge heroic or ignoble behavior. Every social system, every culture, has both sin and grace, pathology and virtue, and needs to be monitored by effective sanctions, both positive and negative.

Third, *culture is a meaning-making system.* Supported by standards and rules, every culture makes intelligible communication possible among its members. Outsiders therefore must learn the code or struggle with partial communication and mutual misunderstandings. Theoretical linguistics distinguishes contextual criteria for identifying three levels of communication: *grammaticality* (strict and consistent conformity to grammatical

---

[6] These descriptive components are gleaned from many sources. Culture is a topic that has generated a vast amount of easily accessible literature. I offer a simplified but multifaceted description.

rules); *acceptability* (less formal but appropriate and intelligible communicative interaction); and *meaningfulness* (simple, basic, but adequate information transfer). Though interlocutors may experience hilarious or embarrassing misunderstandings, they *can* communicate meaningfully, if not always with the perfect grammaticality of the pedant or perfectionist—something to remember in intercultural living. Linguistics also speaks of the paradoxical rule-governed creativity that allows a virtually infinite number of utterances to be produced *and understood* from a limited core of grammatical rules (English has 150). Every speaker routinely produces utterances never before articulated in an identical way yet understood by people who have never before heard exactly the same sequence of words. Likewise, intercultural community members produce creative behavior from their common stock of beliefs, convictions, and virtues, which can be understood and accepted—or resented—by others.

In chess, the moves are limitless but the rules are few. Not knowing the rules, we could watch players forever without being able to understand the game. Likewise, without a grasp of underlying cultural rules and rationality (which require serious study), members of intercultural communities will never become as proficient as even novice chess players.

Fourth, *culture might be compared to skin.* Grafting it is difficult and sometimes impossible. If the skin is severely burned, death may be inevitable. And yet skin can tolerate multiple scars, blemishes, wrinkles, and dermatological conditions. We cannot be literally in someone else's skin, and if ours were to be stripped or flayed, we would certainly die. Cultures, like skin, need not be perfect and can tolerate both wear and tear and some trauma, but the overall integrity of the skin is as necessary for life as is the overall integrity of a culture and its members. If that is thoroughly compromised, cultures—like the people who constitute their social reality—will atrophy and die.

Fifth, *culture is an enduring social reality.* Cultures gradually rise and decline, flourish and die, and none is static or immortal; implications for intercultural living should be obvious. Culture is transmitted over time through the generations—an ongoing process rather than a simple social fact. Some cultures (often referred to as traditional) may appear to be in stasis or equilibrium, but all cultures are in the process of change, at varied speeds, and always "contested" by their members. Some cultures are more resilient than others.

Reality is culturally and socially shaped: people are born into a community that has already interpreted the world and identified the meaning of things, events, and relationships.[7] Socialization or enculturation extends through the first decades of life, as a person is aggregated to the preexisting world of meaning; once adequately socialized, people are quite resistant to thinking that their thoughts or ways are wrong.

With such an understanding of culture, the challenge facing us all is to respond to the demands of intercultural living. The broader community must engage with the cultural identity of newer members and abandon the crude assimilation model as no longer fit for the purpose. Individuals will respond to the challenge by embracing intercultural living wholeheartedly or halfheartedly, or by resisting and waiting for death. But everyone must stand and be counted; the future, viable or not, is at stake.

IDENTIFYING THEOLOGICAL IMPLICATIONS

Because every mature person is a person of culture, and because spirituality (that is, lived faith) can only flourish in a cultural context, we must ask how faith and culture coexist. Saint Jerome coined the word *spiritualitas* (spirituality) in the fourth century, defining it explicitly as life in the Holy Spirit given at baptism to guide our faith journey. It might be described as a way of being in the world with God, where every variable (way, being, world, God) is shaped by each individual's and every community's experience. During a lifetime a person may embrace a number of possible *ways* (single, married, widowed, celibate, and so on), experience different states of *being* (from youth to dotage, health to sickness, safety to peril, as citizen or refugee and so on), live in several different worlds (rural, urban, tropical, arctic, peaceful, or warring), and relate in different ways to God (Creator, Wisdom,

---

[7] We only need to consider the *reality* of witchcraft, eucharistic presence, heaven, resurrection, metempsychosis, or ghosts to make the point here: one person's reality may be another's fantasy.

Lord, Father, King, Warrior, Spirit—or the Jesus of the Manger or Golgotha, the miracleworker or faith healer).

Spirituality is not a set of formulated beliefs; rather, it shapes and is shaped by how we relate to God and creation, pray and express our embodied selves, respond to suffering and well-being, and make life choices. From different cultural environments and experiences human beings have generated myriad legitimate expressions of Christian spirituality. People in a multicultural community, attempting not just to live their faith separately, but to do so in an explicitly intercultural way, will encounter many opportunities and challenges, similarities and differences, with respect to liturgy, prayer, ritual, music, silence, privacy, dress, diet, conformity, and so on. Each person must discover a new *modus vivendi* amid cultural differences, learned behaviors, and personal preferences. Some of the most contentious issues and initially unintelligible responses may prove—if approached sympathetically and creatively—to be mutually enriching.

Following are four areas—out of many—of contested culturally shaped topics with particular salience for intercultural community members. Failure to learn from one another and adapt accordingly can destroy the integrity of a community.

Social location refers to our enduring world and our place in it—from Pacific atoll to forest enclave, from isolated settlement to crowded high-rise, from tight-knit extended family to free-wheeling independent citizen. Serious thought should be given to the formative power of each person's social location and to how much individual variety and preference are compatible with the demands of the religious community and its mission. Understanding others' social geography, socialization, and social mobility is a prerequisite to formulating appropriate responses. Sadly, some community members know less about their fellow members after decades than they do about celebrities or politicians. No intercultural community can be built on such foundations.

Body tolerance describes culturally diverse ways people treat and display their bodies and interact with others. It points to different people's comfort levels. A relaxed and spontaneous (Dionysian) attitude no more indicates immodesty than a controlled and disciplined (Apollonian) posture indicates modesty. Cultural differences in body tolerance cannot be grossly correlated with morality, as virtue or vice. Culturally diverse people in an intentional community must become mutually sensitive to what is considered appropriate dress and demeanor, interaction, and affection. The "noble simplicity of the Roman Rite" may be revered, especially in colder climates, yet people from the tropics may find it ill-suited to worship through appropriate displays of affect and temperament and constrained by too many rules and rubrics. Compare the image of a day-long, open-air liturgy under an African sun with a hurried forty-minute Sunday mass with a congregation that neither sings nor emotes, the difference between Dionysian exuberance and spontaneity and the clock-governed "Sunday obligation" of Apollonian discipline and control becomes obvious. In matters of common prayer, liturgy, music or silence, movement or stillness, different levels of comfort and body tolerance will constitute significant points of concern within an intercultural community.

Health and sickness are culturally coded. Many northern people with highly developed health systems rarely see a dead body, and serious sickness is understood to be a matter for hospital isolation for a medical or surgical solution before a rapid return to the community. But in many parts of the world death and dying are constant visitors, sickness is attended to domestically, and medical/surgical solutions are rare. Rather than sickness isolating patients from family, it integrates them; when death nears, family solidarity is critical, whatever the expense or distance involved. But many members of conventional religious communities have had to make a real break with their families, had no further involvement with sick or dying relatives, and were prevented by distance, finances, or rules from attending funerals or assisting with family needs. Intercultural living demands a radical rethinking of what is appropriate or demanded in justice relative to each member personally and to members' kin.

Finally, attitudes to *time* and *space* are so culturally variable that any diverse group will need to address them explicitly. We have all heard pejorative references—by people enslaved by clock or watch—to "African time" or "Mexican time," but clock watching can also produce hypertension, frustration, and intolerance. Think again of those open-ended, timeless Sunday liturgies of African communities compared to clock-ruled, time-starved, and rushed liturgies. In some cultures time is seen as a gift, to be used freely without reference to chronology. In others it is a scarce resource, treated as a commodity, with the very same vocabulary we use for commercial transactions; time can be saved or spent, gained or lost, and even wasted. When daily life is structured by the clock, there is little "time" left over for spontaneity, creativity, or simple availability. Intercultural living calls us to address the use (and abuse) of time. And, as with time, so with space: attitudes to space—personal, open, private, common, or sacred—are not simply whimsical but culturally shaped. In an intercultural community interpersonal space must be negotiated, not without some discomfort or pain, and certainly requires compromise.

CLARIFYING THE CHALLENGE

Ethnocentrism is a fact of life: we see and interpret through culturally conditioned eyes. It is immoral only when we inflict our own perspective on others, imagine it is the only true perspective, or act as if it were actually God's way of seeing the world. We are all ethnocentric, but with maturity and training we can identify and address this bias. Ethnocentrism judges other people and worlds as inferior reflections of our own. The "other" then becomes the problem—to be avoided, demeaned, attacked, or perhaps converted or assimilated. Intercultural living exposes everyone's ethnocentrism. The narrower and more prejudicial our shared world of meaning, the more we will identify with "people like me" and discriminate against the "other" or "them." The challenge is to create a new culture from the various cultures represented in our communities, so that there is no longer an us/them opposition. But this noble thought is undermined in practice by what I call the *cultural flaw*—what some call original sin.

God's idea of a community—from the mythical Genesis story, to the historical Jesus community, and down to our own day—is one of radical inclusion and radical equality, explicitly modeled by Jesus. But while God wants to unite, every culture is limited by a perverse tendency to stratify, separate, diminish, and exclude; no human society has achieved radical inclusion or equality. Every attempt to form an inclusive community of "we" very soon results in alienation, the creation of hierarchy, or drives a wedge between people. An ideally inclusive community of *we* becomes polarized into *us* and *them*. It is precisely this situation that Jesus encountered. The Letter to the Ephesians describes humanity's self-inflicted wound and the Jesus solution. It describes the polarized world of Jews (us) and Gentiles (them), and God's plan to reconcile humanity to itself and to God as an all-inclusive *we*.

> But now in Christ Jesus you who once were far off have been brought near by the flood of Christ. For he is our peace; in his flesh he has made both groups into one and has broken down the dividing wall, that is, the hostility between us. (Eph 2:13–14)

This is a stunning articulation of Jesus's radical plan for humanity. Pauline writings also declare three times that there is henceforth to be no moral *distinction* or political *division* erected on the obvious *differences* between men and women, Jew and Greek, slave and free (see Gal 3:28; Col 3:11; 1 Cor 12:13). This vision must be the foundation and justification for every attempt to build intercultural communities. Jesus chose to become a person of the margins, a stranger rather than a person of power and influence. Influential people occupy central positions where power and authority lie. But Jesus chose the most effective way to encounter the people marginalized by circumstance and society: outreach to "them" or the "other," separated by gender, ethnicity, religion, lifestyle, or social or moral standing. For him, margins and boundaries were points of engagement rather than marks of separation or discrimination. Since the primary purpose of intercultural communities is greater commitment to the mission of Jesus, every member is called to *kenotic* living: self-emptying service of, and among, the least or the other. The only sure way of doing this is the way of Jesus, the way of the cross. Intercultural living not only calls us to a countercultural, faith-based lifestyle within the community, but it stands as a public example of how to live with diversity beyond our immediate communities, as Jesus did.

Good will alone is insufficient; it has produced sin and scandal (from the Crusades, slavery, or burnings, to the marginalization and abuse of women, to excommunications, and to an odious lack of due process). Some would-be disciples of Jesus have been stumbling blocks rather than honest witnesses; good will needs to be complemented and shaped by ongoing conversion.

Because our vocation is not just a rational game plan but a faith-driven and lifelong undertaking, it is the foundation of the life project of every Christian disciple. In the face of frustration and failure it may be our faith alone that sustains us and others. Mature faith sharing, appropriate correction, reconciliation, and mutual encouragement are essential; we know the corrosive effects of gossip and slander and of a lack of encouragement from peers and leaders.

But even personal faith is insufficient unless supported by the actual *fruit* of people's good intentions: the ongoing commitment to acquiring appropriate skills and virtue. Not that everyone must become super efficient, but everyone must persevere in the effort. In ministries that require a new language, the most effective are not always the most fluent or brilliant, but rather those most dedicated to the learning process and to never giving up in the face of difficulty. While learning the art of intercultural living, perseverance may be the most effective tool.

The constant challenge is to become virtuous. Virtue is moral good repeated until it becomes a habit (and vice is its opposite). Intercultural living demands a litany of virtues, such as the virtue of practical respect for personal and cultural differences, and the virtue of commitment to seek truth through dialogue. Truth is not a commodity but a goal to be sought with others, and it will change us all. Then, because marginality and downward mobility constitute the apostolic strategy of Jesus, disciples must strive for the same, lest we fail to encounter poor and forgotten people. We are also called to cultivate the virtue of being continuous learners—the very meaning of the word *disciple*. And we must learn from the best of theology and tradition: intercultural living is really as old as Christianity, and we have much to learn from the past.

EVALUATING THE PROSPECTS

Since intercultural living is a faith-based commitment to the vision of Jesus, to see it primarily as a problem would be strategically and psychologically wrong. Rather, it is an opportunity, a challenge, and a grace. Not everyone needs to be young and active. The moral support of those who are less active is of incalculable value, while a polarized group is self-defeating. But intercultural living is not a natural arrangement, though it is possible in a *supernatural* context: "Jesus looked at them and said, 'For mortals it is impossible, but not for God; for God all things are possible'" (Mark 10: 27). Diplomacy, compromise, and a common vision must inspire a common effort and provide appropriate means to sustain it. Even in established international communities most of us remain rather monocultural attitudinally. Intercultural living is costly for viable international religious life, but it is obligatory if the dry bones of ministry are to live. If successful, it will revolutionize our lives and the Christian mission. Not everyone will accept the challenge, and it does require a critical mass of committed supporters lest the apathetic or resistant compromise its realization.

As membership of international institutes continues to decline in the Northern hemisphere, communities that survive with integrity in the coming decades will do so in and through their diversity. They will be characterized by "fusion," the integration of culturally diverse personnel. The alternative is "fission," the fragmentation of international congregations so that they become no more than loose aggregations of culturally discrete groups. They would remain international entities, but at the cost of their intercultural witness to the gospel. This happens through individualism, tribalism, factionalism, or the loss of the founding charism. The future of international religious life depends significantly on the ability of each community to think and act interculturally. Failure to do so in a global church will lead to terminal decline.

Intercultural living is a much more persuasive witness than cheap rhetoric about loving one's neighbor. But new wine cannot be put into old wineskins, and we cannot build such communities by recycling old material or uncritically employing obsolete ideas. The classical model for community building was assimilation: new members were welcomed into a preexisting and largely *monocultural* community with its established rules and expectations, standardized dress, food, and forms of prayer. Those able to adjust accordingly might be admitted, while others would soon leave; there were always plenty of aspirants. The unspoken message was "come join us and share our ways and religious tradition." This

	Invitation	Inclusion	Radical Welcome
The Message	"Come and join us, and share the riches of our cultural and religious tradition."	"Come and join our community and help us to diversify internally and Internationally."	"Bring your cultural and religious values, your voice and yourself: help us to become an intercultural community."
The Purpose	Assimilation: We invite new people to become one of us as part of our community.	Incorporation: Marginal "others" are welcome but the community's style and practices remain.	Incarnation: The community will be transformed by each person's talents and faith commitment.
The Cost	Little cost to the community: Structures are set and newcomers incorporated into them. Resisters are marginalized or removed.	Some cost to the community: It preaches inclusivity but does not practice power analysis or self-analysis. Individuals sink or swim.	Significant cost to the community, striving to practice real inclusion and be mutually enriched through the infusion of new and culturally different ways of living the faith.
The Outcome	Encouraging numbers, but the community is very monocultural. Those who are different are marginalized or overlooked.	High turnover of members. Whoever is not mainstream is muted or made to leave. Community remains largely monocultural, with few exceptions.	The community evolves organically. Difference is dignified and valued. Authority does not dominate but respects all. There is a common spirit and missionary commitment.

Radical Welcome © 2006 Stephanie Spellers. Adapted by Anthony J. Gittins, CSSp, and used by permission of Church Publishing Incorporated, New York, NY.

Figure 2–2. From Invitation to Radical Welcome

cost the existing community very little; life could go on while potential newcomers were being formed, assessed, and then accepted or not. Potential incomers different from the norm were either marginalized or rejected by a community administration that held the authority in all matters.

Since Vatican II and the increase of women and men religious from the global church, this model has given way to a more inclusive approach in some long-established communities. Now the message is clearer: "come join our community and help us diversify internally and internationally." This is a significant advance, indicating a desire not only to speak and teach but to listen and learn. But mere inclusion of the "other" does not go far enough. Unless customary behavior is changed, a marginal outsider merely becomes a marginal insider. Many cultural "others" still feel ineffective and invisible in their own communities. Without a careful power analysis and self-analysis of the established community there will be no radical inclusion. Such analysis would show whether the traditional decision makers and privileged personnel have remained as before, or whether incoming members are treated as equals—notwithstanding the critical process of formation. So intercultural communities must reject both assimilation and token inclusion, and develop an attitude of radical welcome. Then the message is "bring your cultural and religious values, your voice and autonomous self, and help us together to build a new community." This facilitates the authentic incarnation of each member, which means that everyone will be affected by the cultural diversity and called to an ongoing conversion to God, to each other, and to the authentic cultural values that shape the lives of our fellow Christians. People will not be able to hide behind their own cultural conventions or play the "culture card." Rather, each will need to examine cultural habits, bad and good, and learn to compromise some comfort for the sake of the new community. The cost will be spread vertically and laterally and not only borne by new or incoming members. But an authentic, faith-based undertaking will survive.

Three principles might help us move forward. First, we are called to build a home, a home away from home because "here we have no lasting city" (Heb 13:14). But this is no mere proliferation of houses, where different individuals subsist under the same roof. That is living together separately, not intercultural living. Second, integrated communities evolve gradually, organically, and not without pain. Therefore, we must truly value difference, *because God created difference and saw that it was good.* The cultural flaw uses difference to justify discrimination and disrespect. That is sinful. We must learn to live with and be respectful of our differences, and not despite them. And third, we must rethink the way we think. We are called to repent, not by feeling bad but by thinking—and acting—differently. This is the cost of conversion, and it is much more challenging to think and act differently than it is to feel bad but do nothing.

In a classical rabbinic story the teacher asks the disciples,

"When do you know it is dawn?"

One says, "When you can distinguish a white thread from a black one."

"No," says the teacher.

"When you can see the outline of a tree against the horizon," ventures another.

"No," says the teacher—to this and all other efforts to answer the question.

Finally, the teacher says, "When you can look into the eyes of a stranger, an 'other,' and see a brother or a sister, then it is dawn; until then it is still night."

May we have the grace and good sense to look for, and to live in, the light of a breaking dawn!

3

Intercultural Living in Consecrated Life in the United States

Teresa Maya, CCVI

Consecrated life in the United States began a profound transformation in the 2000s, marked by critical transitions. The large number of cohorts that led the implementation of the Vatican Council are beginning to retire in big numbers; sponsored ministries are being transferred, merged, or dissolved; and big questions about what is ours to do as we face the future have engaged our conversations, assemblies, and imagination. Some of the transformation is happening quietly, one member at a time, in one institute at a time. This more subtle transformation is related to the new members attracted to our life, to simple inter-congregational collaborations, to local care-of-creation initiatives, or the call to renewed advocacy for persons who are vulnerable or in need in the face of political turmoil. The realization that younger entrants to religious life come from more diverse backgrounds than ever emerges among these gentle, but steady, aspects of transformation. This new presence challenges our assumptions about race, culture, and ethnicity.

The diversity trend, barely noticeable just a few years ago, began engaging vocation ministers and eventually formators. As always, the latter have been on the frontline of the changes to religious life. The National Religious Vocation Conference (NRVC), which had been addressing the challenge of recruitment among ethnic and racial minorities for several years, has gradually shifted its attention to intercultural competencies, like almost every area of the Catholic Church in the United States. The Religious Formation Conference soon followed, scrambling to prepare formators for more diverse entrant classes. *Interculturality* has become the buzzword among our peers. Books, conferences, and workshops have emerged that seek to train and prepare us to live and minister in this new reality.

The transformation of the US Catholic Church also offers a context for this new paradigm. The V (Fifth) National Encuentro of Hispanic/Latino Ministry began calling for us to notice, adjust, and welcome the gift of Latinos/as to our church.[1] The Secretariat of Cultural Diversity of the US Conference of Catholic Bishops (USCCB) began an intense effort to train ministers in intercultural competency.[2] The shift took a long time in coming, but religious institutes slowly began to recognize that they needed to engage with the challenge of diversity in different and meaningful ways.

The debate began with questions that have been brewing for decades and have a strong relation to our historical understanding of diversity. The story of one of our Incarnate Word sisters can serve as a backdrop for the reflection of how to engage our call in this new reality. Sister Rosa María Icaza was born in Mexico City in 1925 and entered our community there in 1941. Shortly after, she was sent to the novitiate in San Antonio and spent her entire life of ministry in the United States as an educator (a teacher and then a college professor). Her personal journey and discernment eventually brought her to the burgeoning Mexican American Catholic Center (MACC, now a college) to become an

---

[1] "The main goal of the V *Encuentro* is to discern ways in which the church in the United States can better respond to the Hispanic/Latino presence, and to strengthen the ways in which Hispanics/Latinos respond to the call to the New Evangelization as missionary disciples serving the entire Church" (V Encuentro, "Fact Sheet," 2016, vencuentro.org).

[2] The intercultural competency program states that "one cannot preach, teach or form persons in the Catholic faith adequately without attending to the ways in which Catholic faith and identity become embodied in culture. Proficiency in matters of culture and intercultural relations is an essential feature of the ongoing process of conversion by which the Gospel becomes life for people" (USCCB, "Issues and Action," September 15, 2011, usccb.org).

advocate and formator for Hispanic ministry. Sister Rosa María could easily be counted in the diversity narrative of any religious institute; she was foreign born and a migrant. She certainly experienced all the challenges of the assimilation model beginning in her novitiate, where she was constantly told, "You are in America, speak English!" She suffered discrimination both by her North American sisters, for being Mexican, and her Mexican sisters, for living in the United States. Like most Latinos she lived the painful reality of "ni soy de aquí, ni soy de allá" (I am neither from here nor from there). Her story reflects the challenge offered by older members in our institutes who claim that diversity is not a new thing in religious life.

Borrowing again from my own institute's story, I feel compelled to acknowledge that the challenge of embracing diversity is both a new story and an ongoing story. When I look at the sepia-toned pictures of our founding years in San Antonio, I am not surprised to find sisters from all over the world in the first cohorts of valiant women who journeyed to the frontier to serve and evangelize. One painful story comes to mind. The sisters founded the Saints Peter and Joseph Orphanage in San Antonio, which had a tragic fire in which several children and five of the sisters died. All five were from different nationalities, none from the United States. Over the years other photographs tell similar stories, sisters serving on the San Antonio Mission parochial school system, Mexican Americans, Irish or Polish Americans. The photographs tell a compelling narrative of diversity that assures me that this is an unfolding story, not just a new one. This narrative challenges us further when I consider the complexity of the Irish presence in our congregation. I will return to this critical aspect of our story later in this chapter, but undoubtedly the Irish gift, along with those of the German, Italian, and Polish religious, suggests that cultural diversity has always been an integral part of the story of North American religious.

As we acknowledge this legacy of diversity, the growing diversity today in our ranks and in the people we serve, both in and out of our church pews, must also be named as a new moment that requires fresh approaches and new insights. We must engage the diversity we face today from a new cultural paradigm and with a whole new set of cultural lenses. We are experiencing a new moment. Here is why.

REFLECTING ON THE NUMBERS

North Americans love to count. We count everything—people coming to church on Sunday, number of responders to phone calls, number of calories, number of cars, and so on. Technology has only affirmed this counting obsession with more powerful tools: the number of *likes* and *clicks* and *new followers*. This fascination with counting is not always successful because we could be counting but not noticing. Certain cultural blind spots prevent us from noticing some of the shifting demographics happening right in front of us. White privilege and unconscious bias can play tricks on our numeric mind and make us either see fewer than there really are, or worse still, raise our fear factor with a sense of overwhelming numbers. We need to be careful to understand that we are not exempt from the political climate that surrounds us. When the US Catholic Bishops made statements defending DACA immigrants, for example, Steve Bannon, still leveraging a lot of influence in the media in 2017, was quick to say that the bishops were simply after more resources.[3] Our reactions need to be recognized and challenged: "Why are all these people coming to our parish?" or "I wish they could just learn to speak English!" I applaud the efforts the National Religious Retirement Office (NRRO) has been making by intentionally showing in its photographs in its annual reports the growing diversity—generational, racial, cultural, and ethnic—in our ranks.

The statistics are revealing, even if we account for the bias inherent in all of them. My first clue came from John Allen's book *The Future Church*, in which he talks about the "browning of the Catholic Church." I realized later that, while he was talking of the church at a global level, this "browning" was also noticeable in North America and Western Europe.[4] Studies have continued to confirm this trend. Research from CARA, the Center for Applied Research in the Apostolate, confirms the increased diversity of the church, both in studies commissioned by NRVC and by the

---

[3] CBS Interactive Inc., Charlie Rose interview, *60 Minutes Overtime*, "Bannon Criticizes Catholic Church's Response to Trump's Plan for DACA" (September 10, 2017).

[4] John Allen Jr., *The Future Church: How Ten Trends Are Revolutionizing the Catholic Church* (Crawfordsville, IN: Penguin Random House, 2009), 15.

USCCB.[5] The GHR Foundation funded a study of international sisters serving in the United States in 2017.[6]

An overview of any of these studies confirms the trend of increased diversity. The 2010 CARA study on diversity in the church, reporting on US Catholics by race and ethnicity, showed that white non-Hispanics were a 54 percent majority, with Latinos representing 38 percent, with an even higher percentage among younger Catholics.[7] The NRVC/CARA study of recent vocations to religious life published in 2009 showed a stark contrast between the diversity of sisters in perpetual vows and those in initial formation.[8] It showed that sisters in perpetual vows are 94 percent white, whereas women in initial formation are 57 percent white. Latina, Asian, and black vocations are a growing 40 percent of those in initial formation.[9] The crossroads of race and ethnicity, in particular, are affirming this trend toward growing diversity. This is a different moment for religious life in the United States.

The trend toward greater diversity should also be contrasted with the increased average age of men and women in our institutes. According to CARA statistics, there were 47,170 religious sisters, 4,119 religious brothers, and 11,432 religious priests in

---

[5] See Mark Gray, Mary Gautier, and Thomas Gaunt, SJ, "Cultural Diversity in the Catholic Church in the United States" (Washington, DC: CARA, June 2014).

[6] Trinity Washington University and CARA, "International Sisters in the United States," GHR Foundation (2017). Since its presentation at CTU (Catholic Theological Union) in 2017, this study has become a book. See Mary Gautier, Mary Johnson, Patricia Wittberg, and Tran Thu Do, *Migration for Mission: International Catholic Sisters in the United States* (Oxford: Oxford University Press, 2019).

[7] Gray, Gautier, and Gaunt, "Cultural Diversity in the Catholic Church in the United States," 4.

[8] NRVC/CARA, "Study of Recent Vocations to Religious Life" (2009). This study on new generations of women in religious life was part of the ground work for Mary Johnson, Patricia Wittberg, and Mary Gauthier, *New Generations of Catholic Sisters: The Challenge of Diversity* (Oxford: Oxford University Press, 2014).

[9] NRVC/CARA, "Study of Recent Vocations to Religious Life." See also Mary L. Gautier, Jonathon L. Wiggins, and Jonathon C. Holland, *Incorporating Cultural Diversity in Religious Life: A Report for the National Religious Vocation Conference* (Washington, DC: CARA, 2014).

the United States in 2016.[10] But the average age is getting higher among these cohorts. The NRRO, created by the USCCB to aid religious institutes in facing the retirement of their members, publishes annual data that are representative of the trend. The 2017–27 NRRO projections are showing that by the end of this period, more than 80 percent of all religious will be older than seventy-five years of age. The older age groups are more homogenous—at least racially, though some would argue ethnically as well—than current entrants. The reason we need to pay attention to this trend next to the increased diversity of men and women in formation is that in the next few decades, as our current older members complete their mission, the new generations will be so diverse they will have a completely different profile than what we have grown accustomed to in religious life. The next twenty years will begin to color our lives in ways that we have not seen in the last half century. And if we consider the International Sister Study sponsored by GHR, we can argue that international sisters, women born outside the United States, along with women of diverse cultural and ethnic backgrounds, will completely reverse our current trend.[11]

There is no doubt that this is a new moment. Janet Mock, a Sister of St. Joseph, is adamant about the importance of naming this reality:

> Naming anything as prophetic is dangerous and fraught with the potential for hubris. The Spirit of God and time determine whether our acts are prophetic or corporate ego run awry. There are trends in our age, however, that demand our attention. How we women religious address them can create an environment for the activity of God to flourish.[12]

---

[10] The 2016 numbers are no longer online, but the 2015 and 2017 numbers show the trends (see "Frequently Requested Church Statistics," cara.georgetown.edu).

[11] See Gautier, et al., *Migration for Mission*. See also idem, "International Sisters and Priests in the United States," in *Pathways to Religious Life*, 159–74 (Oxford: Oxford University Press, 2018).

[12] Janet Mock, CSJ, "Surprised by Joy: Springs from the Great Deep Illuminating Religious Life," keynote address, LCWR Assembly, 2015.

This new reality begs the question: How are we going to welcome this growing diversity?

CALLED TO ASK THE RIGHT QUESTIONS

The story needs to return to the affirmation that while this is a new moment, some of the lenses through which we are looking at it are conditioned by our history. How can we even begin to engage the growing diversity among us if we have not even reflected on how we lived with diversity in the past? One of the most significant migrant experiences of religious life in the United States, for both men's and women's institutes, is that of our Irish brothers and sisters. We run the risk of missing the importance of this reflection because we sometimes fail to embrace all diversities, focusing only on racial differences. In the case of our Irish sisters I also turn to my congregational story to illustrate the challenge. As a Mexican sister, it took me a long time to "see" a difference between the American and the Irish sisters; after all, they are all white women of about the same age. As I got to know them better, however, I began hearing the Irish accent and noticing the ongoing complaint about lukewarm tea. It was not until my first trip to Ireland that I finally had the privilege of encountering their experience. One of the sisters shared the story of the day her ship sailed from Ireland: "As I saw the Irish coast disappear on the horizon, I wanted to die. I knew I would never see Ireland again. It was devastating." She narrated that soul-wrenching moment with such intensity and pain that I could hardly believe it had been over fifty years since her ship set sail. My interest encouraged her to tell the rest of the story, about arriving in America, encountering strange food (yes, like hotdogs), and being sent to "accent school" to polish her Irish brogue. Her story is only one of many. Throughout my first years in religious life I heard rumors of the Irish American tension; any reference to abuse of power or creativity always carried an ethnic label, "They are more. . . . We are less."

Recently, my congregation began preparing for its sesquicentennial celebration by compiling information and archives from the fifty years of Vatican Council II renewal to understand how that process moved us toward greater unity. The historian charged with the task called me one evening to say: "Do you realize that you never had an American vocations problem? All you had was an Irish vocations problem." Puzzled, I asked her to elaborate. She explained that the Irish sisters were 44 percent of the total number of women who entered my congregation between 1869 and the present—almost half. American sisters were only about 29 percent, and while there were more entrants in the 1950s, as in every other congregation, they grew but never peaked like the Irish entrants during that period. Slowly pondering these historical numbers, the tension and rivalry began to make more sense.

What did we learn from this historic diversity? I suggest that our institutes might as well take a loving, honest look at the way we integrated the vocations of women from cultural and ethnically diverse backgrounds. We need to do the work of reconciliation with our history before we can pretend to develop intercultural competency. The assimilation model that prevailed in the United States was uniquely ours. Some historians would even argue that especially among Catholic migrants, men and women religious were the most important advocates of assimilation into the United States. As our institutes were being founded or consolidated, all of us had ministries that helped migrants integrate into American society; some of us were even founded specifically to aid migrants. The climate of the time required assimilation for survival, for belonging, and ultimately for acceptance by the rest of America. The assimilation model of our ministries crept into our communities. This was the paradigm in which we engaged the first diversity among us, and our formation programs paralleled this model. Local or American culture was the norm, and English—not just any version of English, but proper, well-pronounced "American" English—was to be spoken among us. The Irish might have struggled with accent schools, but German and Polish migrant sisters were relegated to menial domestic duties because of their poorly spoken English. To this day, challenges with pronunciation plague our relationships, as we constantly interrupt people from other countries to correct their pronunciation even though we understand what they are saying.

I return to the introductory story of Sister Rosa María Icaza. Her life in the United States was never easy. One of my sisters published an article in *US Catholic Historian* about the treatment of Hispanic Sisters in our congregation. The stories she collected are heart-wrenching. For example, she writes:

Many times the inability to communicate in English was confused with ignorance or lack of intelligence. Upon entering the convent, Hispanic women had to forget their roots and their language so as to be able to enter the culture of religious life, which was uniformity, the strength to repress emotions, submission so as to give up what is most sacred of a person, one's proper dignity. During the summer for special celebrations of the Congregation, Mexican Sisters generally came to San Antonio. The Sisters from the United States would say: "put everything away and lock your things because the Mexicans are coming and they are thieves."[13]

Many of these sisters are still alive. How could we possibly be talking about engaging diversity among younger entrants if we have not engaged the difficult work of reflecting on and reconciling our history? Unpacking our history will help us understand why the assimilation model is still present among us, boycotting any efforts at growing our intercultural sensitivity and joyfully embracing the competencies that the present moment requires. Nothing short of an examination of conscience is necessary to unpack our racism and discrimination toward minority groups. How else can we unlearn the paradigm of the past that continues to inform the present moment?

Learning from the present moment will also be critical for religious life meaningfully to embrace its growing diversity, and noticing how diversity is also changing the society where we live and serve is just as critical. The lessons from the present are many. We might be living amid a backlash toward the diversity we thought we were beginning to embrace and celebrate with the election of President Barack Obama, but the transformation of American society cannot be reversed. The portrait that *The Next America* paints requires our attention and reflection.[14] One of the

---

[13] Maria Luisa Vélez, "The Pilgrimage of Hispanics in the Sisters of Charity of the Incarnate Word," *US Catholic Historian* 9, no. 1/2, *Hispanic Catholics: Historical Explorations and Cultural Analysis* (Winter-Spring 1990): 190.

[14] Paul Taylor, "The Next America: Two Dramas in Slow Motion," Pew Research Center (April 10, 2014). This research has since become a book: Paul Taylor and the Pew Research Center, *The Next America*, updated pbk. ed. (Philadelphia: PublicAffairs, Perseus Books Group, 2016).

reflections in the study is on the Coke commercial that aired during Super Bowl 2014.[15] The commercial features Americans of all backgrounds, ethnicities, generations, races, and religions singing "America the Beautiful" in different languages. The observations made in *The Next America* about what this reflects in American society need to be part of our noticing the growing diversity among us. I could not imagine what my elementary schoolteachers would have said about a song so tied to American identity being sung in a language other than English. The projections proposed in *The Next America* merit careful analysis—projections about diversity, racial intermarriage, and generational differences, all of which help us understand our environment of diversity.

We need to notice and listen carefully to these signs of the times. Our social context is both one of greater diversity and increasing tension. We are living in a particular sociocultural context, in a particular time in history that will only make this hyper-diversity more real, more challenging, and certainly more like the world God created. We are also called to notice and wonder what is ours to do. We live in a country that continues to be the number one destination for migrants in the world, in a country where xenophobia continues to rise. The papal visit to the United States in 2015 highlighted this moment. When Pope Francis addressed the Joint Session of Congress on September 24, he reminded lawmakers that the United States is a nation of immigrants:

> In recent centuries, millions of people came to this land to pursue their dream of building a future in freedom. We, the people of this continent, are not fearful of foreigners, because most of us were once foreigners. . . . When the stranger in our midst appeals to us, we must not repeat the sins and the errors of the past. We must resolve now to live as nobly and as justly as possible, as we educate new generations not to turn their back on our "neighbors" and everything around us. Building a nation calls us to recognize that we must constantly relate to others, rejecting a mindset of hostility to adopt one of reciprocal subsidiarity, in a constant effort to do our best. I am confident that we can do this.

---

[15] The commercial, available on YouTube, is worth watching.

Church leaders across the United States have been challenged to address this situation and the growing tension it is creating. Among the reflections worth paying attention to, the pastoral letter of July 18, 2017, from Bishop Seitz in El Paso, Texas, *Sorrow and Mourning Flee Away*, is notable for its comprehensive approach to a very complex issue. Bishop Seitz also addresses the honorable men and women who daily work for ICE (Immigration and Customs Enforcement). We need to notice much more, even beyond ethnic and racial diversity. We need to notice the way our own congregational culture is embracing all diversities—generational, gender, interracial, religious, and environmental, to mention a few.

Engaging this hyper-multidimensional diversity—one of the most significant signs of the times in which we have been called to live—needs to become an intentional effort in all our institutes, whether we have new vocations or not. Simply living during this time obligates this deliberate engagement for the sake of the gospel. The first step to embrace diversity and move into intercultural living is to address our own story with honesty and integrity. Addressing the realities of unconscious bias and white privilege is a great place to start. Beginning the difficult and painful conversation about racism will likewise make our embrace of interculturality more authentic. I agree with Bryan Massingale, who states that racism is the subtext of almost every social concern in our nation. He writes, "Catholic failure to engage adequately the pivotal issue of racial injustice decisively compromises its theology of justice and renders its praxis of justice ineffective."[16] We are called to an examination of conscience.

Unless we are willing to risk the vulnerability and often shame related to how we have historically engaged diversity, we cannot move into the intercultural mission we are being called to model in today's reality. Certainly, the times were different and we are all products of our social context, but today a reconciled memory is an essential first step. Consider all the places where commissions of memory and reconciliation have been created precisely to engage this historical legacy so that we can learn and so that

---

[16] Bryan N. Massingale, "James Cone and Recent Catholic Episcopal Teaching on Racism," *Theological Studies* 61 (2000): 700.

we can ensure we are not repeating anything that diminishes the common good.

THE RESPONSIBILITY:
INTENTIONAL INTERCULTURALITY

Living with people from other cultures, backgrounds, generations, and ways of thinking does not automatically create an intercultural community. Interculturality is intentional gospel witness, as Anthony Gittins affirms.[17] Religious institutes are called to model living into this diversity in a way that goes beyond the cultural competency corporations have been promoting to improve their bottom line. We need to embrace a spirituality of diversity that celebrates and understands that God's intent for creation is this beautiful diversity that weaves the tapestry of life itself.

Interculturality requires intentional formation and training; it needs leadership. Simply inviting men or women religious to live together is never enough. We need to develop a nuanced understanding of culture. Despite the increasing literature available on this subject, I still appreciate Divine Word missionary Antonio Pernia's simple but illuminating definitions as he distinguishes among internationality, multiculturality, and interculturality:

- *Internationality*, that is, "the mere presence in the congregation or community of members from different nationalities or cultures."
- *Multiculturality*, that is, "the ability of members from different nationalities or cultures to simply co-exist side by side [with] each other."
- *Interculturality*, that is, "a congregation or community which allows the different cultures of community members to interact with each other and thereby mutually enrich the individual members and the community as a whole."[18]

---

[17] Anthony J. Gittins, *Living Mission Interculturally: Faith, Culture, and the Renewal of Praxis* (Collegeville, MN: Liturgical Press, 2015), 4.

[18] Antonio M. Pernia, SVD, "Challenges to and Opportunities for Religious Life from the World and the Church of Today," *UISG Bulletin* 146 (2011), 40.

International communities need to be particularly discerning of the nuances of each of these processes. Multicultural liturgies where every culture brings its native dress is a great beginning, but it is not enough. We need to examine where power and resources are concentrated in our international communities. We often say we are multicultural, but the cultural norm has always been set in the global North. Having a presence in other countries or members from other countries is not enough. Furthermore, we need to also understand all the nuances of diversity—generational, ideological, regional, and theological—and recognize that congregations have their own culture, one we unconsciously intend everyone to assimilate into. How can we allow and encourage these new cultures, entrants, and diversity to transform our congregational culture? What would our communities look like?

Intercultural competency needs to become a goal of all of our ongoing formation programs and aspirations. Interculturality must touch every aspect of our institute´s life. Our understanding of the vows, community, ministry, and our spirituality should be transformed as we engage this process honestly and intentionally. We are preparing our members to enter fully into the encounter with today's reality, with the hyper-diversity of today's world, and nothing short of a transformation of the heart is required. This culture of encounter, which has become one of the signature messages of Pope Francis, provides the framework for our intercultural living. Pope Francis explains in *Evangelii Gaudium* that

> becoming a people demands something more. It is an ongoing process in which every new generation must take part: a slow and arduous effort calling for a desire for integration and a willingness to achieve this through the growth of a peaceful and multifaceted culture of encounter. (*EG*, no. 220)

We are never done. I often hear from sisters in different institutes that they have already done these multicultural workshops. Attendance at workshops several decades ago does not mean that we have "done" or "checked off" our integration of cultures in our congregations. We must heed Pope Francis's beautiful message toward the end of *Evangelii Gaudium*: "Whenever we encounter another person in love, we learn something new about God" (no. 272). We are all in the process of entering fully into our Catholic identity. Thomas Groome explains that we all know the term *catholic* means universal, but that we should revisit the Greek word to recognize that it means "inclusion." *Katha holos*, he explains, should be understood as "gathering in the whole," or more beautifully expressed, "all are welcome."[19] Hospitality for diversity will be the hallmark of our intercultural living.

Intercultural spirituality necessarily points us to Jesus. We need to return to and read the Gospels from the perspective of this call to gather in the whole. The incarnation, in fact, took place in Palestine, one of the most diverse regions of the ancient world. Jesus grew in grace and wisdom in a crossroads of the Roman Empire, a frontier. North American religious are living in a "modern-day Palestine," a crossroads of people and ideas. Pope Francis has referred to this often; for example, at the *Angelus* in Saint Peter's Square on January 26, 2014, he said:

> Galilee . . . is a borderland, a place of transit where people of different races, cultures, and religions converge. Thus Galilee becomes a symbolic place for the Gospel to open to all nations. From this point of view, Galilee is like the world of today: the co-presence of different cultures, the necessity for comparison and the necessity of encounter.

Jesus, too, had to learn to live in this reality.

Jesus encountered the diversity of his time and had to enter into a process of intercultural conversion that inspires our journey. We find him struggling with diversity when he confronts the Canaanite woman. His response sounds xenophobic to modern ears: "I was sent only to the lost sheep of Israel." The woman does not retreat, but rather causes Jesus to change, to begin an intercultural dialogue, and by the end, we find him saying, "Woman, great is your faith!" (Matt 15:24, 28). What a conversion! Indeed, this was a transition into an intercultural spirituality, which recognizes the gift of someone who is different, of a different gender, and of a different culture. A similar encounter happens with the Roman centurion. No need to elaborate on the resentment against the Roman Empire that was breeding in Palestine; suffice it to

---

[19] Thomas Groome, *What Makes Us Catholic: Eight Gifts for Life* (New York: HarperCollins, 2002), xvii.

say that we should pay attention to the fact that Jesus bothers to engage with a Roman officer. The narrative of the encounter shows the profound respect the centurion had for Jesus, as he models an intercultural spirituality: "Lord, I am not worthy to have you come under my roof." Then we are told that Jesus "was amazed," surprised, perhaps even converted, and responds: "Truly I tell you, in no one in Israel have I found such faith" (Matt 8:8, 10). Many other such encounters are found in the Gospels; we need to return to Jesus to discover how he moved during his life away from a closed understanding of the salvation for Israel to a universal embrace of all peoples.

This movement into intercultural living should be our journey as consecrated men and women. Contemplating Jesus today in order to respond with his mind and heart to the call of our time needs to be at the center of our missionary discipleship. Nancy Sylvester affirms this call: "Facing breakdown or breakthrough we, people of faith, are challenged to put on the mind of Christ. To transform our own consciousness so that we can take a long loving look at the real and see our connectedness, our unity, so that we can imagine new ways of responding to the crisis of our time."[20] The encounters in the gospel narratives offer examples of transformation and conversion, as they show us a Jesus who is willing to enter into these conversations. Are we ready to follow?

---

[20] Nancy Sylvester, IHM, presentation, International Assembly, Sisters of Charity of the Incarnate Word, April 2016.

4

Interculturality and Leadership in Consecrated Life

Antonio M. Pernia, SVD

Much has been said in this conference about interculturality, intercultural living, and intercultural communities. I believe it is clear that central to interculturality is the encounter with the "culturally other," the one culturally different from us.

Instead of elaborating on interculturality as such, I offer here a reflection on what I believe is the theological significance of interculturality or of our encounter with the culturally other and, in this context, explore the question of leadership within consecrated life. Indeed, as institutes of consecrated life and societies of apostolic life today become more and more intercultural, the question about how leadership should be exercised in religious congregations acquires a certain urgency.

THE THEOLOGICAL SIGNIFICANCE OF INTERCULTURALITY

The theological or spiritual significance of interculturality is that our encounter with the culturally other is an invitation to seek the other face of God. This insight comes from Mary Jo Leddy, founder of the Romero House in Toronto, a residence for refugees and migrants. Let me begin, then, by summarizing the main points of her book, *The Other Face of God*.[1]

An Ancient Biblical Belief

Leddy says that it is an ancient biblical belief, which the Hebrew people constantly recalled, that God is not like us. God is always more than our thought of God, more than what we make of God. Again and again the prophets of the Old Testament reminded the people that God is not an idol, the work of our hands and imagination. God is always stranger and less familiar than we think. God is the totally Other, the radically New. In other words, God always has another face. And this other face of God is revealed to us when we are faced by one who is different from us, by one who is other than us. It is when we come face to face with the "culturally other" that we get a glimpse of the other face of God.

This other face of God summons us to newness. As Saint Augustine writes, "God is nearer to me than I am to myself but different enough to make me more than myself." Thus, the invitation of the culturally other is to reflect on the mystery that draws us from the familiar face of God to the other face of God that summons us to become more than ourselves, the mystery that moves us from our customary experience of God to an encounter with God who is different enough to call us to a different way of being, the mystery of how the culturally other, if we stay with that other long enough, can lead us to a new sense of the nearness of God.

This capacity to see the other face of God is a particular need in today's world, where the general tendency is to enfold what is different into what is familiar. The temptation is to create an image of a god who is friendly and familiar, a god who is like us. This becomes a domesticated and manageable god, one who can be called upon for all kinds of personal and political solace. Such a god is thoroughly predictable and totally lacking in surprises, a god who can be asked to guard us from those who are not like us, to protect us from strangers.

Indeed, we live in a world where we fear strangers. Strangers are a threat to us. Strangers are a danger to our security. We tell

---

[1] Mary Jo Leddy, *The Other Face of God: When the Stranger Calls Us Home* (Maryknoll, NY: Orbis Books, 2011).

our children not to talk to strangers. But unless we allow strangers to face us, we will never see the other face of God. Unless we come face to face with them, we will never experience the "about face" so necessary for us to hear God's call to a different way of being and God's summons for us to become more than ourselves.

A Biblical Story

I would like to illustrate this point with a biblical story, namely, the story of the stranger on the road to Emmaus (Luke 24:13–34).

As the Gospel of Luke narrates it, toward the evening of the day of the resurrection two of the disciples of Jesus were making their way from Jerusalem to Emmaus. They were conversing about the things that had happened the previous days. Disappointment and discouragement were deeply etched into their faces. Their dreams were shattered, their hopes crushed. Their master had died an ignominious death on the cross. After all that had happened, there was nothing to the great dreams of their teacher. Everything had failed. It was finished.

Apparently, they were going home, turning back to their former way of life. Then a stranger entered their lives. "Are you the only stranger in Jerusalem who does not know the things that have taken place there in these days?" they asked him. They welcomed the stranger and walked side by side with him on the road. They allowed this stranger to explain the scriptures to them. This was very unusual—two Israelites allowing a "stranger in Jerusalem," probably a non-Jew, to interpret the Hebrew scriptures to them. But as he spoke, their hearts began to burn within them.

They invited the stranger to stay and share a meal with them. It was at table, when they were face to face with him, that their eyes were opened and they recognized the Master. They saw the other face of Christ—not the familiar face of the earthly Jesus, but the unfamiliar face of the risen Lord. That was when they made an "about face." "That same hour they got up and returned to Jerusalem," where they rejoined their companions. No, it had not ended. It was not finished. It had only just begun. A turnaround from home in Emmaus to mission in Jerusalem, and from Jerusalem to the ends of the earth.

This was all because they allowed themselves to face, and be faced by, a stranger. All because they agreed to walk side by side with the stranger and stayed long enough to eventually be face to face with him.

This is what the culturally other does to us, that is, puts us into contact with that part of ourselves, of our world, and of God that we have never experienced before.

MYSTERIUM TREMENDUM ET FASCINANS

In a similar way the eminent German Lutheran theologian Rudolf Otto (1869–1937), in his book *The Idea of the Holy* (1917), speaks about God as *mysterium tremendum et fascinans,* a mystery that is both terrifying and fascinating, a mystery that both repels and attracts.

We are comfortable with our own images of God, but we are ill at ease with the *mysterium tremendum et fascinans*—the unfamiliar face of God that emerges out of God's hiddenness. Our usual tendency is to do away with mystery by trying to understand it with discursive philosophical and theological language. Once "understood," we can then file it away in a folder and archive it. Then we go on with business as usual, never bothering again about the mystery we have understood and filed away, or better, never allowing the mystery to bother us again.

And yet, I think what the world today needs to see is not the familiar and customary face of God, the image of God that is very often created according to our own image. I believe what the world needs to see today is the unfamiliar and mysterious face of God, the image of God that is beyond our ideas and imagination. Not the face of God that makes us complacent and comfortable, but the face of God that challenges and disturbs us.

What we need today is not an evangelization that can explain away the mystery of God through discursive philosophical language, but an evangelization that can lead people into the very mystery of God through the language of signs and symbols. We need a mystagogic approach and language, or what Pope Francis calls in *Evangelii Gaudium* a "mystagogic initiation" or a "mystagogical renewal" of evangelization (*EG*, no. 166). What is needed in the new evangelization is for people to encounter the God of mystery.

This is what our encounter with the culturally other can demand of us, that is, the courage to encounter the *mysterium tremendum et fascinans*, allowing it to lead us beyond our customary selves toward encountering our own unfamiliar selves. As Palmer Parker puts it:

> It is no accident that this God is so often represented by the stranger, for the truth that God speaks in our lives is very strange indeed. Where the world sees impossibility, God sees potential. Where the world sees comfort, God sees idolatry. Where the world sees insecurity, God sees occasions for faith. Where the world sees death, God proclaims life. God uses the stranger to shake us from our conventional points of view, to remove the scales of worldly assumptions from our eyes. God *is* a stranger to us, and it is at the risk of missing God's truth that we domesticate God, reduce God to the role of familiar friend.[2]

A SIGN OF OUR TIMES

It would seem that the current interest in and search for intercultural communities is a veritable sign of our times. It is the Spirit stirring in us, urging us to seek the other face of God and thereby show to the world the other face of the church, of theology, and of the consecrated life. Pope Francis is leading the way in this regard.

The Other Face of the Church

Here I am not speaking of the church in "conservation mode," but rather in "missionary mode." Not the church as an institution concerned about its self-preservation, but as a community-in-mission at the service of humanity. Not a bureaucratic institution, but as Pope Francis says, "like a field hospital. . . . This is the mission of the Church: to heal the wounded hearts, to open doors, to free [people], to say that God is good, God forgives all, that God is our Father, God is tender, that God is always waiting for us."[3] Not a church that is inward looking, busy with issues *ad intra*, but a church that is outward looking, concerned with affairs *ad extra*.

---

[2] Parker Palmer, *The Company of Strangers: Christians and the Renewal of America's Public Life* (New York: Crossroad, 1981), 59.

[3] Vatican Radio, "Pope at Santa Marta: Servants of the Kingdom," February 5, 2015.

As Pope Francis writes in *Evangelii Gaudium*, "We need to move from a pastoral ministry of mere conservation to a decidedly missionary pastoral ministry" (no. 15). Elsewhere in the exhortation he notes, "'Mere administration' can no longer be enough. Throughout the world, let us be permanently in a state of mission" (no. 25). And again, "Missionary outreach is paradigmatic for all the Church's activity" (no. 15). Pope Francis, quoting Pope John Paul II's 2001 *Ecclesia in Oceania*, states, "All renewal in the Church must have mission as its goal if it is not to fall prey to a kind of ecclesial introversion" (no. 27). In his other discourses Pope Francis refers to this as a self-referential church, that is, a church whose identity and mission are defined in reference to itself rather than in reference to the world. Thus, we need not a self-referential church, but a world-referential church.

The Other Face of Theology

We need not only a theology that proves that faith in God is right and true, but one that shows that faith in God is beautiful and joyful. Not just a theology that employs the *via rationis*, or the way of reason, but one that uses the *via pulchritudinis*, or the way of beauty. Not just a theology that answers questions of the mind, but one that responds to desires of the heart. Not just a theology that demonstrates the reasonability of faith, that faith is compatible with the demands of reason, but a theology that reveals the beauty of faith, that faith corresponds to the longings of the heart.

We need not only a theology built on faith seeking to understand the mystery of God, but one that arises from faith seeking to experience the God of mystery. Not just *fides quaerens intellectum* (faith seeking understanding), but *fides quaerens sensum* (faith seeking experience). Not just *credo ut intelligam* (I believe so that I may understand God), but *credo ut sentiam* (I believe so that I may experience God). Not just discursive language, the language of rationality, but mystagogic language, the language of mystery. To quote Pope Francis on this point:

> So a formation in the *via pulchritudinis* ought to be part of our effort to pass on the faith. Each particular church should encourage the use of the arts in evangelization, building on

the treasures of the past but also drawing upon the wide variety of contemporary expressions so as to transmit the faith in a new "language of parables." We must be bold enough to discover new signs and new symbols, new flesh to embody and communicate the word, and different forms of beauty which are valued in different cultural settings, including those unconventional modes of beauty which may mean little to the evangelizers, yet prove particularly attractive for others. (*EG*, no. 167)

The Other Face of the Consecrated Life

We need not the consecrated life that, in the words of Pope Francis, is identified with the practice of religious exercises, but one that is characterized by "encounter with others, engagement with the world or a passion for evangelization" (*EG*, no. 78). Not a consecrated life where followers of Jesus are merely disciples, but a consecrated life where followers of Jesus are "missionary disciples" (*EG*, no. 120). Not the comfort and security of the religious house or convent, but the insecurity and discomfort of missionary service. Not the order entailed by monoculturality in consecrated life, but the disorder implied by interculturality in consecrated life.

Indeed, interculturality in consecrated life calls for accentuating its other face. On the one hand, sharing intercultural life among a culturally diverse membership is an invitation to seek the other face of God and an opportunity to deepen the mystic dimension of consecrated life. On the other hand, sharing intercultural mission among the poor and marginalized is an invitation to view reality from the peripheries and an opportunity to deepen the prophetic dimension of consecrated life.

THE CALL TO MYSTICISM AND PROPHECY
OF THE CONSECRATED LIFE

Allow me to elaborate a little bit more on this other face of the consecrated life. Some years ago the German theologian Johann Baptist Metz spoke about the evangelical counsels as having both a mystic-religious and a prophetic-political dimension.[4] This implies that fundamental to the consecrated life is the call to mysticism and prophecy.

Mysticism in the Consecrated Life

The mystical dimension of the evangelical counsels refers to the profession by consecrated persons of God as their only treasure (poverty), their only love (chastity), and their only freedom (obedience). It refers to the consecration to seek God alone and to love God above all. This consecration, in turn, is rooted in the attraction to the mystery of God.

While most people are ill at ease with mystery, mystics are attracted to and at home with mystery. They sit with it, contemplate it, and live it in such a way that it begins to manifest in their own lives. The ineffability of mystery leads them to seek another language with which to speak about it. Often they can speak of it only in the language of signs and symbols. Mystagogic language, rather than discursive language. The language of mystery rather than the language of rationality.

Mysticism is built on the conviction that God is not like us, that God always has an other face. This is the unfamiliar, mysterious face of God, the face of God that is revealed to us when we come face to face with the one who is different from us, namely, the poor, the stranger, the foreigner, the refugee, the migrant, the displaced people, the indigenous people, the unwed mother, the single parent, the person with HIV/AIDS, the faith seeker, the unbeliever, the non-Christian.

Mysticism begins not in the silence of our chapels, or in the sacredness of our religious houses or convents, or in the comfort of our rooms, but in the places where we encounter the ones who are different from us—in the slums and barrios, the inner city, the marketplace and the workplace, in schools, hospitals, and orphanages, or, as Pope Francis would say, in the "peripheries." It leads us to the moment of contemplating the mystery of God, gazing at the other face of God, and encountering the unknown

---

[4] Johann Baptist Metz, *Followers of Christ: Religious Life and the Church* (London: Burns and Oates, 1978).

and unfamiliar God. In doing so we are summoned to newness and are led out of our customary selves. Gazing at God's face, we acquire the heart and the eyes of God, so that we begin to gaze at the world with the eyes of God.[5] When we do so, we see the world in a new way—enemies become friends, separating walls become open doors, strangers become brothers or sisters, borders become bridges, diversity leads not to differences and conflict but to harmony and unity. So mysticism, which arises out of mission, leads back to mission.

Prophecy in the Consecrated Life

On the other hand, the prophetic dimension of the evangelical counsels refers to solidarity with those for whom poverty, chastity, and obedience are not virtues but imposed conditions of life. That is, solidarity

- with the poor, for whom poverty is not a virtue but a condition in life;
- with the marginalized, for whom celibacy is not a virtue but a social destiny;
- with the oppressed, for whom obedience is not a virtue but a sign of oppression.

As we know, there is a certain "unreality" to our religious vows, for they are attempts to live in the present the values of the future. In a certain sense the evangelical counsels are not yet "real," which is why they are vows or promises. We vow to be poor, chaste, and obedient because we are not already poor, chaste, and obedient. If we were, there would be no need for us to vow to be these things. But there are those who by force, not by choice like us, are actually poor and are already obedient—these are the poor, the marginalized, and the oppressed. And so, in becoming one with those for whom poverty and

---

[5] See Donna Orsuto, "Dialogue: Optional Activity or Way of Life," in *The Religious: A Person of Dialogue* (Dialogue in the Church and with the Church), Semestral Assembly of the USG (Union of Superiors General), May 28–31, 2003, Rome.

oppression are realities of life and not just vows or promises, consecrated persons acquire a certain dose of reality in living out the evangelical counsels.

The option for the poor is not just a sociopolitical strategy but a recognition of God's own preferential option. As Pope Francis puts it in *Evangelii Gaudium*: "God's heart has a special place for the poor, so much so that he himself 'became poor' (2 Cor 8:9)" (no. 197). So, the option for the poor is God's own perspective, God's own way of looking at reality. As such, it constitutes a hermeneutical key, that is, a key for the interpretation of reality. In an interview with the Jesuit Italian magazine *La Civiltà Cattolica*, Pope Francis said the following:

> I am convinced of one thing: the great changes in history were realized when reality was seen not from the center but rather from the periphery. It is a hermeneutical question: reality is understood only if it is looked at from the periphery, and not when our viewpoint is equidistant from everything.[6]

So, the call to prophecy is an invitation to seek the other face of God—not the familiar face of God as seen from the "overside" of history, that is, from the standpoint of the victors and the powerful, but the unfamiliar face of God as seen from the "underside" of history, that is, from the standpoint of the victims and the marginalized.

Mystics are those who seek the other face of God and prophets are those who view reality from the other side or the underside of history. What is required today in the new evangelization is the development of a mystagogic language and the adoption of the perspective of the periphery. This, it seems to me, is the challenge of interculturality in the consecrated life today.

LEADERSHIP IN CONSECRATED LIFE

If what we have seen earlier is the other face of the consecrated life, and if interculturality requires that living the consecrated life

---

[6] Pope Francis, in "Wake Up the World! Conversations with Pope Francis about the Religious Life," an interview with Antonio Spadaro, SJ, *La Civiltà Cattolica* (2014): 13–17.

today should be directed toward revealing its other face, then how should leadership be exercised within consecrated life?

Leadership in the consecrated life has always been a profoundly spiritual exercise. Its purpose has always been to create an atmosphere in the religious community wherein each member not only remains faithful to but also grows in his or her vocation to follow the Lord and share in his mission. Indeed, the leader or superior is called to form a community that helps to mediate God's call to every member and facilitate the member's response to this call. This is the reason why often today people speak of the superior's role as primarily that of spiritual animation. Indeed, there is something sacred about the ministry of service that a religious leader or a superior of a religious community is called to provide. The leader or superior is invited to enter into the sacred sanctuary of each member, namely, his or her intimate relationship with God.

This notion of religious leadership acquires an added dimension in the context of intercultural communities in the consecrated life. I offer three brief points on the characteristics of intercultural communities and how leadership may be exercised in them, under three pairs of adjectives: (1) diverse and varied, (2) unfamiliar and new, and (3) mystic and prophetic.

Diverse and Varied

First, the leader will need to be aware that his or her image of God, the face of God that he or she has seen, may not be the image of God that his or her culturally diverse members bring along with them. The leader needs to be aware that an encounter with a culturally diverse membership is an invitation to seek the other face of God. This, in turn, makes it possible for the leader to help members to be open to seeking the other face of God in their encounter with their culturally diverse brothers or sisters.

Indeed, leadership is an invitation to enter into the "sacred sanctuary" of each member. The leader will need to take off his or her shoes because the ground on which he or she stands is sacred.[7] This requires an attitude of profound respect for each

---

[7] Echoing Max Warren, "Preface," in John V. Taylor, *The Primal Vision* (London: SCM Press, 1963), 10.

member of the community and particularly respect for the diversity that each member brings. Only with the attitude of respect will the leader be able to ensure that the fire of interculturality that blazes in the community does not burn the members into uniformity.

A recent document from the Congregation for Institutes of Consecrated Life and Societies of Apostolic Life (CICLSAL), *New Wine in New Wineskins*, puts it in this way:

> [Interculturality] should turn all institutes . . . into places of sympathetic hospitality where different sensibilities and cultures can gain strength and significance. . . . This sympathetic hospitality is built through honest dialogue among the different cultures so that everybody can convert to the Gospel without renouncing their own distinctive traits. The aim of consecrated life will not be to maintain itself in a permanent state in the different cultures it meets, but to maintain the permanence of evangelical conversion in the heart of the progressive creation of an intercultural human reality.[8]

Unfamiliar and New

Second, the leader will also need to be aware—and to create the awareness among the membership—that the interculturality of the community is a call to the unknown, the unfamiliar, and the new. In a certain sense interculturality preserves the call to newness that the consecrated life is meant to embody. *Keep Watch* is the title of a letter of CICLSAL on the occasion of the Year of Consecrated Life in 2015. It says that "religious families are born to inspire new journeys, suggest new routes."[9] This letter likens the consecrated life to a journey into the unknown,

---

[8] CICLSAL, *New Wine in New Wineskins: The Consecrated Life and Its Ongoing Challenges since Vatican II* (Vatican City: Libreria Editrice Vaticana, 2017), 40.

[9] CICLSAL, *Keep Watch: A Letter to Consecrated Men and Women Journeying in the Footsteps of God*, no. 14 (Kenya: Paulines Publications Africa, 2014), 48.

like Abraham travelling to the land of Canaan (cf. *Gn* 12:16), or Moses towards a mysterious land linked to the patriarchs (cf. *Ex* 3:7–8), or Elijah to Zarephath of Sidon; each of them going to mysterious lands glimpsed only in faith.[10]

In this context *New Wine in New Wineskins* warns against the consecrated life getting entangled with managing emergencies and finding strategies to address them instead of viewing horizons and imagining new paths. It reads:

> It is not an easy task to go from the simple administration of a well-known situation to leading others towards unknown destinations and ideals with a conviction that generates real trust. It is not enough to focus on strategies of mere survival, but requires the necessary freedom to launch processes, as Pope Francis continues to remind us.[11]

Interculturality in consecrated life is an impulse toward change, transformation, and renewal. It is like "new wine" that is fermenting as today's religious communities search for intercultural life and mission. Religious leaders are thus called to facilitate the discovery or creation of "new wineskins."

Mystic and Prophetic

The notion of the consecrated life as a journey into the unknown underlines its call to mysticism and prophecy. It is the mysticism of gazing into the unknown, searching the horizon, and recognizing even the little signs of God's presence. It is the prophecy of "pitching our tents at the crossroads of untrodden paths."[12] As *Keep Watch* puts it:

> We are . . . called to pitch our tents at the crossroads of untrodden paths. We are called to stand at the threshold,

---

[10] Ibid., 11.
[11] CICLSAL, *New Wine in New Wineskins*, 8.
[12] CICLSAL, *Keep Watch*, 15.

like the prophet Elijah, who made the geography of the periphery a resource of revelation: to the north at Zarephath, to the south at Horeb, to the east beyond the Jordan into penitent solitude and, finally, to the ascension into heaven. The *threshold* is the place where the Spirit groans aloud: there where we no longer know what to say, nor what to expect, but where the Spirit knows the *plans of God (Rom* 8:27) and hands them over to us. There is the risk, at times, of attributing our long-established maps to the ways of the Spirit, because we find it reassuring always to travel by the same roads.[13]

As we can see, the letter uses the figure of the prophet Elijah as a model for mysticism and prophecy—mysticism because of his life of solitude and asceticism, and prophecy because of his audacity in defending the rights of the poor (see 1 Kings 17–18; 21).[14] The letter further employs the images of borders, frontiers, margins, crossroads, and thresholds in speaking about the consecrated life, suggesting the call of the consecrated life to the unfamiliar, the unknown, and the new. Thus, it speaks about the "mysticism of encounter" and the "prophecy of watchfulness."[15] On the one hand, this means encountering and listening to other people, those who are different from us, unlike us. On the other hand, it means being like "watchmen" who keep the longing for God alive in the world and reawaken it in the hearts of people. Quoting Pope Francis, the letter says that consecrated persons are "like antennas ready to receive the smallest innovations prompted by the Holy Spirit."[16]

The leader, then, will need not only to welcome but also to foster, encourage, or even create opportunities for the encounter, in the peripheries of society with the culturally other and with those who are different from us.

---

[13] Ibid., 15.

[14] See ibid., 6.

[15] Ibid., 13, 10.

[16] Ibid., 13. The quotation from Pope Francis is from his audience with the participants of the encounter organized by the Italian Conference of Secular Institutes, Rome, May 10, 2014.

We are not called to a preoccupied and administrative leadership, but a service of authority that, with evangelical clarity, guides the journey to be undertaken together and in unity of heart, within a fragile present in which the future is waiting to be born. We do not need "simple administration," what we need is to "walk after them, helping those who lag behind and—above all—allowing the flock to strike out on new paths."[17]

In the end, leadership in intercultural communities entails creating the conditions whereby consecrated persons may become men and women with the spirituality of mystics and the lifestyle of prophets.

---

[17] CICLSAL, *Keep Watch*, 12.

PART TWO

LAYING THE FOUNDATIONS

5

The Intercultural Journey of Jesus

Adriana Carla Milmanda, SSpS

I am honored to have the opportunity to share what I have come to see as an intercultural journey for Jesus. In order for you to understand what I mean by this, I explore two biblical texts where Jesus encounters two women who are both foreigners. We know them as the Canaanite or Syrophoenician woman and the Samaritan woman at the well.

The texts are complex and long. However, by highlighting the aspects that are relevant to our conversation and theme, I hope to provide some pathways to explore these biblical texts through the lenses of intercultural living. My goal is that, after reading this chapter, you come away not with answers but with new questions and challenges. Along with a desire to explore and reflect on this theme within your own contexts, my approach to the texts is also informed by my own cultural and social location of origin, and enriched and challenged by my own experiences of cross-cultural living and mission.

As we know, culture is everything for us. It is like our own skin. It is the lens through which we see and make sense of our surroundings. It is what provides us with the sense of identity, cohesion, inclusion, and protection that all of us need as human beings. However, culture also stratifies us and divides us into "us" and "them"—insiders and outsiders, natives and foreigners, conquerors and subjugated, included and excluded, privileged and unprivileged, those who are high on the social scale and those who are invisible to the dominating system. "We" and the "others"—those who are not "like us." Wherever we place ourselves into the social, economic and political stratification of our world, the list of "others" who are excluded from our in-groups is often much longer than we can imagine, even within our Church, congregations, and communities.

In my approach to the biblical texts I identify and highlight two types of "others." First, there are the *outsider others*, such as those with a different nationality, ethnic origin, language, religion, and so on. And second, there are the *insider others*, such as those from a different social class, level of education, generation, theological stance, sexual orientation, and so on.

We are quite familiar with Jesus's subversive attraction to those who were in the lower strata of his own society, the insider others—the sick, outcasts, women, and children. However, his option for the poor (as we would say in Latin America) and for the margins of his own "in group," developed—as we will see—hand in hand with his encounter with the stranger—the "outsider other." I invite you to read some of Jesus's encounters through the lenses of cultural dynamics. Let us see where these encounters led Jesus and how they may challenge us today.

First, let us remember and become fully aware that Jesus of Nazareth was born and brought up in a specific culture. He was a Jew who spoke Palestinian Aramaic and was conditioned by a Semitic way of speaking and thinking. One must realize that Jesus dressed like a Jew, prayed like a Jew, and taught and argued like a Jewish rabbi. His life, mission, and teaching were totally rooted in the Jewish culture and identity. The evangelist John puts it very plainly, "And the Word became flesh" (John 1:14). This simple yet profound statement indicates that the Word found human expression in a Jewish culture. Jesus was a Jew, and it is within his Jewishness that he found his identity and sense of belonging.

Moreover, Jesus's mission was primarily to his people and normally took place within the Jewish territory. He did not travel to far-off lands or learn foreign languages. Furthermore, he clearly said that he "was sent only to the lost sheep of the house of Israel" (Matt 15:24), and when he sent the twelve in mission, he instructed them to "go nowhere among the Gentiles, and enter no town of the Samaritans" (Matt 10:5). Like us, the Jewish Jesus was conditioned and even limited by his human culture. Like us, the incarnated Word had to face his ethnocentrism in order to align himself with God's all-inclusive plan for humanity. Like us, Jesus had to turn away, to convert, from the various forms of exclusion and barriers his own culture had taught him. Like us, Jesus was challenged to move counterculturally in order to become interculturally sensitive and thus witness to us God's kingdom.

We also know that Jesus did heal both Jews and Gentiles. He did meet foreigners and outcasts. We know that he also invited women to be his disciples. He even came to engage some outsiders in theological conversations, as when he admired the faith of a Canaanite woman (Matt 15:28) and of a Roman centurion (Matt 8:10). Furthermore, he even used the Jews' historic enemies as an exemplary model in one of his best-known parables, the Good Samaritan (Luke 10:25–37). So how did a culturally biased Jesus move from an ethnocentric mindset to an intercultural mindset—from ethnocentrism to ethno-relativism, from exclusion of the other to the radical and egalitarian inclusiveness of God's kingdom?

JESUS AND THE CANAANITE WOMAN (MATT 15:21–28)

We begin with Matthew's account of the encounter between Jesus and the Canaanite woman:

> Jesus left that place and went away to the district of Tyre and Sidon. Just then a Canaanite woman from that region came out and started shouting, "Have mercy on me, Lord, Son of David; my daughter is tormented by a demon." But he did not answer her at all. And his disciples came and urged him, saying, "Send her away, for she keeps shouting after us." He answered, "I was sent only to the lost sheep of the house of Israel." But she came and knelt before him, saying, "Lord, help me." He answered, "It is not fair to take the children's food and throw it to the dogs." She said, "Yes, Lord, yet even the dogs eat the crumbs that fall from their masters' table." Then Jesus answered her, "Woman, great is your faith! Let it be done for you as you wish." And her daughter was healed instantly.

For most of us this is a very challenging passage for a number of reasons.

- The Canaanite woman is an outsider to Jesus's cultural and religious group;
- As an insider, Jesus responded to her call with indifference and hurtful silence: "He did not answer her at all";
- When the disciples became annoyed because of her persistence, Jesus finally spoke with an overtly ethnocentric remark: "I was sent only to the lost sheep of the house of Israel";
- Jesus added later a stereotypical statement: "It is not fair to take the children's food and throw it to the dogs."

We are shocked that our sweet Jesus, meek and mild, would have such an offensive attitude and allow such cruel words to come from his mouth. Somehow, we tend to think of Jesus as transcending all the complexities of communal living and loving all peoples regardless of skin color or culture of origin. When we read the Gospels, we usually look at Jesus as if he were color blind, unbiased by his own culture's prejudices. Maybe we want Jesus to be color blind because that's what we want to be or think we should be. But is this possible?

A number of Bible scholars try to soften Jesus's words by explaining that perhaps Jesus wanted to test the woman's faith in order to bring out the best from her. Others emphasize that the word for "dog" that Jesus uses isn't the typical strong language usually associated with this racial insult. They explain that the word Jesus uses takes the diminutive form, implying perhaps a beloved pet or a lap dog, and therefore takes the sting out of the racial offense.

Actually, it does not really matter what kind of exegetical tap dance we create to avoid Jesus's uncomfortable words and reaction. There's no real way to whitewash this passage. If we ever needed proof that the Son of God is also the Son of humankind—that Jesus is indeed fully and completely human—we have it with this apparent demonstration of ethnocentrism.

This is good news! Jesus, given his embedded culture, could not be color blind. And neither can we. The non-edited, impolite words that Jesus addressed to the woman encourage us today to confront ourselves with honesty. His willingness to let her question and broaden his vision is a challenge to our own ethnocentrism and a call to conversion.

This, I think, is the critical lesson of the Canaanite woman. It teaches us the dynamics of the exclusion of the other, of how even the best of humanity—the incarnate Word himself—can get caught up in systems of oppression, in a culture of supremacy. As a good Jew, Jesus would have been raised to give thanks daily that he was born a Jew and not a Gentile, a man and not a woman. Jesus could not help but become entangled by such racist and sexist traps.

However, being caught in evil structures does not make one an overt racist or one who acts in a discriminatory way. It is what happens afterward that makes the difference. How we respond when confronted with the narratives of the stranger, the outsider, and the excluded reveals who we truly are and want to be. Do we continue to ignore or deny these realities of exclusion? Mock them? Disregard them? Continue to brush aside the others as dogs, monkeys, uncivilized, underdeveloped, terrorists, criminals, or whatever labels our cultures teach us to use? Whatever culture(s) we belong to, whether we belong to the dominant group or not, ethnocentrism is present in all of us.

Let us now turn to the woman. I have grown to love her. She is the *only* person in the Gospels who argues with Jesus and wins, who gets him to change his mind. While in Matthew she is portrayed as annoying the disciples, in Mark, where the other version of her story appears, she is shown as interrupting Jesus's rest. In Matthew, she's the Canaanite woman; in Mark, she's the Syrophoenician woman. In both accounts we know her only by her label, her nationality, her otherness. She is portrayed as a bothersome person and as an outsider. We never learn her name.

This woman is desperate. She is in an asymmetrical position, and she's fully aware of it. But she chooses not to play the cultural card or the victim's card. She chooses not to get hooked into the cultural game of exclusion and power. We can imagine the courage, the inner strength, the commitment, the guts, and the wit she must have had. These very traits reflect the divine gifts that are needed in order to bring about God's all-inclusive and egalitarian project.

And Jesus listens to her. He comes to his senses and remembers who and what he is. He may be the Son of humankind—fully human, culturally biased—but he's also the Son of God. This woman, in her weakness and need but also and particularly with her inner strength, clear vision, and courageous sharpness, shows Jesus God's dream for humanity. Jesus opens himself to the challenge—and changes his mind. He listens to the Spirit, awakening in his humanity God's all-inclusive and egalitarian dream.

In this transformative encounter Jesus moves from ethnocentrism toward being more interculturally sensitive. It is a conversion, an "aha" moment that is always mediated by the stranger, the outsider in our lives. This conversion is not only a decision we make in our heads; it must be mediated by the encounter with the other. We need the other, the one not like us, to challenge our ways and broaden our horizons. As a countercultural movement, however, it will surely be an awkward, uncomfortable, and even a frustrating but extremely precious event. Whether we find ourselves as insiders or in a position of power, or whether we are an outsider or in a powerless position, we are all called to conversion. We are called to move out of our comfort zones. But how? Where to?

Before continuing, I invite you to take some quiet time to let this encounter touch you, affect you. You may also recall such a special encounter with the other in your life.

- How do you feel when you see Jesus facing you in the "other" and converting you from the prejudices and stereotypes of your culture?
- What challenges does this reading pose for you today?

Let me unfold the second question into four others:

- When have you been confronted with the blindness of your vision because of your prejudices against the other?
- What prejudices, cultural blindness, or barriers were exposed through the event?
- What is the other asking you? What are the other's needs?
- When *you* are the other, how do you act in order to advance the all-inclusive and egalitarian kingdom of God?

I encourage you to take a moment to reflect on one or more of these questions and perhaps later share this with someone else.

THE SAMARITAN WOMAN (JOHN 4:1–42)

Let us look at Jesus in yet another encounter. Once again, it is an encounter with a nameless and foreign woman: the Samaritan woman at the well. Jesus is sitting there when she comes. This time it is Jesus who takes the initiative; he is ready. This time he is the one in need; he's tired and thirsty. But the woman does not trust him and puts forward two questions that help us read this encounter with our intercultural lenses. She questions Jesus's intentions on two points: (1) why is he speaking with a *Samaritan*, and (2) why is he speaking with a Samaritan *woman?* These two questions get combined into one: "How is it that you, a Jew, ask a drink of me, a woman of Samaria?" (John 4:9). It is historically helpful, however, to look at them separately.

First, why would a Jew speak to any Samaritan? Jews and Samaritans were bitter enemies. Jews did not recognize Samaritans as true Israelites. They also accused them of false worship. According to the Jews, all proper worship to Yahweh had to be made in Jerusalem. Yet, Samaritans persisted in worshiping on Mount Gezarim—in the land of Jacob, home of their ancestors—as seemed appropriate to them. Eventually, Jews avoided travel through Samaria, and any interaction that did happen between the two groups would be heavily charged by the geographic, ethnic, and religious conflicts that divided them. The Samaritan experience was one of oppression, marked by discrimination and violence against their people. In other words, the Samaritan woman at the well had every reason to be distrustful of Jesus.

Second, how could it be possible that a Jewish man would speak with a Samaritan woman? The rabbinic warning against contact with women of any kind was extreme: "He who talks much with womankind brings evil on himself. He neglects the study of the Law and at the last will inherit Gehenna" (Mishnah Aboth 1.5). If speaking with a woman can cast one into Gehenna, how much more will drinking from the same cup? So, Jesus is doing much more here than asking for a drink of water from a stranger—he is very boldly breaking Jewish taboos, with a purpose.

Becoming interculturally sensitive is always an intentional and ongoing undertaking. As theologian David Daube articulates it, "By asking the woman to give him to drink, Jesus showed himself ready to disregard that hostile presumption respecting Samaritan women *for the sake of a more inclusive fellowship* [emphasis added]."[1] Jesus showed himself ready for an intercultural dialogue. An intercultural encounter always entails a countercultural movement.

What about her? In contrast to Nicodemus (John 3:1), she comes to Jesus in the brightest light of day (4:6–7). When he approaches her asking for water, she points out to him his transgression of decorum. When he offers the living water of Spirit and Wisdom, she responds freely: "Give me this water" (4:15)—and having received it, leaves her water jar behind. When he asks for her husband, she is told by Jesus "everything I have ever done" (4:29). But she does not hear an accusation of sexual sin; she does not repent, and Jesus sees no need to forgive her. Because he knows her, she knows him—he is a prophet. She is now ready to trust him and to make her move by asking him the theological question that has separated his people and hers. Like him, she made herself ready for an intercultural encounter:

> The woman said to him, "Sir, I see that you are a prophet. Our ancestors worshiped on this mountain, but you say that the place where people must worship is in Jerusalem." Jesus said to her, "Woman, believe me, the hour is coming when you will worship the Father neither on this mountain nor in Jerusalem. You worship what you do not know; we worship what we know, for salvation is from the Jews. But the hour is coming, and is now here, when the true worshipers will worship the Father in spirit and truth, for the Father seeks such as these to worship him. God is spirit, and those who worship him must worship in spirit and truth." The woman said to him, "I know that Messiah is coming" (who is called Christ). "When he comes, he will proclaim all things to us." Jesus said to her, "I am he, the one who is speaking to you." (John 4:19–26)

---

[1] David Daube, *The New Testament and Rabbinic Judaism* (Salem, NH: Ayer Co., 1984), 374.

True interculturality develops when both interlocutors are able to overcome the either/or way of thinking and move to a both/and alternative—a new and more inclusive space where both meet and where both are, at the same time, out of their comfort zone but also, somehow and at the same time, at home. Rather than God being worshiped either in the temple (Jews) or in high places (Samaritans), both are called to worship God in Spirit and in Truth. However, these spaces of both/and are not static but dynamic; they prompt us to create more questions rather than to find quick answers. In these spaces of both/and we are called to hold to the many questions and paradoxes of intercultural life.

Furthermore, throughout this dialogue at the well Jesus not only crosses national, cultural, religious, and gender barriers, but he also engages the Samaritan woman in a theological quest through which they reveal to each other their deepest and true identity and call. In John 4:26, Jesus reveals himself for the first time in the Gospel of John as the Messiah, "I am he"—while the Samaritan woman finds herself the source of new life for her own people.

Through the call to ongoing conversion from all forms of ethnocentrism, the Spirit inspires us and moves us toward new spaces of encounter, dialogue, freedom, and mission, where God meets us in God's boundless mystery and countless faces. That is why, when we welcome and befriend difference, intercultural encounters enrich and expand our image of God. Crossing the boundaries of culture is a lengthy process during which misinterpretations will surely be plentiful and expectations—from both sides—can be confused or misrepresented. Sometimes this crossing may not even be welcomed. However, it is through the experience of this cultural expansion that the disciple has a unique opportunity to deepen, clarify, and grow in the vision and commitment to God's kingdom.

THE PARABLE OF THE GOOD SAMARITAN
(LUKE 10:25–37)

Finally, the parable of the Good Samaritan helps us envision the synthesis reached by Jesus in his intercultural journey. Let us see how this conversation between Jesus and a legal expert begins:

Just then a lawyer stood up to test Jesus. "Teacher," he said, "what must I do to inherit eternal life?" He said to him, "What is written in the law? What do you read there?" He answered, "You shall love the Lord your God with all your heart, and with all your soul, and with all your strength, and with all your mind; and your neighbor as yourself." And he said to him, "You have given the right answer; do this, and you will live."

But wanting to justify himself, he asked Jesus, "And who is my neighbor?" (Luke 10:25–29)

Jesus replies to the lawyer's question with the parable of the Good Samaritan. The lawyer's question points to the limits of the circle to whom he owes a love comparable to his love of God and self. It is not a simple question. The scenario for the answer is set in a journey between Jerusalem and Jericho, known to Jesus's audience as a dangerous road. The crux of the parable occurs with the introduction of the Samaritan, who, contrary to the priest and the Levite who were traditionally thought to be righteous, was the only one who responded to the plight of the victim lying on the side of the road. Such a characterization of their cultural enemy must have been a shock for Jesus's audience. Even the lawyer could not bring himself to pronounce the name of such a despised group. When Jesus asked him, "Which of these three, do you think, was a neighbor to the man who fell into the hands of robbers?" his response was, "The *one* who showed him mercy." Jesus then commanded him: "Go and do likewise" (Luke 10:36–37).

Why did Jesus choose these characters to answer the lawyer's question? Reading the parable with intercultural lenses, the lawyer was expecting clear guidelines that would clarify the limits of identity, belonging, and solidarity within his group. However, Jesus reversed the terms of his question and challenged his location, his religious worldview, and the context from which the lawyer was asking the question. With the parable Jesus dared him to cross the boundaries of his privileged position and follow a countercultural logic.

Instead of reinforcing religious, cultural, and national boundaries by carefully delimiting the category of neighbor, Jesus challenged the lawyer and drew his attention to the victims of the system, the excluded ones. What made them invisible to the system? Moreover, what kind of religious rationalizations prevented a compassionate response from the Temple officials? These questions refer to issues so ingrained in cultures that they are very difficult to see by insiders, whether out of plain fear or due to the blind spots that every culture has. Jesus then presents the Samaritan, one of the them/strangers group, as the example to be imitated. Implied in the story is a crucial clue that the lawyer did not miss: it was compassion that made the Samaritan's boundary-crossing possible.

The eyes of the other broaden our vision and enable us to see what our cultural lenses—the system in which we grew up, our stereotypes, our patriarchal and postcolonial prejudices, and so forth—hide from us. Intercultural sensitivity and prophetic commitment to the victims of our cultural stratification go hand in hand.

CONCLUDING COMMENTS

Jesus's mission to the outcasts of his society was clear from the start. However, it was in the encounter with the stranger, such as the Samaritan woman at the well or the Canaanite woman, that Jesus was challenged to clarify and expand his own identity and, therefore, his vision of God's kingdom. Both encounters initiated a confrontation and a dialogue that led Jesus and, in these cases, the two women, to change and grow beyond their own boundaries.

We see similar encounters experienced by the first Christians, as told in Acts: Philip and the Ethiopian (8:26–40); Ananias and Paul (9:10–19); and Peter and Cornelius (10:1–49). Only when the nascent church was finally convinced that "God shows no partiality, but in every nation anyone who fears him and does what is right is acceptable to him" (10:34), did the history of the Christian community emerge with all the strength and vitality of the Holy Spirit.

The option to be open to encounter the stranger, however, is not a one-time option. It was not so for the church (not even in Acts), and it is not so for the individual disciple either. It is at the same time a radical option and a gradual process. But today it is an option that cannot be delayed. As Anthony Gittins puts it, it is the option that transforms us into true Jesus's disciples:

> Because humanity has become so scandalously separated and opposed, we (individually and corporately) must make a choice. Either we choose to continue sinning—by exclusion, separation, and boundary maintenance—and every day eat and drink judgment to ourselves; or we resolve, today, to embrace God's radical option for humanity, and—with God's help and our steadfastness—to change our lives. There is no third way. This is what [intercultural] discipleship entails.[2]

The future of humanity, our congregations, and the church may depend on this intercultural discipleship. It is only when we dare move outward, to the margins and the stranger, that we will truly discover who we are and what we are called to be as disciples of Jesus in mission. In the encounter, as illustrated in the parable of the Good Samaritan, both persons meet in a new place: the place of God's compassion for all. At the radically inclusive and egalitarian table of God's kingdom it is the disciples' challenge to move outward, making themselves neighbors. However, it is their privilege and grace to be received as neighbors when their boundary crossing makes them strangers in other people's situations or lands. As with the road between Jericho and Jerusalem, it is a dangerous but life-changing journey.

---

[2] Anthony J. Gittins, *Called to Be Sent: Co-Missioned as Disciples Today* (Liguori, MO: Liguori Publications, 2008), 13.

6

An Intercultural Spirituality

Dancing to the Rhythm of the Spirit

Jung Eun Sophia Park, SNJM

In the Catholic faith the Holy Spirit is the driving force behind the church. It guides us into full commitment to gospel values, in general, as well as our congregational charism, in particular. This charism is always on the move, constructing our identity as religious men and women. It is never static; the Holy Spirit shapes, urges, challenges, and transforms us. Each community carries founding stories filled with the actions of the Holy Spirit. Thus, religious life and charism must be understood within the frame of the movement of the Holy Spirit.

Each congregation has its own unique charism that is expressed in a distinct way. The charism of each congregation, which functions as a unifying force, contributes to the beauty of the church as the body of Christ, through its diverse gifts. However, it is remarkable that even the same charism implanted in different cultures is always differently expressed and appropriated. If we only emphasize the unifying force, out of a fear of losing control, we could suppress the movement of the Holy Spirit. On the other hand, if we emphasize only its extension, we might lose the charism itself. We must hold the tension between the unifying force and the diversifying force within the dynamic of the Holy Spirit.

Thus, it is crucial to understand the direction of the Holy Spirit in a discerning manner. The Holy Spirit visits our souls as a guest, mending problems that impede our journey to the unknown by washing, bending, melting, and guiding us. It is the Holy Spirit who sheds light in the midst of darkness and provides comfort in the middle of confusion. It is not hard to imagine that all Christians who stand on the edge of newness and at moments of transition seek the Holy Spirit.

Regarding religious life in the United States, we face—either nervously or excitedly—a new reality that fosters intercultural living. This chapter addresses this reality, in relation to the movement of the Holy Spirit. First, I briefly examine the immigration history in the United States and explore the multicultural, cross-cultural, and intercultural dimensions of living in today's society. Next, I read chosen pericopes of the Acts of the Apostles as a text that reflects the process of intercultural living in the early Christian community, highlighting the movement of the Holy Spirit. Finally, I propose a spirituality of intercultural living.

A BRIEF IMMIGRATION HISTORY IN THE UNITED STATES

Throughout US history, we can see how immigration policies influenced the understandings of race and culture in religious life. There are distinct differences among the waves of immigration: the first (1790–1820) and second (1820–60) waves were composed mainly of Western European immigrants, while the third (1880–1924) and fourth (1965–present) include non-Western Europeans as well as many Asian and Latin American immigrants.

The First and Second Waves of Immigration

In the first period of immigration (1790–1820) nationalization was limited to those already residing in the United States.

> The first statute in the United States to codify naturalization law ... the Naturalization Act of 1790 restricted citizenship to "any alien, being a free white person" who had been in the United States for two years. In effect, it left out indentured

servants, African slaves, and most women. This implied that black and, later, Asian immigrants were not eligible to be naturalized.[1]

In this environment we can see white supremacy at work, re-pressing the voice of non-white residents. Along with the first twelve Ursuline sisters, who arrived from France in 1727, women religious from various communities from Western Europe began to work in the United States, often in full habits.[2] These early homogenous communities maintained a white ethnicity.

The second wave (1820–60) was composed of immigrants from Northern and Western Europe—countries such as Germany, England, Switzerland, Scotland, and Ireland—who were com-ing for economic reasons. With the arrival of the Irish, by 1850 Catholicism had become the largest Christian denomination in the United States. Many religious congregations then emigrated from their home countries to serve these European immigrants and paved the way for American Catholicism through their work in education and healthcare. As much as the European immigrants were forced to assimilate to the American way of life, so too were these immigrant religious communities. In this way US congregations were congruent with American culture, and this situation was solidified through the joining of new American members.[3]

We know from the chronicles of immigrant religious com-munities that they made the decision not to pray in their native tongues. For example, the Sacred Blood Sisters, who came from Switzerland for mission in the nineteenth century, gave up speak-ing German as a way to assimilate with US culture and the church. This situation mirrors the immigration policy of the United States, in which all immigrants were supposed to speak English and were discouraged from keeping their culture.

---

[1] Shiho Imai, "Naturalization Act of 1789," Densho Encyclopedia, encyclopeida.densho.org.

[2] Jung Eun Sophia Park, "Religious Life in the US: A Vocation of Border Crossing," *New Theology Review* 27, no. 1 (September 2014): 51–52.

[3] Ibid.

The Third and Fourth Waves of Immigration

The third wave of immigration (1880–1924) was deeply related to the rapid urbanization and industrialization of the United States at the time, and the largest groups of immigrants were Central, Eastern, and Southern Europeans, including Italians. Legislation against Asian immigration, such as the Chinese Exclusion Act (1882) and the National Origins Act (1924), was passed, prohibiting Chinese students and Chinese wives of US citizens from entry, thereby applying an uneven quota system between Europeans and non-Europeans.

During this time most religious congregations became predominantly "Americans only" communities in which the segregation laws were applied. However, some sisters wanted to serve the growing population of African American enslaved persons. Mother Mary Elizabeth Lange and Saint Katharine Drexel each founded an order specifically to help African Americans. Mother Mary Elizabeth Lange, who was a French-speaking Creole from Haiti with a partially Jewish heritage, struggled with her own hybrid ethnic identity. From this struggle she tried to form her own order of Catholic sisters with women of color who would educate impoverished people of color. Thus, the first African American religious community, the Oblate Sisters of Providence, was founded in 1882.[4]

In 1917, the Code of Canon Law limited women religious ministries to suburban schools and parishes. Many Catholic girls from the parochial schools entered congregations where sisters taught, and these communities experienced rapid growth in numbers.

The fourth wave of immigration (1965–present) began with the Immigration and Nationality Act, which allowed immigration from beyond European countries. As a result, Asians and Latin Americans successfully came to the United States, although Mexicans had a different history of immigration.[5] NPR journalist

---

[4] John Fialka, *Sisters: Catholic Nuns and the Making of America* (New York: St. Martin's Press, 2003), 7, 9, 107–8.

[5] The history of Mexican Americans in the United States began with the annexation of parts of Mexico in 1848. Approximately eighteen thousand became citizens and, although they mainly stayed in the Southwest, they kept their identity, struggling with equality and fairness. Large numbers of Mexicans moved into the United States during the Mexican Civil War in the 1910s, and in recent years many Mexicans have crossed the border seeking economic benefits and security.

Jennifer Ludden notes that the 1965 immigration law significantly shifted the composition of the US population.[6] By the 1980s, Europeans had decreased to only 10 percent, while Asians had become one-third of all immigrants, and Mexicans were a whopping 50 percent.[7] After the Second Vatican Council, women religious began boldly to serve minority groups, including Native Americans and poor African Americans in urban areas, yet through it all each community maintained its own homogenous identity.

During the wave of immigration in the latter part of the twentieth century, many new immigrants carried their native cultures with them, and the range of these cultures became more diverse. Chinatown is an example of how Asian immigrants protected their ways of living, despite discriminatory immigration policies against non-Europeans. This movement of immigrants bringing their cultures into hosting countries has been accelerated by globalization.

Globalization in the twentieth century stressed mass immigration, leading to border crossings on a grand scale. Currently, any congregation that has new members will recognize that most of them are from non-European countries and that they carry their own distinct cultures. This reality emphasizes the importance of encountering the "other" and has become an internal matter regarding the constituency of the community rather than external missionary activities.

In apostolic religious life mission is one of the most important aspects in defining the identity of religious women and men, and the interpretation of the word *mission* has shaped the ways of living out our charism. The classical term *mission,* which is derived from *missio,* implies an action to send out—*ad gentes.* Now *mission* is more often perceived as "being a missionary" who attempts to live out gospel values rather than having mission tasks and going out to meet the other. This new approach emphasizes mission as an inner mode or orientation toward mission rather than as tasks to perform.

Robert Schreiter, a professor at Catholic Theological Union, argues that in our current global era national boundaries have

---

[6] Jennifer Ludden, "1965 Immigration Law Changed Face of America," NPR, May 9, 2006.

[7] Alden Analytics, "Waves of Immigration in America," Preceden, preceden.com.

blurred and the notion of people's identity being based on geography has lost much of its meaning. In this climate, he suggests, the notion of *ad gentes* should be replaced with that of *ad extra*—simply going outside of one's framework—as well as that of *ad altera*—emphasizing going to the other.[8] Thus, today's mission is to live the gospel values, focusing on leaving our own framework, *ad extra,* and encountering the other, *ad altera.* Both *ad extra* and *ad altera* indicate an interior journey rather than an exterior one *(ad gentes).* This new understanding could be well applied to the congregations in the United States.

INTERCULTURAL DYNAMICS

Regarding a new perspective toward the other, it is useful to understand the characteristics of being multicultural, cross-cultural, and intercultural as a process of encountering the other. Here, the dynamics are examined analogously in relation to the movement of the Holy Spirit.

Being Intercultural as a Process toward the Other

Today we talk about interculturality with a deep sense of fear, along with a sense of excitement, because it might require a loss of order, power, and independence—letting go of the old ways and bravely inviting new ones. By nature, human beings seek stable meanings of the self, the world, and God, although no such stable meanings exist. In communication there is a signifier that indicates the meaning, or the signified. Psychoanalysis theorist Jacques Lacan states that the signifier fails to deliver the intended meaning, or the signified.[9] Actually, very often, the signifier refers to another signifier, and the meaning is just deferred. The meaning could instead emerge through the process of referring by approximation. In the same vein, culture—as a system

---

[8] Robert Schreiter, "Challenges Today to Mission *Ad Gentes,*" paper presented at the meeting of the Superior General of Societies of Apostolic Life, Maryknoll, New York, May 1, 2000.

[9] See Jacques Lacan, *Écrits: A Selection* (London: W. W. Norton, 1997).

of language—is so elusive that it is inappropriate to define it as a set way of living. As such, culture is an ongoing process and an organic system that include referring, deferring, and transferring, and through this process, only approximate meaning can be constructed. Through the whole history of human society there have been no eras with only a single monolithic culture. Instead, we have had various subcultures in which each cultural norm fights for acceptance. There may be a hidden curriculum, which is the process by which the dominant cultural values and attitudes are informally transmitted and found in rules, routines, and regulations.[10] The subcultures involve generations, ethnicity, gender, race, political view, education, and so forth.

This analysis of cultural dynamics provides a clue to understanding religious life in the United States today. For example, in women's religious communities the gap between younger and older generations is wide and a cause of discomfort and tension. Also, a high percentage of newer members come from other cultures, which also intensifies the generational tension. A set of subcultures carries distinct ways of decision making and modes of communication aside from language.[11] In each religious community one must identify the norm of the community and its assumed way of living. For example, is the way of running the meeting comfortable for you? How about for other members?

Multicultural, Cross-Cultural, and Intercultural Living

Although the terms *multicultural*, *cross-cultural*, and *intercultural* are often used interchangeably, their respective meanings carry distinct characteristics. The term *multicultural* signifies that society acknowledges the existence of the other, those who are different from my own culture. For example, in the small city where I live, there is both a Buddhist temple and an Islamic mosque in proximity to a Catholic parish. But the multicultural approach does not force cultures or religions to interact; by holding onto

---

[10] Diana Kendall, *Race, Class, and Gender in a Diverse Society* (Boston: Allyn and Bacon, 1997), 145.

[11] Leo Parvis, *Understanding Cultural Diversity in Today's Complex World* (New York: Lulu Press, 2005), 9.

one's own values, lifestyle, and mission, there might be no serious attempt at engagement with others. However, it is almost impossible to not engage with people from other cultures or to keep from acknowledging the other. Acknowledging differences is the first step toward accepting those differences and breaking the myth of the so-called melting pot.

The next process involves facing cross-cultural realities. The term *cross-cultural* emphasizes the notion of engagement and necessitates the crossing of one's own boundaries. It creates a borderland—a liminal space—in which one does not belong to a certain culture but does not belong to the other culture either. This may lead to the creation of a new culture, something which the postcolonial theorist Homi Bhabha describes as a "third culture," an alternative and new space created by the crossing of different cultures.[12] In the borderland, people suffer from a loss of belonging, certainty, and security, yet they also enjoy a great opportunity to be transformed. Chicana feminist Gloria Anzaldúa, who claimed her own identity as a borderlander in her seminal work *Borderlands/La Frontera,* emphasizes the power of being hybrid, which confers a freedom to create one's life destiny and overcome one's weakness by choosing new cultural elements.[13]

As a consequence of border crossing, the intercultural dimension emerges. This intercultural living pushes one into the unknown future, to take an evolutionary leap, to be open to mutual enrichment among cultures. It would be helpful to think about where your community is located on this cultural map. As a group, is your congregation in the multicultural stage, the cross-cultural stage, or the intercultural stage? This process can be judged by the level of *ad extra* and *ad altera*—how easily can you leave your own framework and embrace the other?

---

[12] Homi Bhabha, *The Location of Culture* (New York: Routledge, 1997), 37. Drawing on Frederic Jameson's notion of the "third space," Bhabha writes, "The non-synchronous temporality of global and national cultures opens up a cultural space—a third space—where the negotiation of incommensurable differences creates a tension peculiar to borderline existences" (217).

[13] See Gloria Anzaldúa, *Borderlands/La Frontera: New Mestiza* (San Francisco: Aunt Lute Books, 1987).

A READING OF ACTS AS MULTIFOCAL DRAMA

To demonstrate an intercultural mode of living, I read the Acts of the Apostles. Acts was often seen as one of the most important texts for missionaries. But surprisingly, the preferred, externally focused way of reading Acts was an invention of the nineteenth and twentieth centuries, and a reflection of Western missionary zeal—*ad gentes*. Ancient and medieval texts do not emphasize missionary work—the idea that Acts is made up of Paul's "three missionary journeys" is "the creation of the modern missionary movement."[14] Biblical scholar Benny Liew states that Acts has two parts: (1) a sketch of the formation of the Christ(ian) community, focusing on community integration, and (2) the community's evangelization to various people.[15] The first part provides data for the Jerusalem Council, which proclaims Gentile entry into the church (Acts 15). Since the experience of Pentecost the early Christian community had evolved into a Gentile church from a Jewish religious sect. The Acts of the Apostles reveals the intercultural dynamics undergirding both *ad altera* and *ad extra* movements, and thus it provides a model for twenty-first-century religious life. In the text the Holy Spirit often extends beyond geo-cultural categories and breaks through the old ways to create a new paradigm.

I am limiting my study here to Acts 1—11 as a literary unit that reveals the episodes of the expanding movement of the Holy Spirit, an eruption of Spirit-inspired, prophetic border-crossing activity.[16] The early Christian movement is a good example of conspiracy. The word *conspire* is made by combining the Latin terms *con* (with) and *spirare* (breathe). Therefore, although the word

---

[14] Justo L. Gonzalez, *Acts: The Gospel of the Spirit* (Maryknoll, NY: Orbis Books, 2001), 152.

[15] Benny Tat-siong Liew, "Acts," in *Global Bible Commentary*, ed. Daniel Patte (Nashville: Abingdon Press, 2004), 419–28.

[16] Robert P. Menzies, "The Development of Early Christian Pneumatology: With Special Reference to Luke–Acts," *Journal for the Study of the New Testament*, Supplement Series 54 (Sheffield: JSOT Press, 1991), 244. Although Robert Menzies emphasizes mission, I read it as referring broadly to prophetic mission rather than to being a missionary in prophetic mission.

conspire has a negative connotation today, its original meaning suggested that everyone breathed the Spirit together and convened something that perhaps has not yet reached legal status. When Christianity emerged, it would have been a conspiring adventure against the norms of Jewish law, possibly even against Roman rule, through the practice of negotiating and confronting, in order to proclaim the availability of the Holy Spirit to everyone.

My chosen pericope does not pay attention to just one or two main characters. Instead, many bright stars appear and disappear on stage. The whole mood of the narrative is quite busy, and the rapid pace gives readers a vivid sense of movement and action rather than of position and authority. I read this text by examining the multiple foci of the setting through which the narrative negates the notion of the center and affirms the margin, or the periphery. The focal point moves quickly and continuously—wherever the Holy Spirit is, that space becomes the center, and in this way, the narrative has multiple centers, implying an anticolonial perspective.[17] The center could be Jerusalem, or Antioch, and so on. Let me, then, illustrate the three focal points that suggest multicultural, cross-cultural, and intercultural characteristics.

The First Focal Point: Multicultural Movement

The first focal point (Acts 2:1–11) that indicates a multicultural setting features the Pentecostal experience in Jerusalem, which has theological importance in the Gospel of Luke. It is clear that, although the narrative is still cognizant of the Jewishness of the disciples, it has little interest in either advocating for or annihilating any particular character. Rather, the narrative emphasizes the freedom of the Holy Spirit, just as the church needed to adjust to the Holy Spirit, to be ready to be newly shaped. There is a great amount of surprise and joy in this text.

In this focal point the central figures are Peter and the other apostles who are Galilean Jews, as well as very devoted diaspora Jews from other nations, *ex gentes*. Here they experience *ad extra*

---

[17] See David Pao, "Acts and the Isaianic New Exodus," *WUANT* 2, no. 130 (Tübingen: Mohr Siebeck, 2000).

movements as they go beyond their own frameworks or assumptions. In the Acts of the Apostles, when the apostles experience the Holy Spirit being poured into them, they gain the confidence to express themselves regarding their faith in Jesus as Christ.

When the Holy Spirit comes down to the apostles, the text says, "all of them were filled with the Holy Spirit and began to speak in other languages, as the Spirit gave them ability" (Acts 2:4). We could call this event the gift of speech, or the gift of language, but I argue that it should be called the gift of communication. One could assume, in a theory of communication, that there is a sender and a receiver, and that the communication itself occurs when the message is delivered. But if there is no recipient of the message, the sender would not be able to deliver it, and thus there would be no communication. After describing the apostles as the senders in this drama, the narrative introduces the diaspora Jews as the receivers by saying, "Now there were devout Jews from every nation under heaven living in Jerusalem. And at this sound the crowd gathered and was bewildered, because each one heard them speaking in the native language of each" (2:5–6). Here the narrative signifies that genuine communication must have occurred, although we as readers do not know the exact message. And as biblical scholar Graham Twelftree claims, at this moment the miracle lies in the *act of hearing* rather than in the nature of speaking,[18] that is, in the receptivity. And from this story we can imagine the early Christian community as one in which even minority members, such as Greek-speaking Jews in Jerusalem, could freely express themselves and fully participate in the action of communication. This gift of Pentecost is thus the beginning of the multicultural dimension of the church.

However, some of the native speakers in Jerusalem, likely due to their biases against different tongues, languages, and cultures, were not receptive and attributed the vocalizations of the apostles to too much wine (2:13). In religious communities, certain voices or expressions may be ignored or considered less important because their native language is not English. The text, however, only briefly mentions the negative reaction of the audience members who could not perceive the work of the

---

[18] Graham H. Twelftree, *People of the Spirit: Exploring Luke's View of the Church* (Grand Rapids, MI: Baker Academic, 2009), 73.

Holy Spirit. Rather, the interest is given to the Jesus movement, which unfolds dramatically.

The Second Focal Point:
Cross-Cultural Movement

The second focal point (Acts 8:26–40) shows a cross-cultural engagement in the scene of the Ethiopian eunuch official's baptism. With its characteristics of *ad altera*, which stresses intersection and encounter, this episode happens on the road. In the biblical narrative many spiritual transformations occur on the way. This focal point is deeply related to two episodes earlier in Acts: the election of seven Greek-speaking leaders (6:3–5) and Stephen's martyrdom (7:57–60). First, in Acts 6, the narrator explains how the new small community created in Jerusalem is growing bigger and becoming multicultural as Hellenist Jews of the Greek-speaking diaspora have begun to join the collective.

Multicultural living then evolves into cross-cultural living, which inevitably results in tension and conflict. For example, the need to elect the seven Greek-speaking leaders arose from complaints among Hellenist widows regarding the distribution of bread. However, in light of the Acts of the Apostles, the challenge of pluralism in the church is not the work of the Hellenist Jews but rather of the Holy Spirit of God. The narrative shows no hesitation in addressing this problem, emphasizing that the church is a community of people representing different cultures, because inclusivity is the work and the purpose of the Holy Spirit.[19] In Acts, mission is equivalent to and dependent on the quality of the community of believers, and the narrator explains that the fruit of mission is the increase in numbers. If the church had not facilitated inclusivity, the church could hardly have accommodated those who desired to belong.

As a resolution to the tension of living the mission of *ad altera*, the narrative tells readers that the church has decided to elect seven leaders to handle the distribution of food to the Greek-speaking

---

[19] Gonzalez, *Acts*, 92.

widows, while the apostles focus on prayer and serving the word.[20] This decision was well intended but still biased against the others: *we*, the twelve apostles, do the important work, and *you*, the others, do the minor work. However, in the second scene the narrative (6:12) introduces an ironic situation in which Stephen, one of the seven Greek-speaking others, gives a speech, something that is the responsibility of Jewish leaders, that leads him into martyrdom. As a reader it is a surprise to see these blurred ministerial boundaries between the Jewish and Greek leaders.

Finally, as another example of *ad altera* (going to the other), the narrative introduces the story of Philip's mission. In the early part of Acts 8 the narrative describes Philip journeying to Samaria, with Peter and John supervising his mission from Jerusalem. The narrative continues with Philip being given freedom and authority by the Holy Spirit. He even baptizes the foreigner who was not included because the Jerusalem community had not yet decided to accept foreigners. In this way Philip breaks the boundaries of Jewish law and of ethnicity through the total freedom and agency bestowed by the Holy Spirit.

This movement or event indicates the cross-cultural dynamics of *ad altera*, which gave Philip freedom and authority. Philip, who had been included in the leadership circle as the other, extended the mission of *ad altera*. The Ethiopian, who had listened to Philip, states beautifully and evocatively, "Look, here is water! What is to prevent me from being baptized?" (8:37). The role is switched; the action is initiated by the other, and the subject becomes passive. The passivity of Philip is intensified by the narration, "When they came out of the water, the Spirit of the Lord snatched Philip away" (8:39). My interpretation of this passage is that this passivity paradoxically gives Philip authority by emphasizing the power of the Holy Spirit, and the narrative no longer mentions any censorship or supervision by the apostles.

---

[20] Many feminist scholars mention that the narrative describes women only as recipients rather than as active subjects. And indeed, all the elected leaders were males. See Mary Rose D'Angelo, "The ANHP Question in Luke–Acts: Imperial Masculinity and the Deployment of Women in the Early Second Century," in *A Feminist Companion to Luke*, ed. Amy-Jill Levine (New York: Continuum, 2002), 44–69.

This episode shows a border crossing in which the subject becomes the object and the object becomes the subject. Of course, both become submissive to the action of the Holy Spirit. Also, the result of submission to the Holy Spirit is expressed as the bold action of Philip, in which he goes beyond his job description of serving the table and affirms his vocation as missionary. In this liminal space Philip totally listens to the Holy Spirit, discerning himself whether he should baptize the foreigner, yet also giving much of the initiative to the other, the Ethiopian official.

The Third Focal Point:
Intercultural Movement

The third focal point illuminates Peter's encounter of the other in Acts 10. This episode more dramatically manifests mission *ad extra* and *ad altera*. Peter moves beyond his own cultural and faith framework by crossing cultural norms and experiencing otherness. This story constitutes one of the crucial points in the narrative that leads the Jerusalem Council to conclude that the gospel is also for Gentiles.[21]

The plot of the story is complex, with three separate scenes operating as one episode. In the first scene the narrative in 10:1–9a begins with an introduction of not Peter, but of Cornelius, who is a centurion of an Italian cohort in Caesarea. Obviously, Cornelius is a foreigner, an other. By introducing Cornelius, the narrative seems to give the impression that Cornelius is a leading character, rather than Peter, who receives an invitation and struggles against his own framework. The narrative tells us that Cornelius had a vision in which he clearly saw an angel and received a message from God. As a consequence, he sent his people for Peter. In the first segment it is Cornelius and God who interact as subjects, while Peter is the object, the other.

The second scene is located where Peter is living, in Joppa (10:9b–23a). Here Peter enters into a trance in which he sees animals descending from heaven. These animals are prohibited from being eaten, according to the kosher code, but the voice of heaven invites Peter to kill and eat them, affirming that some-

---

[21] Gonzalez, *Acts*, 130.

thing God created as sacred should not be considered profane. Although the narrative does not directly mention the dietary code, it implies that he would break the boundary of the eating code, as a consequence of a cross-cultural encounter. Also, the narrative states that just after Peter experiences his mystical vision, he suddenly encounters strangers. Although Peter is still perplexed by the meaning of the mystical vision, he puts the practice of hospitality above his inner confusion.

In the cross-cultural discourse hospitality is one of the most important concepts. Philosopher Jacques Derrida says that hospitality can only be a poetic action. Often, radical hospitality indicates the level of the exchange of positions between the guest and the host. The hospitality that was the tradition in Hebrew culture implied that hosts took the risk of losing their life.[22] This action of hospitality is an action of the provider, since the receiver does not have to worry about defilement or pollution, and it is a great step toward the other.

The final scene (10:23b–48) includes Peter's encounter with Cornelius and the Gentiles being baptized by the Holy Spirit after they listen to Peter. It is remarkable for Peter to go into the Gentile's house, breaking all kinds of ethnic and cultural boundaries. Peter says that it is unlawful for a Jew to associate with or visit a Gentile, but that God has shown him that he should not call anyone profane or unclean. Here we can see how Peter extends his understanding of his vision from food to people. Of course, sooner or later, he must eat food by staying with them.

In this scene Cornelius is very humble, as if he were the guest, and Peter seems to take the role of the host in giving baptism by water. By visiting Cornelius, Peter becomes a guest. This activity of being a guest brings mutual transformation: Peter eats with the Gentile and breaks the dietary code by eating the food offered and, in so doing, he understands his vision and crosses his own framework of the sacred and profane *(ad extra)*; and Cornelius, as a person who is more free to follow God's will, officially becomes a member of the Christian community.

---

[22] Jacques Derrida, *Of Hospitality: Anne Dufourmantelle Invites Jacques Derrida to Respond* (Stanford, CA: Stanford University Press, 2000), 67.

The third focal point strongly suggests mutual transformation. Through the process of hospitality Peter understands his vision more clearly, while Cornelius affirms this faith and finds new belonging.

AN INTERCULTURAL SPIRITUALITY

I read closely these three focal points in the Acts of the Apostles, paying attention to the movements of *ad altera* and *ad extra*, which manifest various aspects of the border-crossing process. From this reading I can delineate the spiritual disciplines of intercultural dynamics: examining assumptions, active listening, negating the concept of the center, and letting go and letting come. This could be a reflection of how we should live our current intercultural reality.

Examining Assumptions

In intercultural or cross-cultural living many conflicts arise from different assumptions. For mutual transformation it is crucial to examine assumptions as a way of pursuing justice. In encountering the other a major challenge is being aware of our own assumptions. What are our unspoken expectations? Every culture carries certain assumptions that are taken for granted. Unless we examine these assumptions, we can easily misunderstand, misjudge, and blindly force our assumptions onto the other. It is only through engaging with the other, who carries different assumptions and sets of culture, that we can examine our own assumptions. We have to commit ourselves to creating a safe environment to encounter the other and to make mistakes with a discerning spirit. Dissonance and disagreement are driving forces in this process.

Active Listening

Although the Acts of the Apostles is one of the most active and dynamic texts in the Bible, its teaching as a whole is about listening, not about preaching. Pentecost should be understood as a listening event rather than a speaking event. In 2:6, the narrative clearly describes the event as giving all people the freedom to express themselves, and people understood one another. When those who carry a different language and culture—others—express their faith, we should be ready to listen with an open heart. The Acts of the Apostles stresses that people who listened experienced the Holy Spirit.

Also, many characters, such as Peter, Philip, the Ethiopian official, and Cornelius, all listened to the Holy Spirit through prayer as well as through listening to others with an open heart. Philip listened to the Ethiopian's deep thirst for the truth, and the Ethiopian official listened to Philip. Finally, when the Ethiopian official suggested his own baptism, Philip listened to him and followed him. Similarly, Peter listened carefully to what Cornelius said to him as the voice of God, even though Cornelius was the other.

In fact, in Christian spirituality active listening is one of the most fundamental principles in being transformed through God's grace. Contemplation does not mean just being silent, but rather being open-minded toward others, leaving out one's own understanding. The skill of listening is to surrender to God, in the spirit of obedience. Listening to others and to oneself is a prerequisite for intercultural spirituality, based on mission *ad altera* and *ad extra*.

Negating Concept of Center

As I indicated, the whole narrative of the Acts of the Apostles lacks any particular center and instead has multiple focal points. These multiple focal points emphasize the decentering force of the Holy Spirit. As a literary strategy for conveying this theme, the whole narrative continuously puts various characters' ethnicity, class, and gender on stage, after which they disappear. Although the narrative begins with Jerusalem as the center, it does not keep this community as the permanent center. Rather, the narrative conveys the meaning that any place where the Holy Spirit acts is the center. Thus, the concept of the center does not belong to any geopolitical territory but is rather a space where people experience the Holy Spirit. As a consequence, they then move out toward others.

Therefore, we can say both that the center is plural, and the periphery can easily become the center. The literary tool of multiple focal points in Acts suggests that intercultural living can negate all notions of the center and admit any periphery as one of the centers. Dissonance and difference are fully acknowledged, and networking among the communities is strongly recommended in any multi-centered community living.

Letting Go, Letting Come

In reading the Acts of the Apostles through the lens of mission toward others and from our own framework, we can find the freedom to let go of the past and let come a new reality. Under the guidance of the Holy Spirit, Philip had to let go of his own ministry of serving the table and let come the new ministry of preaching and baptizing Gentiles. Very often people emphasize the importance of letting go as a way of gaining freedom, but the act is incomplete unless there is letting come. To accept new members from other cultures can be a letting go of the old ways of the congregation, operated in the North American way. With that, let come can be an invitation to struggle for an alternative way of living as a congregation, guided by the Holy Spirit.

During the letting go stage, conflicts, dissonance, and discomfort will be part of the process. However, we will be safe as long as we listen to the Holy Spirit, and to others, as well as to ourselves—figuring out any unarticulated assumptions by sharing and making mistakes. Then we will gain a glimpse of the future to which the Holy Spirit will guide us. Now, shall we dance?

7

Reconciling Presence and the Sounds of Silence

Robert J. Schreiter, CPPS

In what follows I explore two interrelated themes. The first theme involves understanding consecrated life as a reconciling presence, both in its forms of community living and in its apostolic ministries. The second theme is the ways of understanding silence in intercultural communication. At first sight these two themes may seem to be unrelated. But I hope to show that there are points of interconnection. A ministry of reconciling presence is particularly sensitive to the fissures and fragments that emerge among those who are suffering and who live under repressive circumstances. Understanding silence within the framework of intercultural communication also has to do with pauses, interruptions, and an inability to articulate what people have been experiencing. Both the ministry of reconciliation and intercultural communication have to deal with silences that can arise from deep pain, but also from awe.

The first part of this chapter deals with the Christian understanding of reconciliation and the spirituality that underlies its practices. The second part turns to the different realms of silence in intercultural communication as silence relates to those neuralgic points in the healing processes of reconciliation that call out for both respect and response.

UNDERSTANDING CHRISTIAN RECONCILIATION
AS A RECONCILING PRESENCE

In the explorations of consecrated life that have appeared in recent years, the intersection of living in consecrated life and the Christian ministry of reconciliation has gained special attention. For religious institutes that are primarily apostolic in their charism, how one should interpret and engage the world have been of special significance. The growth of interest in reconciliation over the past thirty years has proven to be an especially fertile field for exploration and cultivation of ways of living out institutional charisms.

The Rebirth of Christian Understandings of Reconciliation

Reconciliation is, of course, both an ancient and a central theme in Christian faith. In the scriptures it is lifted up especially by the apostle Paul in his writings—so much so that I have called his interpretation of the good news the Gospel of Reconciliation.[1] The narrative of God's having created the world as something good, that human beings have alienated themselves from God, and that God has chosen to reconcile the world to God's own self through the death and resurrection of God's own Son is for Christians the central story of God's action in the world (cf. Rom 5:1–11). The message and ministry of reconciliation have in turn been entrusted to the followers of Jesus to carry out in a broken and alienated world (2 Cor 5:17–20).

This ancient and central theme of Christian faith has shaped the church's self-understanding and ministry throughout history, seeking the conversion of human beings and their incorporation into the church, as well as their forgiveness when they have sinned. It has also inspired much of the church's caritative activity toward those who are poor and marginalized in their societies and are seeking justice and genuine human flourishing. The theme of

---

[1] See Robert Schreiter, "St. Paul's Vision of Reconciliation," *Origins* 38 (April 30, 2009): 725–32.

reconciliation, however, has taken on a new significance in the past thirty years as the world has experienced wrenching political change, revelation of grave injustice, and now threats to the very survival of the planet itself. On the religious front this has reopened reflection on the theme of reconciliation and Christian practices to foster not only humans' reconciliation with God (sometimes called vertical reconciliation) but also reconciliation among individuals, societies, and threatened creation itself (horizontal reconciliation).

Emerging from this renewed thinking about reconciliation, a set of five axioms can be proposed that shape the Christian ministry of reconciliation:

First, *God is the author of true reconciliation. Christians are called to participate in God's work.* The complexity of wrongdoing and its devastating effects on human life are such that only God has the breadth and depth of view to grasp the extent of wrongdoing and its possible resolution. Christians are called upon to carry out the work of reconciliation as agents of God's action. To do this effectively requires a deep spiritual communion with God, since what needs to be done usually far exceeds what any individual or group can achieve. Effective spiritual practices nurture and sustain Christians' work of reconciliation; chief among these is contemplative prayer—prayer that depends upon God speaking to us rather than our addressing God.

Second, *God begins the reconciling process with the healing of the victim.* Common sense would indicate that reconciliation should focus on changing the wrongdoers, on bringing them to repentance and conversion. True as this may be, most often the wrongdoers do not repent. Where does this leave the victim? Is the victim to be held hostage to the wrongdoing of the past forever? Christians believe that God can begin the healing of the victim—a restoration of the victim's humanity that has been wrested away by injustice—without the agency of the wrongdoer. This is consistent with the biblical understanding of a God who is on the side of the poor, the orphaned and the widowed, the prisoner, and the alien.

Third, *in reconciliation both victim and wrongdoer become a "new creation."* This means that reconciliation does not restore victims and wrongdoers to some original state before the transgression. They are brought to a new place, one that includes healed memories of the past and the prospects of coming together once again.

Fourth, *the work of reconciliation requires dealing with the redemption of suffering.* Suffering in itself does not make us better persons; rather, it degrades us and isolates us. Suffering can only be endured if the story of our suffering can be included in a larger narrative of purpose. For Christians, that narrative is the story of the suffering, death, and resurrection of Jesus, who entered into our suffering world even though he did not deserve to suffer.

Fifth, *the work of reconciliation in the world will only be complete when the Lord returns at the end of time, so that "God may be all in all" (1 Cor 15:28).* Every effort at reconciliation remains incomplete because of its being embedded in dense networks of human relationships that cannot be untangled easily. Consequently, Christians look to the consummation of all things in Christ as the moment when full reconciliation will take place. In the meantime, Christians cultivate hope in God's work and celebrate the "small victories" along the way that mark movement toward that final reconciliation.[2]

In sum, the Christian vision of reconciliation is about becoming a "new creation" (2 Cor 5:17), living in the promise given by God to the world in the resurrection of Jesus. This vision is in the first instance a spirituality, that is, a way of living and engaging the world from the perspective of what God is doing to heal a broken world. Strategies are necessary for this healing process, which involves the healing of memories, the pursuit of justice, and the challenge of forgiveness; however, no set of strategies is applicable to every situation calling out for healing and reconciliation. The cultivation of this spirituality requires a deep communion with God, one marked especially by contemplative practices that acknowledge our dependence upon God's action, but also reinforce our capacity to listen to the stories of suffering and build deeper solidarity with victims.

---

[2] These axioms are worked out in more detail in Robert Schreiter, *The Ministry of Reconciliation: Spirituality and Strategies* (Maryknoll, NY: Orbis Books, 1998).

Reconciling Practices: Healing Circles and Building Relationships

What then does this vision of reconciliation mean concretely for the work of reconciliation? It means, first of all, forthrightly continuing to deal with the brokenness of the world in all its myriad forms, from the lives of individuals to the suffering of whole societies. The work of reconciliation can be construed as having four moments: (1) the healing of memories, (2) truth telling, (3) the pursuit of justice, and (4) paths toward forgiveness. There is something of a sequence to these moments, but in reality working at each of these moments calls for visiting the other moments again and again.[3]

Healing of memories has to do with how victims tell the story of what happened to them. This often involves making a coherent narrative out of fragments of suffering and trauma. A sign that a memory is healing is that it no longer holds the victim hostage to what has happened but allows the human dignity and integrity of the victim to be restored.

Truth telling requires overcoming cultures of lies about what happened in the past and cultures of silence that suppress the truth of events. It also involves not only getting the facts correct, but also exploring the meaning of the events and what they mean for victims and wrongdoers now. Truth telling is a prerequisite for pursuing justice, so that "justice" does not become simply revenge.

Pursuing justice involves the punishment of wrongdoers, the restoration of the lives of victims, and making social and structural changes that will impede the injustices of the past from happening again.

Paths to forgiveness are itineraries into the future. Without forgiveness, the rancor of the past can undo efforts to make a different kind of society. In his "2004 Message for the World Day of Peace," Pope John Paul II famously said that justice and

---

[3] These are worked out in more detail in Robert Schreiter, "The Emergence of Reconciliation as a Paradigm of Mission: Dimensions, Levels, Characteristics," in *Mission as Ministry of Reconciliation*, ed. Robert Schreiter and Knud Jorgensen, 9–29 (Oxford: Regnum Books International, 2013).

forgiveness are the two pillars upon which peace is developed. In a similar fashion Archbishop Desmond Tutu said incisively, "There is no future without forgiveness."[4]

These practices of reconciliation must be anchored firmly in the spirituality of reconciliation. There are two enduring features that make these practices of reconciliation possible and feasible. These are creating new social spaces and building relationships.

Reconciliation is in one way a paradoxical activity. Essentially, it tries to bring the past into the present in order that it may be transformed into something new. This is, of course, at one level impossible. We cannot go back in time, nor can we undo the past. This is most evident in facing those who died under the weight of oppression and injustice; we cannot bring back the dead. What we are able to do is enter into a certain kind of social space shaped by ritual and the rules of ritual behavior. Within this space we can revisit the past, at least obliquely, and create a different relationship between the past and the present. These spaces go by such names as healing circles or listening circles. They are called circles because they represent a gathering of people who, as equals, strive to listen to the stories of those who are victims and to work together toward healing the past.[5]

Two principles govern behavior within healing circles: they must be *safe* and *hospitable*. Safety is ensured by two guiding rules: (1) whatever is said in these circles must remain in the circle—no one may speak of what he or she has heard outside the circle without the permission of the one who has spoken it; and (2) people from the circle may not speak together about what they have heard beyond the circle without the explicit permission of the one who has spoken. Safety is extremely important because the need for healing and reconciliation arises from profound breaches of trust. In the hierarchy of human needs, only survival as such

---

[4] *No Future without Forgiveness* (New York: Doubleday, 1999) is the title of Archbishop Tutu's book about the Truth and Reconciliation Commission in South Africa.

[5] Robert Schreiter, "Entering the Healing Circle: The Practices of Reconciliation," in *The Healing Circle: Essays in Cross-Cultural Ministry,* ed. Stephen Bevans, Eleanor Doidge, and Robert Schreiter, 176–88 (Chicago: CCGM Publications, 2000).

is more fundamental to human existence than safety. If persons feel safe, they can become willing to risk trust.

The members of the circle show hospitality by welcoming the contribution and sharing of victims, and they continue to show this welcome in their listening and affirmation of the victims. It is important in this context to recall that gestures of hospitality are culture specific. What this means in intercultural situations is that the hospitality shown must be hospitality the victim understands—not simply the hospitality that the listeners in the circle know how to give. Hospitality in some cultures (such as white US culture) tends to be instrumentalist in nature; it is intended to make a visitor comfortable in the current circumstance. In many collective cultures, on the other hand, an offer of hospitality is a commitment to an ongoing relationship.

In the healing circles of reconciliation the commitment to a relationship is almost always required, since without it, trust cannot be restored. In other words, the participants in the circle must be deemed *"trust worthy"* by victims.

Consecrated Life as Reconciling Presence

Living out the ministry of reconciliation within consecrated life can be understood as a reconciling presence. It must be more than a set of tools that can be brought out to solve a certain problem. It is a presence that becomes a foundation upon which a new set of human relationships can be built. It is a presence among victims that grows out of a contemplative presence before a God who works reconciliation. In the words of German theologian Johann Baptist Metz, it is "a mysticism of open eyes," turned not inward away from the world but rather finding and embracing God in the midst of the stories of human suffering.[6]

Living as a reconciling presence amid the apostolic life of a religious institute requires an acute sensibility to the brokenness of the world around us. It requires an awareness of the gaps, the fragments, and the interstices that grow out of trauma, loss, exclusion, and the sundering of trust. Intercultural living, within

---

[6] Johann Baptist Metz, *Mystik der offenen Augen: Wenn Spiritualität aufbricht* (Freiburg: Herder Verlag, 2011).

religious communities and within their spheres of ministry, can focus on certain aspects of this brokenness. Some of this brokenness comes from sharp fissures in the fabric of human relationships caused by historical forces (such as racism and colonialism). Other forms of interruption and incomprehension arise out of the efforts to communicate effectively in new and unfamiliar situations. For international religious institutes this is where reconciliation practices and the practices of intercultural communication meet. In this increasingly multicultural reality of life within religious institutes, this is equally the case. What makes for a solid spirituality of reconciliation also serves well in addressing the exigencies of intercultural communication that have to negotiate difference and misunderstanding, as well as to build a reverence for otherness.

THE REALMS OF SILENCE

Students of culture and intercultural communication remind us that so much of human communication is nonverbal. It is made up of gestures, facial expressions, tones of voice, and the proxemics of social space.[7] Within the array of all of these forms of nonverbal communication, silence plays a significant role. Given a verbally dense nature of human communication, silence is more than the absence of communication (although it can be that as well). Rather, silence can signal a wide range of communication possibilities: It can mean assent—or dissent—in a verbal situation. It can gesture toward what is not being spoken, what is elusive, or even beyond the reach of words because of its subtlety. Silence can also bespeak a deep sense of familiarity and intimacy that no longer requires words. It can also be a confrontation of exclusion.

Much of the research on intercultural communication has arisen in the West, spurred on initially by the need to create more effective intercultural communication in the business world, and then, later, in educational settings where children and students of different cultural backgrounds worked at learning together. A feature of much of the intercultural communication studied

---

[7] Proxemics is the study of how physical space is organized in communication, such as how close one stands to an interlocutor while speaking and what gestures are considered appropriate.

in these contexts had to do with the effective use of words and gestures. They represented something of the voluble nature of communication in Western (and perhaps one should add colonialist and imperialist) interests.

Communication among some people in oral cultures, and in the great literate cultures of East and South Asia, often places a greater value on silence and on more indirect modes of communication. This sometimes led to a perception by Westerners that such cultures were made up of "inscrutable Orientals" who did not give what were familiar cues to Westerners to understand their patterns of communication. Yet silence can convey many things and reveal a fundamentally different view of the world than the one trumpeted in globalization and the irrepressible expressions of social media.

In what follows I explore three realms of silence that often perplex Westerners. I call them the silence of subordination, silence as a grammar of communication, and the silence of God. All three of these are important for effective intercultural communication in the reconciling presence of consecrated life.

The Silence of Subordination

The silence created by the subordination of individuals or entire peoples is, in effect, a silencing of people's ability to speak. It is interrupted or suppressed speech of marginalized or colonized people, caused by willful exclusionary acts of powerful outsiders. It is an act of power that is in itself violent, inasmuch as it does not respect the human dignity of those who are silenced. Within a culture it can also be a gendered act, as when men suppress the voices of women.

In the work of reconciliation after authoritarian rule, one aspect of truth telling involves uncovering cultures of lies and cultures of silence. Cultures of lies are ideologies propagated by the powerful to justify the oppression of those whom they are marginalizing. A common ideology used in the period of European colonialism was that of the "civilizing mission," whereby conquered peoples were deemed in need of tutelage by their conquerors so as to be liberated from "savagery" or "ignorance." Cultures of silence are developed by the powerful to hide wrongdoing or revelation of what is actually going on. The worldwide struggle with clerical sexual abuse of minors in the Catholic Church has to do with breaking a culture of silence that has protected wrongdoers and their superiors.

Feminist and postcolonial theorists have explored in detail the working of cultures of subjugation and silencing. Subaltern studies in India have been in the forefront of uncovering the silence of subjugation. The term *subaltern,* coined by Italian Marxist philosopher Antonio Gramsci, explores how a people are at once subjugated (thus *sub-*) and made totally other (thus *-altern*). The work of Gayatri Chakravorty Spivak has been pioneering in this regard, showing how patterns of representation and proxy were used in India to silence Indian women and others in the colonial and postcolonial periods.[8]

The silence one encounters among indigenous peoples who have been subjected to colonialism is sometimes such a silence of subordination. It is not uncommon in North America, for example, for indigenous peoples to test settler populations to determine whether they are really willing to listen to indigenous voices by seeing how long settlers will listen before interrupting a native speaker. Indigenous people see settler populations as trying to control discourse and the environment by their endless chatter. To be sure, these indigenous populations often also see silence as a grammar of communication, as will be explored in the next section. At the same time, the silence of subjugation contributes mightily to the "colonized mind" of those who have internalized the ideology of inferiority foisted upon them by colonial rulers.

But the silence of subjugation also functions in highly hierarchical societies—something common among collectivist cultures around the world. Sociologist Geert Hofstede termed these cultures as having "high power-distance," that is, the relative power of agency comes with one's position within the stratification of society. Thus women are subjugated to men, the younger to their

---

[8] Spivak's groundbreaking essay, "Can the Subaltern Speak?" was first presented in 1983 and has gone through a number of editions and expansions. For an oft-cited version of the essay, see Chapter 3 of Spivak's *A Critique of Postcolonial Reason: Toward a History of the Vanishing Present* (Cambridge, MA: Harvard University Press, 1999), 198–311.

elders (in both genders), and strangers to insiders.[9] While high power-distance is most evident in highly stratified societies, it is also at play in any setting where social power is aligned with status and position.

Detecting the silence of subordination is of utmost importance in intercultural communication. As can be seen from the brief description here, it is evident in the aftermath of colonization, and thus of great significance for international religious institutes. As part of a highly hierarchical setting such as the Roman Catholic Church, power-distance issues figure strongly not only between religious institutes and the episcopal structure of the church, but also within religious institutes themselves. A ministry of reconciliation needs to be keenly aware of how the silences of subordination are active in the situations that call out for healing of trauma and brokenness in the world.

Silence as a Grammar of Communication

Silence is not only the result of subjugated speech; it is also an essential part of communication in many cultures throughout the world. Silence is not the absence of communication, but rather a constitutive part of it. This has been most evident in East Asian cultures such as Japan and China. But it is also a fundamental aspect of communication in many indigenous cultures around the world as well.

The Japanese Australian scholar Ikuko Nakane has been one the leading students of the role of silence as part of the grammar of communication itself, especially in Japan and among Japanese emigrants.[10] She notes the importance of the different uses of silence in what Edward Hall has called "high-context" cultures, that is, where much knowledge within the culture is assumed and embedded in the context and so is not communicated to others

---

[9] Geert Hofstede, *Culture's Consequences: Comparing Values, Behaviors, Institutions, and Organizations across Nations,* 2nd ed. (Thousand Oaks, CA: Sage Publications, 2001), 79–143.

[10] See, especially, Ikuko Nakane, *Silence in Intercultural Communication: Perspectives and Performances* (Philadelphia: John Benjamins Publishing, 2007).

by verbal or physical cues.[11] The cultures of Japan and China are prime examples of this, which is what often makes reading communication in those settings particularly difficult for outsiders.

Nakane provides a useful summary of the research on silence by grouping the kinds of silence under four categories. First of all, there are *cognitive* forms of silence, where pauses in speech allow hearers to process what they have heard. Longer pauses correlate with difficult or unfamiliar content that needs to be processed. Second, there are *discursive* forms of silence, which point to what she calls "boundaries of discourse"—the point beyond which language does not convey further or valid information. This is evident in mystical discourse, for example. Third, there are *social* forms of silence that are used to create, maintain, or reduce social distance between interlocutors. These social forms are often quite specific to cultures. Another social form is silence as a form of social control. This is evident in the process of shunning practices in many cultures, where persons to be shunned are treated as though they do not exist. It is also used to render people present as invisible. Another kind of social silence is what Nakane terms "politeness strategies," where silence is introduced in order to save face either for the speaker or for other interlocutors. In cultures where face saving is of prime importance, a special sensitivity to this form of silence is essential. A fourth and final form of silence Nakane calls *affective* silence, which is most evident in the management of strong emotions.[12]

This brief summary cannot explore the ramifications of all these different strategies in the grammar of communication. The meanings of silence, as well as different forms and durations of silence, are deeply embedded in the contexts of a culture. To get to know these forms of silence may require a lifetime of learning for outsiders. Westerners who have gone to work in East Asia have often confronted this reality in their lives and ministries. This can be a daunting challenge, but it is a necessary one to undertake in developing interculturality in religious institutes. I might add that one way for people in US white culture to begin this formidable task may be to come to understand how these patterns of

---

[11] Edward T. Hall, *Beyond Culture* (New York: Random House, 1976), 105–16.

[12] Nakane, *Silence in Intercultural Communication*, 11–15.

communication function in their home culture. Here the work of Deborah Tannen has been particularly useful.[13]

The Silence of God

The third realm of silence that needs to be considered both in a ministry of reconciling presence and intercultural communication might be called the silence of God. It is premised on the awareness of the transcendence of God, which means that it surpasses all forms of human thought and human speech and thus points to more than human finitude. It points rather to a deep "beyond" that is more than the limited capacity of human effort. It represents a qualitatively different realm. Following the theological concept of the analogy of being, the silence of God has similarities to human forms of silence but is greater in its dissimilarity.

In considering the silence of God as it relates to reconciling presence and to intercultural communication, I wish to call to mind here two aspects of that silence. These might be called the absence of God and the divine abyss.

As was noted above in proposing the spirituality of reconciliation, the practice of contemplative prayer opens up a special disposition toward God as the author and end point of reconciliation. In contemplative prayer we do not speak. We wait for God to speak. But as any practitioner of contemplative prayer knows, most often we do not hear God speaking. As we progress in contemplative prayer and move beyond sensory signposts, we come to experience the absence of God. Such absence presents itself in two forms: one, in God as distant and not reachable; and two, in what a world looks like that is utterly devoid of God. The first form is familiar to anyone who has practiced contemplative prayer for some time. It is a kind of pedagogical retreat from reliance on our familiar conceptions of God. It involves what Christian spiritual tradition has called the purgative and illuminative ways. With regard to becoming a

---

[13] Through the years Deborah Tannen has developed a wide range of studies that deal with patterns of speech and silence, but also with gender and generational differences. To begin, one might consult Deborah Tannen, *That's Not What I Meant: How Conversational Style Makes or Breaks Your Relations with Others* (New York: Ballantine Books, 1987).

reconciling presence, it means letting go of how we thought God is or should be acting in a broken situation. It opens up to us a vision of an unredeemed world in all its brokenness and horror. This experience of the absence of God by a minister of reconciliation is important for the minister to be able to enter into closer intimacy with those suffering trauma and acute affliction. By entering the world of those who suffer, the minister is also transformed by being freed from the limited conceptions of a God beyond suffering to a God found in the midst of suffering.

Silence is a prime medium of this experience, since words fail to grasp and deliver meaning in the face of overwhelming suffering and pain. Paradoxically, this sense of the absence of God can become the gateway to a new sense of the presence of God, one that is quite different from what could have been imagined prior to this experience. This experience may not be conveyed adequately by a newfound articulation; it may be found in action, gesture, and embrace. This is the advent of the silence called the boundaries of discourse, as noted above in the summary of Nakane's research on silence.

The second form of the silence of God is an experience of the divine abyss. This is an awareness that before there was divine speech, there was silence. In the first Genesis account of creation we find everything "a formless void" until the speech of God calls forth something else. It is this primordial silence that marks the deepest encounter with God. The world's religious traditions approach this primordial silence that, like an abyss, has no discernible form or limit in itself, but gives new form to those who encounter it. In the Western Christian tradition, metaphors such as the desert (where there are no landmarks of orientation) or the dark night (where darkness obliterates every landmark) are used to describe the experience of this primordial abyss. In exploring the resources for the work of reconciliation, John Paul Lederach has spoken of the limits of the optical metaphors that dominate the landscape of conflict transformation, and he thus calls for a new path through aural metaphors, such as resonance, harmony, and dissidence.[14]

---

[14] John Paul Lederach and Angela Jill Lederach, *When Blood and Bones Cry Out: Journeys through the Soundscape of Healing and Reconciliation* (New York: Oxford University Press, 2010).

It is at the edge of the divine abyss that Christianity and forms of Buddhism may meet each other. In classic Buddhist understanding, true liberation from suffering comes when one reaches the realization that all that one has experienced (including suffering) is illusion. One must enter the realm of *sunyata*, or nothingness. For Western scholars who have approached the practice of Zen Buddhism, this experience of nothingness comes close to the experience of God, and a number of Western authors have tried to articulate this encounter.[15] It is perhaps at this point of encounter between Christian understandings of the divine abyss and the Buddhist understanding of nothingness that Westerners might come to comprehend better the role that living always on the edge of nothingness (Japanese: *mu*) plays in East Asian engagement with silence.

What is the meaning of the silence of God for intercultural communication, especially in a ministry of reconciling presence? First of all, it opens up a space for learning how to negotiate with the different forms and uses of silence in human communication. Silence as a pause in speech, for example, can be a gesture of care and concern for inclusion. Silence as expressing the boundaries of discourse can help call to mind the limitations of all human approaches to profound issues such as recovering from trauma and loss, and of struggling to extend forgiveness to others. Silence can also help negotiate social distance, not simply as something to be overcome, but also to become more fully aware of the limitation that difference places upon every relationship.

Second, the silence of God gives us also a certain permission simply to rest in silence, that is, to avoid the compulsion of filling up threatening or confusing space with words as a way to gain (or regain) control of the game of communication. When silence makes us restless, it is an indicator that we have not come entirely into the embrace of God, bound as we still are to those things that divide us from God. Forms of silent prayer together help school us in this divine silence until we no longer try to dominate it or eliminate it so as to maintain ourselves as the protagonists in the human drama.

---

[15] See, for example, William Johnston, *Silent Music: The Science of Meditation* (New York: Harper and Row, 1974); Hans Waldenfels, *Absolute Nothingness: Foundations of a Buddhist-Christian Dialogue* (New York: Paulist Press, 1980).

CONCLUSION

A ministry of reconciling presence and practices of silence in intercultural communication do indeed intersect at many points. The contemplative practices that lie at the heart of a ministry of reconciliation, and thus make being a reconciling presence possible, require learning about silence as much as about speech and performances. This should help interlocutors understand the differing uses of silence, especially the contextual embeddedness of practices of silence. For Westerners, it opens the horizon of an array of practices where silence shapes and limits discourse. For those who have silence as a constituent part of their grammar of communication, it helps them become more self-aware of how silence is sometimes an act of subjugation, but also a way of negotiating social distance and saving face in difficult situations. And all of this brings people in consecrated life back to the silence of God, out of which all in which we live, move, and have our being has arisen.

8

Conversation as a Methodology for Interculturality, Conflict Transformation, and Reconciliation

SIA NYASARI TEMU, MM

I am Sia Nyasari Temu, a Maryknoll missionary sister born in Tanzania. I have been living for thirteen years in an intentional intercultural community in Nairobi, Kenya, with Sister Giang and Sister Teresa. Things are not always cozy and rosy in our community. As happens elsewhere, we have our fair share of disagreements and misunderstandings. Community life always reminds me of the beautiful rose plant, cherished for its beauty, yet it wouldn't be a rose plant or bear the cherished rose flowers if the sickle-shaped prickles were missing.

That said, I speak from my experience of living in an intentional intercultural community, and I believe that each of us within our own cultural traditions and organizations—religious or secular—needs to be open to other people's stories and to create a space to learn, listen, and be prepared to be surprised by others. We even at times need to be ready to hear of their pains, frustrations, shame, and resentments, and in the process discover that their image of us is anything but our image of ourselves. Jonathan Sacks asserts:

> We must learn the *art of conversation*, from which truth emerges not, as in Socratic dialogue, by the refutation of

falsehood but from the quite different process of letting our world be enlarged by the presence of others who think, act, and interpret reality in ways radically different from our own. We must attend to the particular, not just the universal.[1]

As we struggle with how to live interculturally with differences and yet sustain an overarching community, the response I suggest is conversation. By this I do not mean mere debate but the disciplined art of communicating, that is, making my views intelligible to someone who does not share them, and entering into the inner world of someone whose views are opposed to my own. Each is a genuine form of respect, of paying attention to the other, and of conferring value on his or her opinions, even though they are not mine. Sacks explains:

> In a debate one side wins, the other loses, and both are the same as they were before. In a conversation neither side loses and both are changed, because they now know what reality looks like from a different perspective. It is possible that in conversations each one would hold on to their convictions, and at the same time realize the necessity of making space for another deep held belief, and if my own case has been compelling, the other side may understand and make space too for mine.[2]

This intercultural community is created by a sustained act of understanding and seeking to be understood across the boundaries of difference. As we know, community is built on the willingness to let the "I" be molded by the "we." It is a conversation for many voices. It is through conversations that we become coauthors of our collective future. Sacks underscores that "conversation—respectful, engaged, reciprocal, calling forth some of our greatest powers of empathy and understanding—is a moral form of a world governed by the dignity of difference."[3]

---

[1] Jonathan Sacks, *The Dignity of Difference: How to Avoid the Clash of Civilizations* (New York: Continuum, 2003), 21.

[2] Ibid., 22.

[3] Ibid., 84.

Conversations help us to deal with conflict. This ancient methodology used by communities around the world is one of the communication skills that fosters mutual understanding and respect. People take turns in talking and listening without arguing. They share from personal experiences, are listened to by others, and are able to listen to others; the goal is that everybody feels heard at the end of the conversation. As Margaret Wheatley rightly states, "There is nothing which has happened in this world which did not start with conversation."[4] The Maryknoll Sisters' peacebuilding team, also known as an intentional intercultural community, started with conversations, and twelve years on we continue embracing conversations in all our activities.

The Maryknoll Sisters is an international missionary congregation in the United States. From the beginning, the majority of its members were born in the United States. As such, the values that governed the congregation came mostly from US culture. Founded in 1912, the Maryknoll Sisters had a lot in common with other missionary congregations that were instituted in the nineteenth and twentieth centuries. Similar to these congregations, the values and norms of the Maryknoll Sisters are primarily influenced by Cartesian philosophy, that is, *Cogito ego sum* (I think, therefore I am).

Since the Second Vatican Council the Maryknoll Sisters has, like other congregations, experienced a demographic shift in membership. The diminishment of US-born members and steady increase of new members coming from countries where the sisters had a mission presence have brought a unique set of challenges. For example, these new members primarily came from countries with a collectivist orientation that holds group identity as its primary focus. This is different from the Cartesian philosophy that values individuation. This basic but unacknowledged difference has been a source of misunderstanding, conflict, and pain as newer members try to incorporate into the community system. This difference not only existed in the congregation; it was also a reflection of the wider US society. As new immigrants came into the country they were expected to adapt and assimilate into the

---

[4] Margaret J. Wheatley, *Turning to One Another: Simple Conversations to Restore Hope to the Future* (San Francisco: Berrett-Koehler Publishers, 2002), 54.

normative values with their underlying Cartesian philosophical assumptions. Consequently, the societal model of assimilation influenced how religious congregations organized themselves, and the Maryknoll Sisters congregation was no different. In other words, there has been a cultural shift from those coming from individual-oriented cultures to the majority of new members coming from collectivist-oriented cultures.

MY PERSONAL EXPERIENCE
WITH THE MARYKNOLL SISTERS

Even though Maryknoll Sisters was, from the beginning, open to receiving members from different nationalities—for example, Filipinas, Japanese, Chinese, Koreans, and Irish—and by extension different cultures, they used the assimilation model, since that was the operational model used by all religious congregations in the early twentieth century. Anthony Gittins articulates this model well:

> The classical model of recruitment was that of assimilation: after a suitable period of scrutiny or vetting, prospective members were admitted on the general and specific understanding that they were to learn to accommodate themselves to a preexisting and well-tried way of living. If and when aspirants were admitted to a particular community but brought with them a different culture or first language, the adaptation required would be largely one-way: the new member was simply expected to "fit in," while the community as a whole would continue as before—with a minimum of disturbance.[5]

As many congregations started receiving diverse membership, this model began to fade away. However, there were no explicit efforts in many congregations to identify and change the operating model. So, even though the assimilation model is not explicitly emphasized much today, it still often functions in the day-to-day

---

[5] Anthony Gittins, *Living Mission Interculturally: Faith, Culture, and the Renewal of Praxis* (Collegeville, MN: Liturgical Press, 2015), 2.

life of many communities. It is implicitly expected that the newer members will assimilate to the historical model.

How My Intercultural Living Began

Like many things, my story begins in a very small and almost insignificant way. In 2005, while preparing for my first vows and area studies, two sisters engaged me in a conversation. We were at the Maryknoll campus in Ossining, New York. One of them had worked in Taiwan and the other in East Timor, and they invited me to become a part of an intercultural community. At this time the most common phrase used for this was *multicultural community*. The term *intentional intercultural community*, though very new, was critically necessary and appealing to me, but I needed to understand it more fully.

The community was intentional because we were not simply going to talk about it—we were *deliberately and purposefully* going to put it into practice. The unique plan was that no two people from the same country would be in that community. I did not need any more convincing. I took the plunge, and together we began the new intentional intercultural community. Sister Giang Nguyen was from Vietnam, Sister Teresa Hougnon from the United States, and I came from Tanzania. We were a diverse community in terms of nationality, personality, and other background differences. One thing we were sure of was that to be intercultural, each member would contribute to and participate in creating the community.

This raised understandable concerns from some of the sisters, who thought that we wanted to be exclusive and special, and that we were leaving out other members of the congregation who were already living in multicultural communities. Despite some questions, we continued to pursue our dream. However, one question still lingered in my mind: What had prompted Giang and Teresa to want to start the *intentional intercultural* community?

As Sister Teresa reminded me recently, she and Sister Giang "desired to form an intentional community because they valued diversity and wanted a community where each member was valued, and then to show the congregation it could work." The two sisters had joined the Maryknoll Sisters in 1996. Since then they had experienced much talk about multiculturalism and diversity in the congregation, yet, even with all our diversity, they still experienced the challenges of fully living interculturally. They were thus determined to make a difference by being pragmatic, drawing strength from the fact that although in their first mission assignments each of them had experienced some challenges in their respective communities, they were still living the spirit of multiculturalism.

Having grown up in Texas, Sister Giang experienced the kinds of racism faced by many minority groups. After joining Maryknoll, her ministry was with women sold into marriage. She saw how nationalism can blind people so they do not help even victims of trafficking. These issues around differences also surfaced in the congregation. So, the two sisters felt they needed to try a different paradigm in the congregation. The outcome was the idea of intentional intercultural living. It would provide a safe space where every community member would feel valued and be able to share her cultural values more deeply and in a true spirit of mutuality.

Nonviolent Communication

The process of nonviolent communication was developed by Marshall Rosenberg. Based on the principles of observing, feeling, and sharing needs and requests, it offers a guide for reframing how we express ourselves and how we hear others. Consequently, we perceive relationships in a new light and are able to use nonviolent communication to hear our own deeper needs as well as those of others. "Instead of being habitual, automatic reactions, our words become conscious responses based firmly on an awareness of what we are perceiving, feeling, and wanting."[6]

As they were preparing to work together, Teresa and Giang looked for tools and studied their practicality. Another Maryknoll sister, Norma Angel, worked with us and helped us to create community values. The primary tool for building relationships and fostering conversations is cultivating good communication skills. This involves active listening with the ears, the eyes, and the heart, as well as being able to hear what the other person really means. This kind of listening fosters understanding and elicits feelings of

---

[6] Marshall Rosenberg, *Nonviolent Communication: A Language of Life* (Encinitas, CA: PuddleDancer Press, 2003), 6.

empathy from the listener. We envisioned having between three and six members in the community. Our goal was to start living and putting into practice more intentionally what we had been talking about in the larger congregation.

Thus, the Maryknoll Sisters intentional intercultural community was born.

THE MARYKNOLL SISTERS' PEACEBUILDING TEAM

In August 2006, the three of us were assigned to the Kenya region as the Maryknoll Sisters' peacebuilding team. Some people asked us about this, since Kenya was a peaceful country at the time. Such questions reveal how common it is to associate peacebuilding with conflict. We fail to see the conflicts that frequently occur in our daily activities due to personal differences. Mindful of this disconnect, we wanted to create a diverse team and to have a space to practice our shared values in our ministry. We knew that living in an intentional intercultural community would give us an opportunity to struggle with our differences. In this regard, our experiences from the community would help us and even give us credibility to share our good practices with communities around us, including our work with other religious congregations and the entire Maryknoll family. This meant that if the three of us could create a safe space in our intentional intercultural community to work on our differences, then our combined experiences would inform our ministry. Likewise, our ministry would also inform our community life.

In order to strengthen our skills and to develop a common understanding of peacebuilding, we led several courses at the Eastern Mennonite University's Summer Peacebuilding Institute. We have kept the name Maryknoll Sisters' peacebuilding team as the umbrella under which we would work. We live together and (most of the time) work together in twos or threes, collectively planning our community life and ministry. Our team is also multidisciplinary, with each person bringing her gifts and talents to enrich our ministry. We focus on a number of issues, including conflict transformation, trauma healing, reconciliation, and conversations for social change, centering more on how we want to live together than on what we want to do.

As the peacebuilding team we hope to work with our differences and share the fruits of our daily lives with the people we interact with in our ministry. When Giang, Teresa, and I started, we agreed that we would do our external work as well as our internal and unfinished work. The external work includes being aware of our common call as Christians and women religious in a Maryknoll Sisters congregation and being familiar with the values and norms that govern our organization. The essence of the external work is informed by internal work, which includes comprehending some of our own unresolved childhood and other "growing up" issues, as well as creating time and space to work on transforming ourselves.

I have found that although inner work is paramount in any community, it is the most difficult work, especially in intentional intercultural communities. Living in such a community helps each one of us to reflect more on our individual cultures, traditions, and belief systems. The intentional intercultural model invites us to go beyond our societal culture and move deeper into the culture of our family of origin. In the process we realize that each one's core values are influenced by her family and the community in which she grew up. It is within our families that we first learn that the things we say and do are normal, abnormal, or bad. This helps us to be aware of our biases and prejudices. In addition to individual perceptional and emotional filters, we also have our cultural filters. Often we judge other cultures using our cultural lenses, forgetting that every culture is complex and unique and endowed with both positive and negative elements.[7] These life-giving and life-restraining traits of culture are within each individual and operate in our daily interactions with others. This awareness is fundamental for any person or organization striving for intercultural living as a way of life.

Additionally, both the individuals and the group are invited to have conversations around individual and organizational values. Creating space to articulate and identify these values helps us to be aware of what forms our norms and behaviors. Gittins argues that "once we have matured as members of society and assimilated social rules and expectations, we become relatively ethnocentric:

---

[7] See Anthony J. Gittins, *Ministry at the Margins: Strategy and Spirituality for Mission* (Maryknoll, NY: Orbis Books, 2002), 61.

we see, judge, and act from our cultural perspective."[8] Similarly, Shakil Choudhury states:

> When walking through the field of diversity, pebbled by mistake-making opportunities, our "secret power" is compassion.... It can help us all accept that humans—regardless of background, color, or identity—are imperfect creatures. We are all on a learning curve regarding unconscious prejudice and intergroup dynamics. Accepting this as part of the process may help us move past the internal and external judgments that hinder learning.[9]

As such, being aware of our cultural backgrounds helps us recognize how often we project our way of doing things and unresolved issues to other people.

UNDERSTANDING CULTURAL DIMENSIONS

As a concept of anthropological origin, culture has been evolving over time and can be analyzed from different perspectives. Moreover, culture is more than what we see; its most important aspects are typically not visible. As such, it does not have one clear-cut definition. For our purposes, we define *culture* as "the values, beliefs, ideas, customs, and social behavior of a particular group of people or society."

Every culture has an obvious part as well as a not-so-obvious part. The obvious part, material culture, is visible and includes things like food, clothing, artifacts, drama, music and dance, faith and religion, and language. Anthropologists tell us that this part comprises only 10 percent of a culture. The remaining 90 percent is the unseen part, which includes values, beliefs, attitudes, rituals, and what is embedded in the language. This unseen part, which informs the obvious part of culture, is usually the part for which we need to create more time and space to articulate. Most

---

[8] Ibid., 66.

[9] Shakil Choudhury, *Deep Diversity: Overcoming Us vs. Them* (Toronto: Between the Lines, 2015), 18.

conflicts in intercultural communities happen because the unseen dimension of each culture is not recognized equally.[10]

Even as we focus on understanding a person's culture by articulating cultural values, there are things that will still remain unique to a culture and that may not be wholly embraced by a community. Nonetheless, it is important to be aware of these aspects of culture because it helps us to learn to disagree respectfully with one another. Sacks notes:

> Nature, and humanly constructed societies, economies and politics, are systems of ordered complexity. That is what makes them creative and unpredictable. Any attempt to impose on them artificial uniformity in the name of a single culture or faith, represents a tragic misunderstanding of what it takes for a system to flourish. Because we are different, we each have something to contribute, and every contribution counts.[11]

Ultimately, if we come together and form a truly intentional intercultural community, in time we will influence one another and thereby be transformed by our interactions and our sharing.

MULTICULTURALITY IN RELATION TO INTERCULTURALITY

There is a common but misleading tendency to assume that *intercultural* and *multicultural* mean the same thing and are, therefore, interchangeable.

A *multicultural* community is a group of people of different cultures living together; there may not be much real, in-depth sharing among the members. Sometimes, members are assigned randomly to new communities without being consulted or giving their consent. It is, therefore, important to bear in mind that in many cases people in multicultural communities are not only

---

[10] Open Educational Resources (OER) Services, "Facilitating Discussions about Intercultural Communication Issues," courses.lumenlearning .com.

[11] Sacks, *The Dignity of Difference*, 22.

adapting to the culture of a new place—which, in itself, is already highly demanding—but that they are also interacting with multiple cultures within their communities, which may not be their top priority.

It is unfortunate that sometimes when we form multicultural communities, we do not take time to think about or imagine the complexities that we are getting our members into. Although good relations and proper communication skills are crucial, they are definitely not enough for healthy relationships and for moving beyond mere coexistence. It is therefore advisable to create space for all members to acknowledge the magnitude of this complexity and to find different processes that will support their transition.

Interculturality, on the other hand, is a process that responds to the reality that surrounds and imposes itself on us. A fairly new paradigm, it can be described as a means by which consecrated persons can reread their life and mission in today's world. This model recognizes the diversity of cultural values, belief systems, customs, and norms. It is expected to move us beyond the mere tolerance of differences, seeking instead to deepen our awareness and understanding of them and, in turn, integrating these differences. In short, intentional intercultural community presupposes the willingness of members to create the community together despite their cultural differences. If they are honest, open, and ready to encounter other cultures, these members will eventually collectively create a new culture.

Just as multiculturality and interculturality are different, so they are also different from *acculturation.* In itself, acculturation is a challenging and enriching experience of learning and adapting to another culture that is different from the one in which a person has been socialized. My first acculturation experience was very challenging. Roughly three months after my arrival in New York, I had to attend a week-long workshop on acculturation facilitated by Cross Cultural Service. The goal of this workshop was to acculturate new non-US members to US culture. We had no opportunity to share our cultures of origin; the objective was for us to grasp what was and what was not acceptable in US culture. We were expected to adjust to the host culture and try to fit in as much as we could. As we continued with our orientation to Maryknoll, our coordinators kept correcting what they felt were faults or wrongs.

Surprisingly, even though we had to participate in this acculturation workshop according to US standards and culture, there was a standing conversation within the larger context of Maryknoll Sisters about the importance of embracing diversity and multiculturalism. Even though I struggled hard to adjust to the Maryknoll culture, I always felt that I was in transition mode. I found myself explaining everything I did because there were always sisters who would ask, "What does that mean?" The whole experience was tiring. At the end of the workshop I went to our formation house in Chicago for further orientation. Once there, I observed obvious issues related to power dynamics. In retrospect, I recognize that I also had power then, contrary to my feelings at the time that the orientation directors had a great deal of power over me. Each time we had a meeting, I noticed that whenever I pointed out any perceived inequality, my concern would not be acknowledged. Instead, I felt that I was chastised for not being open to constructive criticism and for failing to adjust my attitude and behavior.

My companion in that orientation was from El Salvador. Together we were trying to adjust to the culture of religious life, to the Maryknoll culture, and to the US culture—all at once. Thankfully, we eventually had two workshops facilitated by a Maryknoll sister who was an expert in organizational and individual cultures and in issues related to deep diversity. There were five of us in the second workshop: two from Tanzania, one from Kenya, one from El Salvador, and one from the Philippines. The facilitator offered us a non-evaluative space to share our personal experiences of living together in this new environment and trying to negotiate life together in the community. This was the beginning of my awareness of the challenges and real complexities of the way of life I had chosen to embrace. I remember our facilitator repeating over and over: "This is abnormal life. Ordinary people do not live this way."

This last workshop made so much sense when I thought of my first year in Chicago, when we were only two sister candidates. It was much easier for us to negotiate our differences and reach an agreement. When three more candidates joined us in the second year, the challenges increased—and that is when the challenges facing the entire congregation dawned on me. Until then, I had thought that all Maryknoll sisters attended these kinds of workshops from time to time. However, after I had completed my orientation and gone back to the Maryknoll Sisters Center in New York, I realized that only those in the orientation-to-mission phase were attending these workshops. As a result, when we as individuals tried to practice what we had learned in Chicago, we did not always get enough support from the Maryknoll system to make what we had learned relevant. It appeared that despite their value in raising awareness and personal growth, these workshops unfortunately did not affect the entire congregation very much.

I believe that developing competencies that support "adult" behavior for managing deep diversity is a necessity for all members—more so for leaders, formators, personnel directors, and financial officers in religious congregations. Moreover, I believe that given the unique structure of religious life—and especially missionary congregations—compounded by the paradigm shift from being monocultural to multicultural congregations, those in leadership positions need additional skills and tools so they can guide and support all members to continue to develop their own competencies. The underlying assumptions that guide the conventional role of leadership in organizations are usually based on the cultural values of the normative or dominant culture, which usually support members to:

- become and remain aware of their core values;
- work toward aligning themselves with these values;
- support members in feeling passionate about these values; and
- make their daily decisions based on these values.

Unlike in the past, when congregations had members who came from the same localities and shared similar cultures with their founders or foundresses, most of the new members who join our congregations today come from different continents and backgrounds. As such, they have varied cultural differences and values; quite often they have the experience of only the world-view that is anchored in their individual cultures and practices. This brings about inconsistent values and priorities, and many congregations are at a crossroads between monoculturalism and multiculturalism. For Maryknoll sisters the dominant way of life

was the New England–Irish-American culture. The congregational
values never had to be explicitly articulated because they were
similar to the values of the above-mentioned majority members.
The Italians, Polish, Filipinas, Japanese, Midwestern, and East
Coast Americans had no choice but to learn, digest, and then
embrace the new culture. However, the possible negative consequences of letting each member incorporate her culture into the
already existing norms should not be lost on us. As such, it is very
important to articulate carefully considered organizational values
in order to circumvent new members perceiving these as simply
the cultural values of the normative group and therefore only as
relative to their own cultural values.

Like the Maryknoll Sisters, everyone can draw crucial lessons
from what has been tried and tested. In our congregational discussions and discernment Sister Norma Angel, a specialist in human
and organizational systems, has often said that leadership can help
the newer community members by using or strengthening the following areas: in-depth understanding of a personal perceptional
filter (worldview); understanding our feelings (what they mean to
us); and developing skills to understand the different ways feelings are expressed, especially at times of conflict. Furthermore,
Sister Norma affirms that Geert Hofstede's work on dimensional
cultures is one of the most important modalities for articulating
issues related to value priority and for teasing out some of the
following organizational dynamics that are central to the well-
being of our community: power-distance, uncertainty avoidance,
individualism/collectivism, masculinity/femininity, long-term/
short-term orientation, and indulgence/restraint.[12]

Experience of Conflict in Intentional Intercultural Community

The uniqueness of each person and the differences of opinion,
thoughts, or desires with others that arise daily make conflict an

---

[12] Geert Hofstede, *Culture's Consequences: Comparing Values, Behaviors, Institutions, and Organizations across Nations* (London: SAGE
Publications, 2003).

inevitable and normal part of life.[13] However, the way people deal with those differences determines the magnitude of the conflict and how long it will last. Differences do not have to intensify to serious fights. We can thwart such an outcome by embracing the positive side of conflict and using it as an opportunity to learn and to grow. Louise Diamond acknowledges: "The greater the threat, the greater the lesson. . . . Let yourself feel gratitude toward her/him, for giving you the opportunity to learn this lesson."[14] However, the vast majority of our community conflicts are not over differing values but rather about our differing interpretations of shared values. Learning to live with others who interpret the same values differently is one of the goals of intercultural living. This calls us to be aware of and to listen to other people's understanding and expression of the same values instead of being reactionary and judgmental.

Storytelling as a Way of Creating a Community

Storytelling is another form of conversation and one of the ways in which members of an intentional intercultural community can create a new culture. Members collectively create a space where they tell their life stories and share their values freely without being interrupted, judged, or evaluated.

When I agreed to join Teresa and Giang in their proposed intercultural community, they had already invited Sister Norma Angel as the facilitator to help the three of us live together. She helped us to look at our personal values and taught us how to revisit and clarify communal values. For example, Sister Norma told us that if someone said she valued commitment, that was not enough. It was simply a word. She had, therefore, to state what commitment meant to her. This would help us to identify and articulate what we felt would be accepted as group or communal values. Had we not created such forums before we started living together, it would have been difficult to negotiate matters when conflicts arose later. And we have, for the past thirteen years, continued to share our stories in our intentional intercultural community.

---

[13] Louise Diamond, *The Peace Book: 108 Simple Ways to Create a More Peaceful World* (San Francisco: Conari Press, 2001), 14.

[14] Ibid., 15.

PROPOSALS FOR
INTENTIONAL INTERCULTURAL LIVING

I find voluntary intentional intercultural living in religious community to be a good thing, because individuals are consciously choosing to live this way. In contrast to being assigned or appointed to a community, those who choose to live interculturally are aware of the blessings and challenges of negotiating their differences harmoniously, as well as the possibility for mutual enrichment. Congregation leaders may encourage members to make this choice by adopting this model for themselves. Like any paradigm shift, things take time to change. Similarly, the desire for intercultural living in our religious congregations will take time before it is fully realized. What we are doing now is a sign that transformation is taking place. This is an opportunity for religious congregations to start thinking along intercultural lines and intentionally to begin to radically welcome new members.

Intentional intercultural community living is worth the investment of time and energy. All persons joining the community bring a different layer of culture from their family of origin and what they have acquired in the process of becoming and realizing their full potential. By making and walking the path repeatedly, we gain experience and become practitioners. The more one makes mistakes and tries to correct them, the more one gains confidence and grows in the process. As we invite people to live interculturally, we need to be compassionate and patient with one another. Although sometimes we may think some people do not want to change, we still need to create a safe space to hold them.

One of the challenges of intentional intercultural living is that we may have to explain ourselves a lot. In the process, however, we gain more understanding about ourselves and the things we value, helping us to develop good intercultural communication skills and a deeper level of self-growth. For example, I have learned to listen to the other person without interruption and to be attentive to the person's feelings and body language. I have learned to seek clarification about what the other person shares and to check my assumptions.

On the systemic level we need to be aware that we are inviting into our organization new members and a whole new culture. This helps us to articulate and share congregational values with the new members. We need to create time and space for them—especially during their orientation/formation phase—to have good conversations. This helps them to integrate these values into their lives, as the coordinator simply guides and accompanies them. It is also helpful to revisit organizational values from time to time to see how they are serving the congregation today.

CONCLUSION

Intentional intercultural living integrates mission, culture, and faith. I am happy and feel privileged that God called me to be part of our congregation's intentional intercultural community for the past thirteen years. Even with challenges here and there, which is normal in life, and despite our divergent ways of expressing our cultural differences, this experience has helped me to have a "communion of intents" and to live, work, and walk together with my two sisters in unity. As I share my values and my way of doing things, I am also open to other people's ways of doing things. Together we seek to know, rather than to interrogate. These values are not rules. They are guidelines that govern our time together as well as what we have agreed to uphold, challenges and differences notwithstanding. For example, it may be normal for a novice to drive a vehicle in the United States, but this is not the case in some parts of Africa, where there may be only one vehicle, which is driven by the superior. We have to be cognizant of the context within which things happen. When we join an international missionary congregation, we are coming to live together. We therefore need to cultivate an attitude of openness and curiosity.

PART THREE

ENGAGING PARTICULAR ASPECTS

9

Intercultural Sensitivity

Building Awareness and Competence

Tim Norton, SVD

This chapter is drawn from a presentation given to a group of religious attending an interculturality program at Chicago Theological Union in November 2017. It aims to address growth in intercultural sensitivity in both community life and ministry. It begins with a discussion of the concept of culture, with a particular focus on traditional and urban environments of cultural development. The idea of how culture becomes a part of us in both individual and group terms is developed using personal experience. Processes are suggested for identifying the need for growth in cultural sensitivity in Christian communities and for developing said processes using a holistic approach. Ideas around difference are discussed with a view to broadening our understanding of intercultural sensitivity. The Intercultural Competency Scale (ICS) is introduced and described as a useful tool in both assessing and improving intercultural sensitivity. It is helpful to begin by defining some terminology used to discuss culture.

In *multicultural communities* we live with one another holding some values of tolerance around our diversity, perhaps acknowledging some of our differences around food, social norms, and dress. Nevertheless, our preference is to keep company with others of our own cultural background.

In *cross-cultural communities* we tend to be more active in listening to and learning from each other. However, there are often tensions around unaddressed power differentials, as well as attitudes of superiority of one culture over another.

In *intercultural communities* we highly value equality, respect, freedom, and mutuality. We intentionally foster reciprocal relationships among people from different cultural backgrounds, working toward a community that shares and trusts. *Intercultural sensitivity* is the ability to develop, as Chen and Starosta put it, "a positive emotion towards understanding and appreciating cultural differences that promotes appropriate and effective behaviour in intercultural communication."[1]

CULTURE: WHAT IS IT AND WHAT DO WE KNOW ABOUT IT?

In order to begin talking about intercultural sensitivity, it is helpful to step back and wonder about culture—what is it and what do we know about it? In 1952, Kroeber and Kluckhohn found more than 350 definitions of *culture*.[2] And certainly that number has increased in the past sixty-plus years. For the sake of simplicity, I use the following definition for *culture* by Anthony Gittins: "The way people in groups react to, form, and shape their environments."[3]

Different people in different parts of our world have found and/or invented a great variety of ways to survive and thrive in the environments in which they find themselves. Some traditional societies have evolved ways of being over time that remain reasonably constant, albeit with modifications to accommodate fluctuations in things like climate, habitat, educational needs, and demography. Urban societies exhibit a much more rapid rate of

---

[1] Guo-Ming Chen and William J. Starosta, "A Review of the Concept of Intercultural Sensitivity," *Human Communication* 1, no. 1 (1997): 5.

[2] Alfred L. Kroeber and Clyde Kluckhohn, *Culture: A Critical Review of Concepts and Definitions* (Cambridge, MA: Harvard University Press, 1952).

[3] Private communication between author and Anthony Gittins on November 2, 2017.

change; indeed, change is expected and often promoted in towns and cities. Keeping abreast of change can be a fulltime occupation. And change both modifies and produces culture.

The rural-urban divide is one that is in constant flux. Significant numbers of people around the world are moving from more traditional rural societies to urban environments, seeking educational and employment opportunities for themselves and their families. "Today, 55% of the world's population lives in urban areas, a proportion that is expected to increase to 68% by 2050."[4]

This growth in urban life and culture affects us in a variety of ways. World poverty and inequality are decreasing in some areas while increasing remarkably in others. As world markets become increasingly globalized, people are moving from one cultural context to another in much greater numbers than ever before, either by chosen or forced migration. In many places where populations were traditionally dominated by one particular ethnic group, significant groupings of people from other ethnic backgrounds are appearing and gradually giving rise to new and nuanced ways of being in those societies. Multiculturalism is becoming a worldwide phenomenon. Our food, literature, educational policies, religion, politics, art, and laws are increasingly affected by ideas and influences from cultural sources that once had little or no impact on us—whoever "we" are, wherever "we" are from.

THE WORLD ON THE MOVE

This is increasingly true for Christian communities that are forming, growing, and declining across the world. This movement of peoples inevitably influences both our understanding of and our response to the mission of God in the intercultural world of today. Religious congregations that once sent missionaries from culturally homogenous backgrounds to locations in other parts of the world are now finding this model of mission to be less effective as they try to accommodate to the fast-changing ethnic makeup of their membership. Some smaller diocesan groups are realizing how heavily invested they have historically been in the cultural

---

[4] United Nations Department of Economic and Social Affairs, "2018 Revision of World Urbanization Prospects" (May 16, 2018).

dimensions of both their membership and ministry selection, as they respond to new ministry horizons with a younger membership from parts of the world well outside their original diocesan boundaries. New questions are arising in multicultural religious life about basic elements of community life and ministry. How do we pray together? What do we eat? What gifts and talents do we bring to the mission of God? What language(s) do we use in our community life? What ministries are we called to, and how do we plan for them? How do we prepare our members to cross cultures in mission, and how do we prepare our members to receive people from other places?

North American sociologist Louis Wirth offers the following insight into culture that is helpful in the consideration of these matters: "The most important thing, therefore, that we can know about a man is what he takes for granted, and the most elemental and important facts about a society are those that are seldom debated and generally regarded as settled."[5]

The phrase *takes for granted,* although challenging to translate into other languages (always an important consideration when talking about intercultural sensitivity), may be viewed as understanding as true without actual proof or further consideration. With this phrase Wirth is referring to the substantial accumulation of knowledge, tradition, ritual, relationships, and experience that groups of people attain over time. The shared nature of this information within a relatively constant population of people lowers the necessity of making it explicit, as everyone is presumed to know it and behave according to this knowledge. Thinking in these terms can help us to deepen our understanding of why it is so complex to move for a significant length of time from one cultural context to another.

When newcomers arrive, they seek information about the new place and new people through what they can see, touch, taste, smell, and feel, as well as by asking questions—a process that is sometimes confined by limitations in a shared language with the locals. Ideally the newcomers have also done some language and culture learning prior to arrival. While these processes of information seeking are important and useful, there is a whole world of

---

[5] Louis Wirth, "Social Interaction: The Problem of the Individual and the Group," *American Journal of Sociology* 44 (May 1939): 967.

information and tradition that local people do not talk about or share in other ways with the newcomers because it simply may not occur to them to do so. These are the matters that all locals know as real for them, and they often assume that they are real for others as well; thus they do not require the effort of being made explicit. The implicit nature of this unexplained information is what Wirth refers to in the above-mentioned quotation and can be exceedingly difficult for newcomers to encounter as they try and discern deeper matters in society such as attitudes, taboos, importance of time, appropriate gift giving, what is safe to share, and ways to share it appropriately.

CULTURE, INTERCULTURALITY, AND US

Culture becomes a part of us without us really being aware of it. As local residents in a certain place and space in the world, we carry within us lots of knowledge about how to behave, how to survive, how to relate, and how to thrive. We consider these to be important elements of our culture. As we grow up in this specific cultural environment, we don't often reflect upon it—and only rarely does it occur to us that life, with its inherent questions and challenges, may be physically, relationally, and emotionally different for others in other spaces and places. Furthermore, we teach culture to others, usually those who are younger than us, without being aware that we are doing it. And as young people ask clarifying questions during this culture-learning process—for example, "Why don't girls play football?" or "Why are the chiefs of the village always from the same family?"—our standard responses may be "that's just the way things are here" or "we have been doing it that way for a very long time."

The process of acculturation described above, in which my first culture becomes a part of me, is a normal human process. Yet culture is so important to living that aspects of a second culture can also be interiorized. Prior to my arrival in Mexico, where I was missioned for seven years from Australia, I read that a hug or *abrazo* was going to be a common form of greeting instead of a simple Australian handshake. I wondered how I would feel about this. Upon my arrival in Mexico, I not only quickly adjusted to greeting everyone with a handshake and an *abrazo*, but

I found that I liked it. Within a couple of months it became so frequent and so normal that I simply forgot about it. Two years later, when I returned to Australia to be met at the airport by my older brother, I shook his hand and naturally drew him into an *abrazo*. He was shocked at this behavior and asked me why I was hugging him. I then remembered that my brother and I did not share the custom of *abrazo*. So, we simply shook hands—but it no longer felt the same for me.

Speaking in metaphorical and corporeal terms, the concept of the *abrazo* had gone from my head (where I wondered if I would like it) to my heart (where I found that I did like it) to my gut (where I forgot about it as it had become part of me). When I returned to my first culture, I had to renegotiate appropriate greetings, as well as my feelings around them. I had to bring the *abrazo* from a subconscious space (gut) to a conscious space (head) in order to think about it and decide if and when to use it. I had clearly changed during my time in Mexico, and I needed to change again upon returning to my first culture.

Culture provides a framework within which we situate most things that we learn or come to know. Music, dance, water resources, food, family relationships, availability of financial and educational resources, hierarchical sensitivities, and development and implementation of rules are some of the many elements that help to give us our sense of who we are and how we belong in the world. New arrivals need to enter into an intense form of culture learning when they cross borders. This form of entry learning is not limited to those who move from one country to another but can also come into play when a person moves within a multiethnic country, or, to a lesser but still significant degree, when a person changes jobs or moves residences. Cultures are created and lived out in different hospitals, schools, office environments, service industries, retail spaces, religious communities, and facilities for the elderly, as well as in different cities, suburbs, barrios, *favelas*, and small towns.

Culture is a dynamic concept. In traditional societies culture may be very slow to change, but cultural change over time is inevitable. As mentioned above, urban societies are known for rapid change. A few years after returning from Mexico to Australia, while staying at the home of my brother, he asked me to take my fourteen-year-old niece and my sixteen-year-old nephew to school. I was happy to do this, but I was surprised to see that when my niece arrived at the gate of her girls-only school, she and her classmates all hugged as a form of welcome. I was even more surprised when I arrived at my nephew's mixed-gender school to see him engage in the same form of welcome with all the boys and girls at the school gate. I was left asking myself, "When did this change come about?" When I went to school some thirty years earlier, we said hello to each other as we arrived at school, but we did not even shake hands, much less hug one another. Things and people change—as do cultures.

Returning to Chen and Starosta's above-mentioned definition of intercultural sensitivity, I am reminded that, as I encounter people with appearances, attitudes, and behaviors that are culturally different from mine, I become more interculturally sensitive in accordance with my curiosity and interest in deepening my awareness of and interaction with these differences. However, Chen and Starosta make the important clarification that "intercultural awareness (cognition) is the foundation of intercultural sensitivity (affect) which, in turn, leads to intercultural competence (behaviour)."[6]

Thinking again about my encounter with the *abrazo* in Mexico, I understand this to mean that my intercultural sensitivity in this area had a capacity to develop through my thoughts about it prior to arriving in Mexico (cognition), my felt encounter of the practice with the people (affect), and my regular engagement in this practice (behavior), which became so much a part of me that I simply forgot about it.

Thus, in our commitment to interculturally sensitive Christian communities, it is important to make use of our whole being, that is, utilizing a holistic approach, with our thoughts and ideas, our feelings, and our subsequent actions.

GROWING IN INTERCULTURAL SENSITIVITY

As Christian communities enter into a commitment to building their awareness and competence in intercultural sensitivity, they may encounter an inertia that goes against the idea of changing

---

[6] Chen and Starosta, "Intercultural Sensitivity," 5.

some very foundational aspects of community life and ministry due to the presence and interactive involvement of newcomers. *We* have understood ourselves and functioned this way for a long time, so why change? Can't the new people simply adjust to *our* way of seeing our lives and commitment? Julien Bourrelle gives three options to communities with this line of thought—confront, complain, or conform.[7] In *confronting* the newcomers, I make clear statements and indications that my behavior is the acceptable one and that they need to conform—thus nothing changes. When I *complain* about the situation, I simply isolate myself and other likeminded individuals into a subgroup that has little desire or ability to respond to a new reality. However, when I *conform* or adapt, I begin to sense the overall positive effects that living diversity can bring. My intercultural sensitivity has a chance to breathe and grow.

When Christian communities reach a point of being open to listening to, understanding, and learning from one another, there are a variety of processes they may undertake to enhance their intercultural sensitivity. Taiye Selasi presents an insightful method with the question, "Where are you a local?" rather than, "Where are you from?"[8] She believes that both the individual and collective natures of our life experiences tell us and others more about us than the country or nation where we were born. Selasi's suggestion involves thinking, writing, and sharing about our lives under three headings, which she helpfully refers to as the three "Rs": *rituals* (consider simple things such as making your breakfast, getting to work, harvesting your crops, and saying your prayers); *relationships* (think of the people who shape the emotional life of your week through personal interactions, phone calls, meetings, and interactive social media);[9] *restrictions* (Where are you able to live? What passport do you hold? Are you restricted by racism, civil war, or governance dysfunctionality from living in the locality where you had your rituals as a child?).

---

[7] Julien S. Bourrelle, "How Culture Drives Behaviours," TEDxTrondheim, YouTube, July 10, 2015.

[8] Taiye Selasi, "Don't Ask Where I'm From, Ask Where I'm a Local," TEDTalks, YouTube, October 20, 2015.

[9] Selasi suggests that Facebook-only friends should *not* be a part of this exercise.

For growth in intercultural sensitivity, processes such as Selasi's are not just for those who are on the move from one place or space to another in order to explain themselves when they arrive, but they are also for members of the receiving community to do the work of understanding and sharing once more who they are and where they are local as they receive new members. Intercultural sensitivity needs to be engaged in by both groups, and indeed the learning processes can be enhanced as the two groups share their learnings and understandings.

Christian communities that are evolving from being multicultural to cross-cultural to increasingly intercultural need to nourish an environment of fraternity, an interest in the new and the different, and a desire for understanding. This is rarely a purely linear pattern of growth. There are always steps forward and back, successes and failures. The consistent intentionality of striving for intercultural sensitivity in Christian communities requires leadership, energy, commitment, and belief that it is to that the Spirit is calling us.

CHARACTERISTICS OF INTERCULTURAL SENSITIVITY

Chen and Starosta identify six personal attributes that a truly intercultural person develops. They are self-esteem, self-monitoring, open-mindedness, empathy, interaction involvement, and suspending judgment.[10] I find these helpful in the discussion of intercultural sensitivity because they model closely my being a Christian person in the world—knowing who I am as a child of God, monitoring my behavior with God-myself-others, being open to the movement of the Spirit through those around me, showing compassion, involving myself in works of charity, and not judging others. This adds further momentum to the desire for increased intercultural sensitivity for the promotion of the reign of God in our communities and our ministries today.

Milton Bennett created a developmental model of intercultural sensitivity (DMIS) that can be used in detecting and explaining

---

[10] Chen and Starosta, "Intercultural Sensitivity," 8.

the reactions of people to cultural difference.[11] The model has six stages of increasing sensitivity to cultural difference. Another way of describing this movement is from ethnocentrism to interculturality. The first three DMIS stages are ethnocentric (I experience my culture as central to my reality and judge others accordingly). These stages are

1. *Denial:* I avoid other cultures by maintaining my own strong cultural boundaries.
2. *Defense:* My world is about "us" and "them." I am highly critical of other cultures.
3. *Minimization:* I accept there are cultural differences; however, I downplay them with the idea that essentially all human beings are the same.

The second group of DMIS stages are ethnorelative (I experience my culture in the context of other cultures). These stages are

4. *Acceptance:* There are other cultures with complex worldviews. I don't necessarily agree with them.
5. *Adaptation:* My worldview is expanded through the experience of other cultural worldviews.
6. *Integration:* I can move in and out of the worldviews of others.

Bennett's stages are useful for interpreting how we see, think about, and interpret events that are occurring around us, and they give us a clearer window into what we only vaguely see or think. They can also be used to provide us with some information about how competent we are in dealing with cultural difference.

---

[11] See Milton Bennett, "A Developmental Approach to Training for Intercultural Sensitivity," *International Journal of Intercultural Relations* 10, no. 2 (1986): 179–95; idem, "Towards Ethnorelativism: A Developmental Model of Intercultural Sensitivity," in *Education for the Intercultural Experience*, ed. M. Paige, 179–95 (Yarmouth, ME: Intercultural Press, 1993); idem, "Becoming Interculturally Competent," in *Toward Multiculturalism: A Reader in Multicultural Education*, ed. J. Wurzel, 2nd ed., 62–77 (Newton, MA: Intercultural Resource, 2004).

CONSIDERING DIFFERENCE

As they critically analyze their ability to deal with culture differences, Christian communities need to think more broadly than simply about differences among ethnic, tribal, and national groups. A second area that deserves consideration is the difference between the culture of being woman and that of being man. There is much work yet to be done to explore and understand gender differences with a view to understanding ourselves and those we are in ministry with, for a deeper and more authentic witness to gospel values in the world. As traditional gender roles are changing in the world around us, so it is within the church. Of course, this cultural change does not have a common pattern around the world and across the church. It takes many different forms, often as a mixture of the dominant culture and Roman Catholic Church culture. All of this requires our attention for increased intercultural sensitivity.

A third area for consideration with respect to intercultural sensitivity is that of generational differences. Many of our communities are cross-generational. Some younger members from so-called Generations X and Y do not have the same understandings of commitment, allegiance, initiative, and face-to-face relationships as those who have gone before them in religious life. Possibly for the first time in history, the majority of young people from across the world share a common formational component in their lives in the form of social media. As this group of younger people moves into intercultural religious life, they require higher degrees of accompaniment, feedback, understanding, and motivation than the majority of their older companions. They also generally have a wealth of competence in the areas of social communication to be unlocked and utilized for mission.[12] This is neither worse nor better than previous forms of religious life; however, it requires careful consideration by leaders and members as generational groups interact on behalf of the Reign of God in the world.

---

[12] Vivian Giang, "Here Are the Strengths and Weaknesses of Millennials, Gen X, and Boomers," *Business Insider Australia* (September 10, 2013).

INTERCULTURAL COMPETENCY SCALE
(ICS)

In any multicultural community there is often a direct correlation between the variety of cultural groups present and the achieved integration. Muriel Elmer developed an Intercultural Competency Scale (ICS)[13] to assess how our personal preferences, our likes and dislikes, can assist in knowing how the characteristics of our personality affect our intercultural competence.[14] The ICS is based on research done by the Canadian International Development Agency on qualities required for competent cross-cultural communication. It was tested and found to be valid for over three hundred missionaries working in seventeen different cultural contexts, and it has benefited from regular and relevant updating. It claims universal validity, but it is known to have a bias toward the culture of North America.[15]

The ICS was later adapted by Muriel Elmer into an intuitive scaling tool for measuring intercultural competence. It identified twelve characteristics that persons—such as missionaries or ministers working in another culture—need in order to be successful in a cultural setting different from their own. The twelve characteristics are identified as approachable, intercultural receptivity, positive orientation, forthrightness, social openness, enterprise, shows respect, perseverance, flexibility, cultural perspectivism, venturesome, and social confidence. The characteristics are briefly described below, along with a few representative suggestions for improving competency in that respective area.[16]

---

[13] Muriel Elmer, "Intercultural Effectiveness: Development of an Intercultural Competency Scale," unpublished PhD diss., Michigan State University, East Lansing, Michigan, 1986.

[14] Jon P. Kirby, SVD, "Intercultural Competence for Religious Communities: Models, Gauges and Guides," *SEDOS Bulletin* 48, no. 5–6 (May–June 2016): 23–37.

[15] Ibid.

[16] Muriel Elmer, ICS (2000), unpublished. An accompanying resource to the test is a tool in the form of skill builders that address the twelve characteristics.

Approachable: Makes Contact with Others Easily

Those who excel in this area usually enjoy relating with others—and others find these people easy to talk with. This is a particularly useful skill for building trust and reducing suspicion when crossing cultures. Without this, people will experience difficulty starting conversations and making new relationships. They may try to learn the approachable habits of some in their friendship group, or they may benefit from reading about how Jesus connected with those around him, as in his dealings with the Samaritan woman (John 4:5–33); practicing "Habit 1" of *The 7 Habits of Highly Effective People;*[17] and viewing the Diversity Films' video "Penny for Your Thoughts" on YouTube.

Intercultural Receptivity: Interested in People, Especially Those of Other Cultures

Those who succeed here are naturally attracted to people who are different, and they are interested in their values, customs, and beliefs. This is a very useful ability to have when seeking to enhance intercultural relationships. Those who find this difficult are encouraged to grow beyond their preference to be with people like them. There is a whole world of joy to be found in discovering how others perceive what goes on around them. They may find encouragement by reading about Abraham and Sarah receiving strangers (Gn 18:1–16), studying *Cross-Cultural Servanthood,*[18] and watching the YouTube video "Cultural Humility."

Positive Orientation: Expects to Be Successful Living/Working in Another Culture

Those who do well in this area expect to adjust and function well in another culture, while those who are lacking this characteristic do not share this belief and, sadly, their negative expectations can be self-fulfilling. Their task is to become more confident and positive, perhaps by reading the encounter of Philip and the Ethiopian

---

[17] Stephen Covey, *The 7 Habits of Highly Effective People: Powerful Lessons in Personal Change* (New York: Free Press, 2004).

[18] See especially "Understanding: Seeing through the Other's Eyes," chap. 9 in Duane Elmer, *Cross-Cultural Servanthood: Serving the World in Christlike Humility* (Westmont, IL: InterVarsity Press, 2006).

eunuch (Acts 8:27–39), Robert Kohl's discussion on stereotypes in *Survival Kit for Overseas Living*,[19] and reflecting on how attitudes in community life affect the way new people are welcomed.

Forthrightness: Acts and Speaks Out Readily

While some restraint in pushing ahead with new ideas and activities is desirable in a new cultural setting, people with this characteristic find that people trust them more easily than they do those who constantly hold back from sharing thoughts and suggestions. Constant hesitation and continued silence may harm relationship building. There is a need to work on being more open with people. The section on message exchange with strangers in *Bridging Differences* by William Gudykunst may help.[20] It may also be helpful to experiment with being more open with people at community gatherings.

Social Openness: Inclined to Interact with People, Regardless of Differences

People who are skilled in this area simply enjoy being with and learning from others who are different from them. Those who are not skilled need to work on why they are uncomfortable with those who are different. Reflecting on Jesus's openness to the centurion whose daughter was ill (Matt 8:5–13) may help, along with reading about intercultural communication in *Dynamics of Intercultural Communication* by Dodd.[21] A simple but effective exercise for improving this ability is to share a common activity with a community member who is culturally or ethnically different from you.

Enterprise: Tends to Approach Tasks and Activities in New and Creative Ways

This can be a real strength when encountering unexpected difficulties in a cross-cultural context. Those who find such encounters

---

[19] Robert Kohls, *Survival Kit for Overseas Living*, 4th ed. (Yarmouth, ME: Intercultural Press, 2001), esp. chaps. 1–9.

[20] William B. Gudykunst, *Bridging Differences: Effective Intergroup Communication*, 4th ed. (Thousand Oaks, London, New Delhi: Sage Publications, 2004), chap. 6.

[21] Carley Dodd, *Dynamics of Intercultural Communication*, 5th ed. (New York: McGraw-Hill, 1998), chaps. 4 and 5.

difficult may rely too much on regular daily routines and may need to consider developing greater flexibility and creativity, which can open their sensitivity to difference. Reading and reflecting upon the meeting between Jesus and Zacchaeus (Luke 19:1–10) may be helpful. Intentionally taking part in an event that is outside one's normal routine can also be a good exercise.

Shows Respect: Treats Others in Ways That Make Them Feel Valued

Apart from being a strong Christian value, this characteristic can prevent the newcomer from appearing superior, and it also facilitates healthy local relationship building. Those who tend to disregard seemingly difficult or quiet people may need to work on their people skills before entering a new culture. Reading chapter 10 in *Cross-Cultural Connections* by Duane Elmer could be helpful.[22] Reading about the woman caught in adultery (John 8:1–11) may also provide a new view on respect. Watching Diversity Films' YouTube video "Name Calling at Masonville" is also recommended for improving this characteristic.

Perseverance: Tends to Remain in a Situation and Feel Positive about It Even in the Face of Difficulties

This characteristic, although often lived out in ambiguous and uncomfortable situations, can lead to growth in understanding. If we always withdraw from difficult situations, we will never be interculturally competent. Thus, we must take deliberate steps to increase tolerance for ambiguity and train ourselves for living with uncertainty. The scripture passage where Saint Paul speaks of running to obtain the prize (1 Cor 9:24–27) is relevant here. Chapter 13 in *Cross-Cultural Servanthood* on living with mystery is a good resource,[23] as is the YouTube video "Ouvaru Pookkal-umea" (Every flower) from India.

Flexibility: Demonstrates Openness to Cultural Learning

This characteristic enhances the ability to see the world through the eyes of others. Those who are weak in this area are possibly

---

[22] Duane Elmer, *Cross-Cultural Connections* (Downers Grove, IL: InterVarsity Press, 2002).

[23] Elmer, *Cross-Cultural Servanthood*.

unsure about the value of learning about language and culture. Their hesitancy requires specific steps to increase their flexibility and openness to other ways of being and doing things. They need to monitor their thoughts when they start thinking negatively about people who speak and act differently. Every culture, including their own, has limitations. It will help to focus on the positive aspects rather than the negative. They may find it helpful to read about the openness of the Council of Jerusalem in its dealings with Gentile Christians (Acts 15:29), as well as chapter 13 about the biblical figure of Joseph in *Cross-Cultural Servanthood*. During his years in Egypt, Joseph was a wonderful example of a culture learner.[24]

Cultural perspectivism: Shows the Capacity to Imaginatively Enter into Another Cultural Viewpoint

Strength in this area assists in communication because of an enhanced understanding of the worldview of the other. Limitation here suggests the need to develop different ways of viewing the world. Those trying to improve in this area can read about the life of the prophet Daniel (Dan 1–6), which focuses on how he learned about Babylonian cultural practice and then sometimes had to take a stand against it, taking note of how gentle he was in those responses and how he gave God the credit for everything good. Craig Storti writes about cultural values in *Cross-Cultural Dialogues*.[25] A practical exercise is to initiate a conversation with a person who has recently come to the community, asking that person what things were surprising in this new context and why.

Venturesome: Inclined toward That Which Is Novel or Different

When this characteristic is well developed, an individual has the capacity to thrive on the novelty of the cross-cultural context, while those without it will struggle to initiate new relationships in new situations. The latter group are encouraged to discover curiosity and adventure. Read about Saint Paul preaching in Athens in the Areopagus (Acts 17), as well as chapter 1 in *Bridging*

---

[24] Ibid.

[25] Craig Storti, *Cross-Cultural Dialogues* (Yarmouth, ME: Intercultural Press, 1994).

Differences, which offers some good reflection questions.[26] Such reflections may help in identifying why it is difficult to be with people who have different habits.

Social Confidence: Tends to Be Self-Assured

Although strength in this characteristic can prevent people from assuming a learning stance, it can be very useful in the early transition phase, encouraging them to take the risk of interacting with new people. They recognize that they do not always receive the expected affirmation in some situations, and they don't become discouraged but remain open and sincere with people in order to boost their self-confidence. Those who lack this characteristic may be helped by reading how Peter risks walking on water to Jesus (Matt 14:32–33) as well as the call of Jeremiah (Jer 1:7). Another resource is *Telling Yourself the Truth* by Backus and Chapian[27] and thinking about experiences in the past that were positive for self-confidence.

CONCLUSION

This chapter has attempted to help Christian communities identify their needs and subsequent processes for building intercultural awareness and intercultural competence as foundational aspects of their intercultural sensitivity. Our Christian lives are intertwined in a tapestry of cultural threads that come from the environments in which we grew up, the people we have grown with, the places and people with whom we have truly lived, the people in our present communities, and those with whom we minister. This tapestry is further wrapped in the ever-changing and ever-new Christian story that touches our minds and hearts in myriad ways. We are all cultural beings with stories to tell and stories to hear. As ministers in this multicultural world we need cultural variation for our own authenticity—being and acting in the world with different eyes and heart. Our growth in intercultural sensitivity will surely open us more to the Spirit that lives in each of us.

---

[26] Gudykunst, *Bridging Differences*.

[27] William Backus and Marie Chapian, *Telling Yourself the Truth* (Minneapolis, MN: Bethany House, 2000).

10

Cultural Frameworks and Concrete Situations

Maria Hong Nguyen, OSB,
and Roger P. Schroeder, SVD

Some years ago we did a joint two-day workshop on cultural frameworks for an international religious female community that was experiencing a significant amount of misunderstanding and tension between the two major cultural/nationality groups within the local community. One group of sisters consisted of Asians and the other of US-born women. Although only one of us was initially asked by the religious community to facilitate this program, the two of us decided to conduct this workshop on interculturality as a team—a Vietnamese woman religious and a white North American priest—to represent the general cultural perspectives of the two groups in the religious community. This process worked very well with them, and it has been a very helpful framework in other contexts since then.

We begin with a working definition of culture, in two parts. First, many are familiar with the iceberg image of culture, whereby 15 percent of the iceberg is visible and the remaining 85 percent is under water. In terms of culture, the upper, smaller section includes food, dress, rituals, celebrations, and language. The lower section, below the water line, includes values, worldview, assumptions, and beliefs. The conflicts between cultural groups appear most often on the surface level, but the heart of the misunderstanding and judgment lies below the surface. Therefore, the development of cultural understanding and sensitivity requires a deep dive into the water. Second, the term *culture* is still often equated only with ethnicity. However, today *culture* is understood in a much more inclusive sense. Borrowing from the work of Stephen Bevans,[1] the current understanding of culture includes:

1. social location: rich/poor, male/female, urban/rural, Global North or Global South, young or old;
2. ethnicity, race, and/or nationality (sometimes multiple associations);
3. social change: position in the cycle of social and technological change;
4. personal and communal experiences among members of the same family or community.

Another thumbnail description of culture is that it is essential for order, meaning, and identity.

DESCRIPTION OF THE FRAMEWORK

We have chosen to use one of a number of frameworks developed by social scientists for understanding the complexity of the cultural iceberg. This organizing principle of cultural worlds distinguishes, but does not separate, individual-centric and sociocentric societies.[2] In an individual-centric society, an "individual attains a healthy sense of self (or individuates) by distinguishing

---

[1] See Stephen Bevans, *Models of Contextual Theology* (Maryknoll, NY: Orbis Books, 2002), 3–7. Bevans uses these components to describe context, but they also adequately capture the broader, postmodern understanding of culture.

[2] Dutch anthropologist Geert Hofstede was one of the first to describe this principle in terms of individualism and collectivism. See Hofstede, *Culture's Consequences* (Beverly Hills, CA: Sage Publications, 1980), 209–78. Hofstede and many others have developed this concept in the past forty years. Rather than using the original terminology, we use the terms *individual-centric* and *socio-centric*.

him or herself from the other and then, with this full self in place or at least in process, freely associates with others for one's own and mutual benefit."[3] Put simply, *the well-being of the individual is of primary importance.* This is not equated with negative individualistic attitudes, nor does it imply that there is no regard for one's family or group. This only points to the central focus in such a worldview, which in turn influences every aspect of a society, as will be demonstrated later in this chapter. Second, in a socio-centric society "one's identity is rooted in the group (first usually with the family). One individuates by accepting and perhaps redefining one's role *within* the group, but never by stepping outside the group."[4] In a few words, *the well-being of the group is of primary importance.* Again, this does not mean that the individual person has no value in such a society, but rather the value of the group takes precedence as the organizing value. For example, in an individual-centric society the choice of one's marriage partner tends to be primarily determined by the individuals themselves, whereas in a socio-centric society, such a decision tends to be determined by the consequences it will have for the well-being of the family or community.

It is very important to note that there are gifts/strengths and precautions/weaknesses in both frameworks and perspectives. Both of them have the potential to embody both gospel values and values contrary to God's reign. This balanced approach will be employed in the next section of this chapter as we focus on selected cultural aspects within generalized socio-centric and individual-centric perspectives—relationships, authority, time, and conflict resolution. In each section we offer parallel descriptions of the two cultural perspectives of the socio-centric (Maria Nguyen) and individual-centric (Roger Schroeder) societies. We also offer concrete examples situated in the contexts of consecrated life.

---

[3] Gary Riebe-Estrella, SVD, "Understanding Cultural Dissonance: Attitudes and Frameworks," in *Word Remembered, Word Proclaimed: Selected Papers from Symposia Celebrating the SVD Centennial in North America*, ed. Stephen Bevans and Roger Schroeder (Nettetal, Germany: Steyler Verlag, 1997), 231.
[4] Ibid.

PARTICULAR CULTURAL ASPECTS AND SITUATIONS

Relationships

Within socio-centric societies, maintaining good relationships is everything. The family is the basic paradigm—vertical relationships between a parent and child, older and younger siblings, and with an authority figure are the most important. Life goals are achieved through communal relationships, and this requires time and hospitality. Maintaining the integrity and coherence of the group is absolutely necessary at all costs. Harmony is an essential value. Rupturing a relationship is a deadly sin and unforgivable. Finally, one's activity and behavior must bring honor and not shame to one's group. These dynamics generally, but not exclusively, occur in the external forum. The giftedness of this perspective for a culture or a religious congregation is that it fosters respect for elders and authority, commitment to group goals and activities, the importance of good relationships, and a strong sense of hospitality. The *precaution* is that a sense of individuality and personal initiative can be discouraged or lost, and an overemphasized sense of ethnocentrism—identity to one's culture—can lead to an attitude of judgment and exclusion toward others.

Within individual-centric societies, relationships are important in light of their importance for an individual's well-being. Individuals are unique and relationships are free associations, especially in urban situations. Many relationships are temporary and short term. Horizontal relationships among peers, friends, and spouses are more important—for example, the relationship between spouses, as possible "soul mates," in an individual-centric society is more important than in socio-centric societies, where the primary relationship is with one's family of birth. Life goals are achieved primarily through individual relationships, and maintaining one's search for and success in personal well-being is primary. Personal integrity is an essential value. While shame in a socio-centric society is caused by not fulfilling the external expectations of the group, in an individual-centric society guilt is the result of a person not fulfilling internal expectations. The *giftedness* of an individual-centric perspective for societies and religious life is that persons tend to strive for self-fulfillment and they demonstrate a healthy sense of freedom, initiative, and creativity. The *precaution* is that this can lead to exaggerated individualism, isolation in community life, and a weak concern for the general well-being of the group/congregation.

Within consecrated life those involved in vocation and formation ministries need to be very aware of how the values associated with socio-centric and individual-centric societies affect potential candidates and those in initial formation. Those with the former perspective may typically choose to enter and stay in religious life based primarily out of a sense of honoring the desire and prestige of the parents, family, and broader community and of not causing others the shame of one's leaving. At the same time, a seminarian may more easily feel obligated to leave religious life in order to financially assist his family. On the other hand, those of an individual-centric society may choose to enter and stay in a religious congregation primarily for the sake of their personal prestige and sense of self-achievement. They may also make a hasty decision to leave consecrated life when they don't feel sufficiently independent and/or fully self-fulfilled.

Authority

The underlying meaning associated with relationships as described above affects all other areas of culture, such as the understanding of authority. We begin again with socio-centric societies, in which the roles of authority are primarily hierarchical and are established by society, church, and/or birth. As mentioned above, vertical relationships are very important—such as with parents, teachers, and elder siblings. Furthermore, authorities should naturally know and respond to what an individual needs. In this context, obedience, respect, and dependence are essential. The *giftedness* of this perspective is that it can produce a healthy respect for authority and a generous spirit for community efforts, when requested. The accompanying *precaution* is that persons will normally not volunteer (or raise their hand in a classroom), since personal initiative or assertiveness is not encouraged. They would be hesitant to raise questions and make suggestions to anyone in authority.

Let us turn to individual-centric cultures, in which the roles of authority accommodate themselves to a more egalitarian spirit, whereby individuals are expected to voice appropriately their needs, concerns, or suggestions to persons with authority, such as asking questions in class. Creativity, initiative, and independence are encouraged. The *giftedness* of this perspective is that it promotes self-initiative and innovation. The *precaution* is that this could lead to an exaggerated critique of or lack of respect for authority figures.

Here is a concrete story of how this could manifest itself in religious life. One of the points of tension within the religious community mentioned at the beginning was around the issue of authority. Within that situation we described the perspective of those of the socio-centric societies (in this case, Asians) who expected the religious superior to know what they needed and thus avoided expressing their needs. Also, at all costs they would not want to shame the person in authority by approaching her directly, which would imply that she didn't know what she was supposed to know and do. On the other side, the religious superior of an individual-centric society (here, US-born) was frustrated that those sisters would not communicate with her directly about these things. Furthermore, this misunderstanding led to judgment on both sides. The Asians thought that the religious superior did not care about them (why wouldn't she assist them, since she should know about their needs?), and the superior thought that they were cowardly and deceitful since they only talked "behind her back" and refused to come to her directly. During our explanation of this issue, the mother superior, who was sitting in the back of the room, "dropped her jaw" out of surprise, and the Asian sisters nodded their heads in agreement. Unfortunately, a lack of cultural understanding often leads to incorrect and prejudicial perceptions of the other.

Time

The meaning associated with time is likewise understood by looking under the surface level. We start with individual-centric societies, in which time is a commodity to be used well and not wasted. The use of time is linked to personal integrity and achievements. The *giftedness* of this perspective is that it can promote efficiency in accomplishing both individual and group tasks. The *precaution* is that there is a danger of overlooking the importance of relationships.

It is quite different for socio-centric societies, in which time is neutral as a value in itself. Rather, time is the "space" within which relationships are developed and maintained. We recall the importance of hospitality. The *giftedness* of this perspective is that it promotes the importance of relationships over the use of time itself. As a *precaution*, this approach can lead to a lack of sufficient attention to making a group decision or addressing the "task at hand."

The following scenario illustrates the potential tension and misunderstanding between these two ways of valuing time. In a multicultural parish of Anglo (primarily individual-centric worldview) and Hispanic (primarily socio-centric worldview) parishioners, a parish board meeting is scheduled to begin at 7:00 p.m. Most of the Anglo members of the board arrive by 6:55 p.m., while many of the Hispanic board members will continue to talk in the parking lot until 7:15 p.m. The former become very angry and consider the Hispanic members to be irresponsible and disrespectful of the other members of the board. The Hispanic members are upset because the Anglos consider the clock to be more important than people and relationships. The good values of both communities clash in such situations. The parish board, or a religious community, needs to understand these values as values, and then agree on a workable solution or a good compromise.

International students in the United States are often confused when they experience an initial warm welcome by Euro-Americans, on the one hand, which is followed later by their unwillingness to take a moment to converse with the international students when they meet, on the other. It seems strange that people don't really want to hear the answer to the question, "How are you?" which is made in passing as they are rushing to be on time for the next event. This applies to religious communities as well.

Conflict Resolution

Social innovator Mitchell Hammer has developed the Intercultural Conflict Style Inventory tool for understanding how different cultures resolve confrontations. It is based on the intersection of two factors or dynamics—direct or indirect, with or without expressing emotions. The quadrant represents four patterns of conflict resolution: (a) discussion (direct and emotionally restrained); (b) *engagement* (direct and emotionally expressive); (c) *accommodation* (indirect and emotionally restrained); and (d) *dynamic* (indirect and emotionally expressive). It is important to note that each of these modes can be very effective and that each can also be misused or manipulated under wrong intentions. While there are a number of factors—such as personality, order of birth, gender, and social environment—that can shape one's preferred style for dealing with conflict, Hammer's tool provides a helpful general framework for our purposes here.

Individual-centric societies normally prefer a linear "getting directly to the point" approach between persons or groups. Northern Europeans and Anglos normally avoid the use of emotions in such situations. The *giftedness* of this approach is that a situation of miscommunication or confrontation tends to be addressed sooner rather than later, and ideally, it allows both parties to express their ideas and concerns from their perspective. The *precaution* is that this pattern may be insensitive, push the process too quickly, and allow the person with more power to dominate the proceedings.

Socio-centric societies are normally indirect; some are emotionally restrained while others are emotionally expressive. This approach is circular, and sometimes a third party may play a role in the reconciliation process. It is extremely important to save face for everyone and to maintain harmony in the relationship. The *giftedness* of this perspective is that it upholds the importance of relationships and allows more time for the resolution of the conflict and for all voices to be heard. As a possible *precaution*, important issues may not receive adequate attention out of fear that relationships may be damaged in the process.

Each of the four patterns of conflict resolution works best when all parties share the same preferred mode of operation. However, when the confrontation or misunderstanding occurs between people of different styles, the resolution is more challenging. For example, those of socio-centric societies often consider those of individual-centric societies to be rude, insensitive, and disrespectful, while the latter see the former as dishonest, cowardly, and "going behind someone's back." Both parties are acting and responding on the level of deep-seated values—located in the section of iceberg below the water line.

Such misunderstandings and practices regarding different styles of conflict resolution can cause major problems in multicultural religious congregations, parishes, and other contexts. One of us, with the assistance of an outside facilitator, participated in a five-hour program on this issue within a culturally diverse formation community of a religious congregation. The program consisted of (a) a theoretical presentation on culture and conflict resolution; (b) completion of the Intercultural Conflict Style Inventory individually by the thirty community members; (c) physical placement by persons within one of the four quadrants (described above) as they were identified by the previous exercise; (d) discussion and reflection by individuals in terms of how they understood their background and placement in that quadrant; (e) a break for supper; (f) storytelling in small groups of a person's positive or negative experience of conflict resolution with someone of a different culture; (g) storytelling in the large group of the one story chosen by each small group; and (h) reenactment of just one of these stories in the plenum through a cultural-drama methodology,[5] which includes the participants changing chairs in the drama—that is, being in someone's else's "shoes"—in order to understand the behavior and perspective of the other party. It was quite interesting near the end of this last stage when the main "actor" (Chinese) responded to the question of how he would now resolve the conflict with his own question, "Should I do it the Chinese way or the North American way?" He knew the difference and could do either depending upon the context.

CONCLUDING COMMENTS

Using Hofstede's cultural framework of socio-centric and individual-centric societies can be very helpful for those striving to foster fuller intercultural living and ministry. It can assist individuals and groups in understanding the worldview of the other, from their

---

[5] See Jon P. Kirby, SVD, "Using Culture Drama for Community Diagnosis and Action Planning," *Compas* 8, no. 40 (September 2004).

perspective. The joint oral and written presentation by each of us presenting socio-centric (Maria Nguyen) and individual-centric (Roger Schroeder) cultures provides a model for this intercultural dynamic, which requires study, trust, and dialogue. And it can lead to mutual enrichment and challenge. Of course, much more can be said about the individual-centric and socio-centric cultural frameworks.[6] Also, other factors affecting the four particular cultural aspects and situations described above include personality and culture, power dynamics, intergender issues, and economic/social positions.

The following three case studies with suggested questions can be used in workshops, group discussions, and/or private reflection to highlight the various factors that could be considered in each of these situations.

CASE STUDY #1

Sister Dorothy and Sister Ann are North American–born women belonging to a religious community in Beaumont, Texas, which has a reputation for being a nurturing environment for sisters of all ages and backgrounds. New sisters coming in are well oriented to the US culture, and the community lives together rather peacefully. Two Japanese sisters, Clare and Liz, for example, are well integrated into the community and they have not affected the culture of the community much since their arrival. However, when two younger Chinese sisters, Yang and Yina, arrived, the dynamics of the community suddenly changed.

There are now four Asian sisters in the community. Sister Dorothy and Sister Ann discover that for the first time in their religious lives, they are ethnically a minority. Cultural differences had never seemed like an issue in the past, but now Yang was cooking "strange" foods in the morning that actually nauseated Sister Dorothy. Sometimes Yang would be preparing dinner early because of her ministry schedule and also preparing her breakfast at the same time. When Sister Dorothy tries to talk to her about the

---

[6] See Patricia Murray, IBVM, "Becoming a Multicultural International Institute," thesis for an MA in theology, Catholic Theological Union, Chicago, 2005, 64–73.

odors, she can hardly understand Yang's response and is not sure how well Yang understands her. This makes it difficult for her to communicate her discomfort without upsetting or hurting Yang.

Sister Mary is also a North American sister in the community, but she is not affected by this situation. Her pattern is to eat breakfast in her room so that she can do her research work. Clare, who would love to prepare fish for breakfast but doesn't have time, strongly supports Yang's right to do so. Liz is more neutral about the issue but feels strongly about everyone's right to be heard.

The community tries to celebrate its diversity and discusses cultural differences. These efforts help in theory within the situations of prayer and meetings, but they don't ameliorate the kitchen issue. Sister Ann starts avoiding the kitchen until the odor has cleared. Sister Dorothy asks that the windows always be opened when cooking, which helps a bit. They resolve it superficially, but it is still an issue during a visitation by an outside religious superior. It had become an "Asian" problem in the minds of the two North American sisters, whereas it is really just Yang who is doing the offensive cooking. Yina was more careful about when she cooked ethnic food because she had been in religious life longer and could see that it was offensive to others.

Questions:

1. What do you think is the real issue in this case study?
2. Do you think that the conflict is more about personal or cultural differences?
3. Could you identify both positive as well as unhelpful reactions and responses to the cultural differences that are found in this case?

CASE STUDY #2

Veronica was thirty-three years old when she entered the congregation. She is originally from Latin America, where she was a successful businesswoman. Since English is her second language, she still finds it difficult to communicate sometimes. After two

years of formation, she went to the Inter-Congregational Novitiate with four other novices and two directors of formation
from another congregation. All of them were born in the United
States. Veronica had looked forward to this experience, especially
after reading the handbook, which emphasizes the building of a
multicultural environment.

After two months into the program, one of the directors calls
Veronica into her office and inquires why she is always talking
about her country. The director says, "Each time we talk to you,
we notice that you often say, 'In my country we do this or in my
country we do that.' Didn't your congregation teach you about
this country?" Then she continues, "You are the one who has to
adapt to our culture, because you are the one who came here. We
don't have to adapt to you." Veronica is in shock. She feels greatly
disappointed. Her intention was not to criticize but to share her
experiences of growing up in her country in order to be engaged
in the conversations. It seems that her attempts to share her life's
stories are not welcomed or appreciated. She doesn't know what
to say. She simply goes to her room and cries.

Questions:

1. What do you think is the real issue in this case study?
1. What caused Veronica (during her two months in the program) and the director to say what they said? Do you think that
what each shared was appropriate?
2. Would you have addressed the situation differently? How
and why?

CASE STUDY #3

Jose is a twenty-three-year-old Mexican American. He was born
in the United States and is the oldest son in the family. He has
seven siblings: four brothers and three sisters. Jose entered the
missionary community four years ago. He is very active in his
community. The brothers and priests in his community like him.

He is charming and likes to be with people. He is a handyman and therefore is helpful around the house.

Jose has not been very happy in the past six months. He struggles with many family issues; for example, his brother got involved with drugs, his sister dropped out of school, and his father got laid off. Jose is very upset and feels depressed. He becomes absentminded and is preoccupied with his family issues. Jose has shared this matter with his formation director. His director recommends that Jose seek counseling, but Jose is very reluctant. He prefers to go home instead of seeing a counselor. The formation team does not know how it can be helpful to Jose.

Questions:

1. What is the real issue in this case study?

2. What aspects of the Hispanic/Latino culture would be important to know in order to more fully understand the dynamics of this case?

3. If you were the formation director, how would you react or respond?

11

Intercultural Communities for Mission

Considerations of Race and Gender

LaReine-Marie Mosely, SND

Unlike internationality and multiculturality, which point to national or cultural origins of persons in heterogeneous groups, interculturality's laser focus is on the *manner* these persons are in relationship.[1] Sharing in the mission of Jesus Christ intercultur-ally in religious life is an emerging, faith-based, and gospel-driven ideal that invites members to be open to the ongoing conversion that results from being communities of "radical welcome."[2] The twofold call of bringing together "the best insights and practices from the founders" and "respond[ing] to and collaborat[ing] with people of different cultures and experiences"[3] creates the founda-tion for intercultural communities for mission. As Anthony Gittins explains in *Living Mission Interculturally,* this type of relatedness is nothing short of revolutionary.[4] Choosing to live in community interculturally signals a willingness to embark on a journey to enter into right relationships with others whose presence will change us. Gittins explains further that interculturality

---

[1] Anthony Gittins, *Living Mission Interculturally: Faith, Culture, and the Renewal of Praxis* (Collegeville, MN: Liturgical Press, 2015), xiii–xiv.

[2] Ibid., 179.

[3] Ibid., 184.

[4] Ibid., xviii.

affects everyone involved, it favors no one, and it demands of each one a transformation. It affects all new recruits, including the recruiters; it affects the way people adapt to new appointments, including their mentors; it challenges members of the dominant culture in any community or group; and it affects the way people within minority groups are treated and respond.[5]

Intercultural living undoubtedly shakes up power dynamics among all members and can provide a forum where evangelical ways of relating can be discerned, tested, and processed. Such a forum can raise the consciousness of members and create a space where all persons can tell their stories and speak their truth with honesty and courage.

In the pages that follow I reflect upon intercultural community living with special attention to race and gender. After sharing my background, social location, and indicators of the signs of the times, I engage select themes from *Living Mission Interculturally* to propose some important responses to these latter realities. I hope to weave a tapestry that showcases the roles of race and gender in twenty-first-century intercultural communities.

MY BACKGROUND AND SOCIAL LOCATION

I am a middle-aged, African American woman religious who belongs to a historically German, international congregation. I joined my Toledo, Ohio, province in 1980, and I am one of only two African American women in our four United States provinces. In the early 1980s I briefly met seven or eight other African American women from our provinces in Chardon, Ohio, and Covington, Kentucky. Over the years all but one of these women have chosen other life paths.

When I was in high school one of my friends, who was also African American, told me that in the 1950s her own mother had asked about joining my community's high-school aspirant program. She was told that the community was not ready to

---

[5] Ibid.

accept negro/colored girls. I have often wondered what, if anything, my community has done to ready itself to welcome new members from the African American community or other underrepresented populations. What do we do now to prepare ourselves to welcome women of color called to share religious life with us?

As the only black woman in my province, I have at times felt frustrated that without being a part of a critical mass with other black women, I have been unable to promote the kind of culture where allies are attuned to issues of racial disparity and pain and are passionate about being change agents. Since working on my master's degree in theology at Xavier University of Louisiana's Institute for Black Catholic Studies during the 1990s, I have been agitating and advocating for deep conversations about race and racial disparities with my community. For the most part, what I have experienced is an allergic reaction to engaging these issues in concrete and systematic ways.

I am a Catholic theologian, and I write from a womanist perspective. Womanist theology is best summed up as indicating "a perspective or approach that places the differentiated (e.g., religious, personal, cultural, social, psychological, biological) experience of African American women in the hermeneutical center of theological inquiry and research, reflection, and judgment."[6] The term *womanist* first appeared in the writings of Alice Walker, most notably in her Pulitzer Prize–winning collection of essays, *In Search of Our Mothers' Gardens,* where she defines a *womanist* as "a black feminist or a feminist of color."[7] The term is derived from the word *womanish,* which is understood as the opposite of *girlish.*[8] A womanist is "Responsible. In charge. Serious."[9] She is committed to her entire community and its ultimate survival and wholeness.[10] "Not a separatist, except periodically,

---

[6] M. Shawn Copeland, "Womanist Theology," in the *New Catholic Encyclopedia,* 2nd ed., vol. 14 (Detroit: Gale Group, 2003), 822.

[7] Alice Walker, *In Search of Our Mothers' Gardens: Womanist Prose* (San Diego: Harcourt Brace Jovanovich, 1983), xi.

[8] Ibid.

[9] Ibid.

[10] Ibid.

for health."[11] My self-understanding and my desire for the full human flourishing of those who are on the margins of society, particularly those in the black community, are greatly informed by womanist theology.

It is hard to overestimate the significance of womanist theology, since it has been a path for many African American female theologians, ethicists, biblical scholars, and scholars of religion to engage their scholarship in fields that have been dominated by white males. All throughout our history in the United States black women have been stereotyped, objectified, and demonized.[12] Womanist theology is the "God-talk" of many African American women as we do our theology on our own terms and in ways that are meaningful for us and that affirm black life in its varied expressions.[13]

SIGNS OF THE TIMES

The UN Refugee Agency (UNHCR) reports that at the end of 2018, "70.8 million individuals were forcibly displaced worldwide as a result of persecution, conflict, violence or human rights violations."[14] In the United States and Europe nationalism in general and white nationalism in particular are on the rise. Immigrants, refugees, and persons of color are being unfairly targeted and scapegoated. A 2016 Pew Research study noted that nationalist parties and organizations were increasingly targeting minority religions in Europe.[15] Political discourse is harsh, polarizing, and increasingly partisan in the United States. Many decry the widening gap between the rich and the poor. Gun violence in the United States continues to make headlines, but a vocal group of young people is boldly pushing back after being traumatized

---

[11] Ibid.

[12] See Delores S. Williams, *Sisters in the Wilderness: The Challenge of Womanist God-Talk* (Maryknoll, NY: Orbis Books, 1993), 60–83.

[13] Se Diana L. Hayes, *Standing in the Shoes My Mother Made: A Womanist Theology* (Minneapolis: Fortress Press, 2011).

[14] USA for UNHCR, "Refugee Statistics," unrefugees.org.

[15] Pew Research Center, Religion and Public Life, "Global Uptick in Government Restrictions on Religion in 2016 (June 21, 2018).

by school shootings.[16] They have made it clear that they intend to oust politicians who rely on the campaign contributions of the National Rifle Association.

The effects of climate change are sobering and are having real-time, deleterious effects on people around the world. Nevertheless, on June 1, 2017, President Trump removed the United States from the Paris climate agreement.[17] A March 2019 article in *Scientific American* makes clear that rising temperatures result in more heat waves, "which enhance conditions for the spread of infectious diseases."[18] Nevertheless, some politicians refuse to acknowledge humanity's influence on this global crisis.

A 2017 Pew Research report indicates that seven in ten US citizens believe that homosexuality should be accepted in society. Globally, more religious societies are less open to homosexuality. A 2018 Pew Research report indicates that 35 percent of Generation Z respondents indicate knowing someone who uses gender-neutral pronouns like *they* and *them,* while 25 percent of Millennials make the same claim.[19] Almost 70 percent of US adults believe that clergy sexual abuse and coverup continue to be problems despite efforts by the United States Conference of Catholic Bishops (USCCB) to develop standards that hold all persons involved accountable.[20]

RESPONSES TO THESE SIGNS OF THE TIMES

Catholic hierarchy, theologians, activists, and others have responded to many of these signs of the times. Of particular interest are a number of noteworthy calls to reach out to those most in need.

---

[16] Martin Vassolo, "Parkland Students Who Became Activists after Shooting Massacre Just Won a Prestigious Global Prize," *Miami Herald,* November 20, 2018.

[17] Michael D. Shear, "Trump Will Withdraw US From Paris Climate Agreement," *New York Times,* June 1, 2017.

[18] Tanya Lewis, "Climate Change Is Having a Major Impact on Global Health," *Scientific American* (March 1, 2019).

[19] Samantha Allen, "Over a Third of Generation Z Knows a Non-Binary Person," *Daily Beast,* January 24, 2019. See Kim Parker, Nikki Graf, and Ruth Igielnik, "Generation Z Looks a Lot Like Millennials on Key Social and Political Issues," January 17, 2019, pewsocialtrends.org.

[20] Clair Gecewicz, "Key Takeaways about How Americans View the Sexual Abuse Scandal in the Catholic Church," June 11, 2019, pewresearch.org.

In an early release of Pope Francis's message to commemorate the September 29, 2019, observance of the 105th World Day of Migrants and Refugees, we read:

> "Take courage, it is I, do not be afraid!" (Mt 14:27). *It is not just about migrants: it is also about our fears.* The signs of meanness we see around us heighten "our fear of 'the other', the unknown, the marginalized, the foreigner. . . . We see this today in particular, faced with the arrival of migrants and refugees knocking on our door in search of protection, security and a better future . . . " (*Homily in Sacrofano*, 15 February 2019). But the problem is not that we have doubts and fears. The problem is when they condition our way of thinking and acting to the point of making us intolerant, closed and perhaps even—without realizing it—racist . . . (cf. *Homily at Mass for the World Day of Migrants and Refugees*, 14 January 2018).[21]

The United States Conference of Catholic Bishops issued a pastoral letter on racism in November 2018 titled *Open Wide Our Hearts: The Enduring Call to Love*, in which they offered this challenge:

> We cannot . . . look upon the progress against racism in recent decades and conclude that our current situation meets the standard of justice. We must be honest with ourselves. Each of us should examine our conscience and ask if the fruits of the spirit (love, joy, peace, patience, kindness, generosity, faithfulness, gentleness, self-control [Gal 5:22–23]) are really present in our attitudes about race. Or, rather, do our attitudes reflect mistrust, impatience, anger, distress, discomfort, or rancor?"[22]

---

[21] Vatican News, "Pope's Message for 2019 World Day for Migrants and Refugees: Full Text," May 27, 2019, vaticannews.va.

[22] USCCB, *Open Wide Our Hearts: The Enduring Call to Love: A Pastoral Letter against Racism* (Washington, DC: USCCB, November 2018), 10, 17.

Last, the Vatican Congregation for Catholic Education states the Catholic Church's views on gender fluidity in this way:

> Gender theory (especially in its most radical forms) speaks of a gradual process of denaturalisation, that is a move away from nature and towards an absolute option for the decision of the feelings of the human subject. In this understanding of things, the view of both sexuality identity and the family become subject to the same 'liquidity' and 'fluidity' that characterize other aspects of post-modern culture, often founded on nothing more than a confused concept of freedom in the realm of feelings and wants, or momentary desires provoked by emotional impulses and the will of the individual, as opposed to anything based on the truths of existence.[23]

In a very lucid and well-written response to this document, theologian Paul J. Schutz makes three compelling arguments that challenge premises supported therein. First, he writes that the American Medical Association states that "gender is incompletely understood as a binary selection."[24] Additionally, the American Psychological Association has defined gender dysphoria as "a genuine condition to be accompanied and treated with therapies and surgeries according to a person's self-understanding."[25] Second, Schutz astutely cites Pope John Paul II's writing that evolutionary theory need not comport with all dimensions of the Genesis story, thus suggesting that using the Genesis language of "male and female he created them" to support the binary nature of gender is disingenuous. Third, Schutz cites the description of erroneous gender theory in "Male and Female He Created Them"—as a sociologically based decision based on feelings and wants[26]—as inviting violence and attacks toward LGBTQ+ persons.

---

[23] Congregation for Catholic Education, "Male and Female He Created Them: Toward a Path of Dialogue on the Question of Gender Theory in Education" (June 10, 2019).

[24] Paul J. Schutz, "A Response to the Vatican Document, 'Male and Female He Created Them,'" NCR online (June 24, 2019).

[25] Ibid.

[26] Ibid.

Issues of gender, including those related to differences based on non-binary gender identities, must be considered important in the context of intercultural community living, because it is a part of how more and more people understand themselves and present themselves to the world. Additionally, what it means to be feminine or masculine in diverse cultures influences all members, whether they are conscious of it or not. How else can we open ourselves to change by being communities of radical welcome if we do not understand the categories that more and more people are using to describe themselves? Since gender identity is increasingly important to Millennials and members of Generation Z, we would do well to engage this issue with openness and a desire to learn.[27]

Many of the themes in *Living Mission Interculturally* are grounded in the seven themes or principles of Catholic social teaching that are often identified as follows: life and dignity of the human person; call to family, community, and participation; rights and responsibilities; option for the poor and vulnerable; the dignity of work and the rights of workers; solidarity; and care for God's creation.[28]

Intercultural living invites community members to enflesh these themes in the daily grind of everyday living together, because these are paths to cherishing those with whom we share community. Engaging these principles of Catholic social teaching on the micro level of community living is just as important as engaging them on the macro level of societies and nations.

MAKING A PREFERENTIAL OPTION
FOR THE OTHER IN THEIR OTHERNESS

Gittins cites an article by German theologian Johann Metz about the making of a culturally polycentric church or an intercultural community, which can happen if two conditions are met:

---

[27] Allen, "Over a Third of Generation Z Knows a Non-Binary Person."

[28] Catholic Relief Services, "CST 101: Themes from Catholic Social Teaching"; text is drawn from USCCB, *Sharing Catholic Social Teaching: Challenges and Directions* (2017).

First, it must be explicitly committed to seeking freedom and justice for all; second, it must be demonstrably "based on the acknowledgement of the other in their otherness." ... Such a "new" hermeneutical culture—one that interprets and explains reality in a new way of endorsing and defending "otherness," "alterity," or the dignity of difference.[29]

This is a bold invitation for community members to move out of their self- or group-centeredness. The language that Metz adopts is important. He suggests that we make a "preferential option for others in their otherness."[30] Gittins then cites theologian David Tracy, who suggests that Emmanuel Levinas's understanding of otherness is inclusive of the transcendent Absolute Other and the human other.[31] The path to the Absolute Other is through the human other. This perspective has the potential of moving comfortable dominant-culture people toward the other in their otherness, since the other has a claim on them. This is indeed revolutionary and bears repeating. The underrepresented other in their otherness has a claim on us.

As an underrepresented other by race and (in the Catholic Church) by gender, whose geographical location in the Global North as a middle-class and well-educated person renders me privileged, I can resonate with Gittins's explanation of what he calls "the stranger in each of us"[32] in a unique way. Nevertheless, all community members are invited to recognize and acknowledge this stranger within. Each needs to "identify and embrace that status and role."[33] This new identity will leave each feeling vulnerable at times, and this engagement can lead to "a progressive development of mutual relationships."[34] I have observed this happening to community members as a result of changes in ministry or in the lifecycle, or when dealing with diminishment, grief, loneliness, or depression. This experience

---

[29] Gittins, *Living Mission Interculturally*, 211–12.
[30] Ibid., 212.
[31] Ibid.
[32] Ibid., 210.
[33] Ibid.
[34] Ibid.

of seeing one's self as a stranger or marginalized member can be an important building block for forming relationships with the other in their otherness.

INTENTIONALITY:
A COMMON/COMMUNITY PROJECT

A path toward forging intercultural communities for mission may be made by all members embracing what Gittins's Congregation of the Holy Spirit calls a common/community project.[35] Gittins reminds his readers that "as a plant or animal will die without water, so a community zeal and focus will atrophy unless its common project is nurtured and tended."[36] What I find particularly instructive in his congregation's common/ community project is that it specifies that the plan "sets down what community life asks of the members, in terms of time and occasions of prayer in common, of deeper sharing of our lives and of periodic evaluation of the community's life and of our apostolic work."[37] Each of these components are important and should increase the likelihood of members having shared common expectations.

This process of a local community articulating such a common project provides a forum for all members to determine the manner in which they can live together. This should be an opportunity for all to speak their truth regarding their hopes for community. Members who are in the minority because of race, ethnicity, age, gender identity, or ministry, together with everyone else, should be able to explain the manner in which prayer, meaningful sharing, and review can take place in life-giving ways. Of course, a collegial give-and-take will likely enable the community to come to a general consensus about this project.

Gittins then proceeds to identify how other shared ideals must also characterize the community to enable members to be committed to the common project. These include individual commitment, mutual tolerance, a forum for articulating frustration,

---

[35] Ibid., 24.

[36] Ibid., 25.

[37] Congregation of the Holy Spirit, *Spiritan Rule of Life* 44.3 in ibid.

appropriate correction, attention to stress and burnout, and clarification of vision.[38]

FORUMS FOR ARTICULATING FRUSTRATIONS

While it can be difficult for community members to name their frustrations and explain them, how else can heterogeneous groups come together to form meaningful relationships? Being vulnerable and sharing oneself is a risk that can be richly rewarded if a critical mass of the community is making good-will efforts to acknowledge the stranger within. Such vulnerability and risk taking can help create a climate where individuals can grow into being their best selves and bonds can be forged between unlikely community members.

Believing in the Possibility of Living Community Interculturally

I was struck by Gittins's statements that intercultural communities for mission are possible. They exist as works in progress "wherever people are intentional about living as a community united in their differences and truly respectful of 'the other.'"[39] Gittins is of the mind that if more people believed that intercultural community living were possible and committed to it there would be more such communities. This commitment would include a willingness to learn and practice "systematically and effectively"[40] how to come together and be together not just for our own well-being, but also for the promotion of God's mission and dream for the human community with its diversity of racial and gender identities.

Becoming Communities of Radical Welcome

Let us return to the image of communities of radical welcome, which Gittins shares and develops from the work of Stephanie

---

[38] Gittins, *Living Mission Interculturally*, 25–29.
[39] Ibid., xxi.
[40] Ibid.

Spellers in *Radical Welcome*.[41] Spellers's book is based on more
than two hundred interviews conducted with members of Christian congregations from around the United States.[42] It is fascinating to me how Spellers analyzes and identifies specific Christian
congregations around the country that are in fact communities
of radical welcome. I hope I have an opportunity to visit some
of these communities in the future to experience what it means
to worship in such a vibrant congregation.

The chart in chapter 12 of *Living Mission Interculturally*,
"From Invitation to Radical Welcome," considers the message,
purpose, cost, and outcome of the respective communities of
invitation, inclusion, and radical welcome.[43]

Radical welcome's *message* is to "bring your culture and
religious values, your voice and yourself: help us to become an
intercultural community." Its *purpose* is incarnation: "The community will be transformed by each person's talents and faith
commitment." The *cost* is significant "to the community, striving
to practice real inclusion and be mutually enriched through the
infusion of new and culturally different ways of living the faith."
The *outcome* is the organic evolution of the community, where
"difference is dignified and valued. Authority does not dominate but respects all. There is a common spirit and missionary
commitment."[44]

Reading and reflecting on this summary of being communities
of radical welcome reminds me of my own involvement with a
cohort of women in our US provinces who will be seventy years
of age or younger in 2025. The age span has been enriching, and
our times of coming together has been a blessing for many of us.
At a gathering in fall 2018 we articulated four goals or commitments that capture a number of the dimensions of communities
of radical welcome:

---

[41] See Stephanie Spellers, *Radical Welcome: Embracing God, the
Other, and the Spirit of Transformation* (New York: Church Publishing,
2006).

[42] Ibid.

[43] Gittins, "From Invitation to Radical Welcome," *Living Mission
Interculturally*, 179. This chart is reprinted in Chapter 2 of this volume.

[44] Ibid.

1. commit ourselves to conversations about authentic living of the gospel, mission, and our vows;

2. develop our readiness for welcoming new members;

3. name, honor, and activate our individual gifts for mission; and

4. stay at the table with God and one another.

I am enthusiastic regarding the manner in which these communally discerned goals and commitments resonate with characteristics of communities of radical welcome. I do believe that the Holy Spirit is at work promoting these evangelical ways of being intercultural communities in religious life, the church, and the entire human family.

CONCLUSION

Communities of radical welcome are inviting and vibrant. Members strive to celebrate the gifts of all who join, and they desire that all persons come as they are so that their talents and faith can contribute to transformative community. Dynamism and genuine inclusion contribute to the ongoing newness of the community that is diverse and/or open to diversity in terms of culture, race, gender identity, and other pertinent categories of difference. The long-term effects of such sustained openness are that the community "will continue to grow in harmony and pluralism,"[45] thus strengthening the commitment of all to the mission of Jesus Christ.

---

[45] Ibid., 142.

12

Striving to Understand the Complexities of Culture and Personality

KEVIN P. MCCLONE, PSYD,
AND CRYSTAL TAYLOR-DIETZ, PSYD

A friend of mine who had damage to her visual cortex as a child grew up seeing the world differently from others. At one point in a conversation she remarked, "You don't see what I see, and I don't see what you see." For my friend, this was the literal truth, but it struck me that her words were a metaphor for the many challenges and complexities of intercultural communication. So often, we fail to understand how others see the world and what factors of culture and/or personality make up that difference as we think we understand culture.

With an increasing number of international religious sisters, priests, and seminarians in the United States, there are often questions that arise during cross-cultural interactions that leave people wondering if culture or personality is the answer for understanding someone's behavior. Identity development, or the way we define ourselves in relationship to the world around us, is influenced by a number of cultural and personality factors. At its simplest, identity can be thought of as the qualities, personality, beliefs, and expressions that make up a person or group; it is shaped by macro-level factors (culture, gender roles, history), individual-difference characteristics, and personal life narratives.[1] An individual's personal identity can be thought of as his or her goals, values, and beliefs, and includes different aspects such as moral standards, social and political beliefs, occupational choice, and family relationships.[2]

CULTURAL IDENTITIES

The development and expression of one's personal identity is influenced by culture. Schwartz et al. explain that the cultural systems in which one resides, and the extent to which one identifies with those systems, direct the ways in which one goes about developing a sense of personal identity.[3] Many things come to mind when one thinks of the word *culture*. For the purpose of this chapter we define *culture* as the "collective programming of the mind that distinguishes the members of one group or category of people from others,"[4] and as individuals grow in their cultural identity development, they develop their sense of personal significance and solidarity with a particular group.[5] There are many different cultural identities that intersect within an individual, such as gender, ethnicity/race, sexual orientation, and spirituality.

In order to understand cultural identities, it can be helpful to explain further some of the cultural identities listed above. *Gender identity* is the process by which individuals come to understand

---

[1] See D. P. McAdams, "Three Lines of Personality Development: A Conceptual Itinerary," *European Psychologist* 20, no. 4 (2015): 252–64; S. J. Schwartz et al., "Identity Development, Personality, and Well-Being in Adolescence and Emerging Adulthood," in *Handbook of Psychology*, 2nd ed., ed. I. Weiner, R. M. Lerner, M. A. Easterbrooks, and J. Mistry, vol. 6 (Hoboken, NJ: John Wiley and Sons, 2012), 339–64.

[2] S. J. Schwartz, "The Evolution of Eriksonian and Neo-Eriksonian Identity Theory and Research: A Review and Integration," *Identity: An International Journal of Theory and Research* 1 (2001): 7–58.

[3] Schwartz et al., "Identity Development, Personality, and Well-Being in Adolescence and Emerging Adulthood," 2012.

[4] G. Hofstede, "Dimensionalizing Cultures: The Hofstede Model in Context," *Online Readings in Psychology and Culture*, Unit 2:1 (2009).

[5] Schwartz et al., "Identity Development, Personality, and Well-Being in Adolescence and Emerging Adulthood," 2012.

their subjective experience of their gender; it includes personal attributes, social roles, social customs, activities, and behaviors. *Sexual identity* is the process by which persons come to understand to whom they are sexually attracted; it includes development of sexual orientation. *Ethnic/racial identity* is the process by which individuals develop a sense of personal investment in and attachment to their ethnic group.[6] It includes individuals' beliefs and attitudes about their group membership as well as the process by which these develop over time.[7] Research shows that often individuals from minority ethnic groups place more emphasis on their ethnic identity than those from majority ethnic groups. *Spiritual identity* is the process by which individuals develop an understanding of their subjective feelings, thoughts, and behaviors that relate to the search for the sacred.[8] This includes their connection to a higher being and can include attachment to a specific religious institution or group.

It is important to note that identity development is not necessarily a linear process. Individual identity develops at its own pace, with the different intersecting variables developing on their own timelines, based on personality and life circumstances. Individuals place emphasis on different parts of their identity at different times, and the diverse aspects of identity all form within a sociocultural context.

PERSONALITY AND IDENTITY

In addition to the influence of culture on our identity development, personality dynamics also play a role in forming our identity and the ways we express ourselves. Personality refers to individual

[6] J. S. Phinney and A. D. Ong, "Conceptualization and Measurement of Ethnic Identity: Current Status and Future Directions," *Journal of Counseling Psychology* 54 (2007): 271–81.

[7] A. J. Umaña-Taylor, "Ethnic Identity and Self-Esteem: Examining the Role of Social Context," *Journal of Adolescence* 27, no. 2 (April 2004): 139–46.

[8] P. C. Hill et al., "Conceptualizing Religion and Spirituality: Points of Commonality, Points of Departure," *Journal for the Theory of Social Behaviour* 30 (2000): 51–77.

differences in characteristic patterns of behaving and includes emotional tendencies, one's general approach to the social world, and dispositional levels of self-control.[9]

There are both universal and culture-specific aspects of variation in personality. The trait approach in psychology has a long and rich history dating back to the work of Gordon Allport.[10] In the past two decades trait approaches to personality have become extremely important in understanding the relationship between culture and personality, and it is the dominant view today.[11] This work has culminated in what is known today as the Five-Factor Model (FFM) of personality. A large body of literature suggests that the "Big Five" personality factors emerge in various cultures.[12]

FIVE-FACTOR MODEL (FFM) OF PERSONALITY

Cross-cultural research generally views personality as something discrete and separate from culture. The FFM is a conceptual model built around five distinct and basic personality dimensions that appear to be universal for all humans. A measure for assessing the FFM is the NEO-Personality Inventory (NEO-PI-R or NEO-PI-III).[13] They are measured on a continuum, whereby an individual may, for instance, be highly extraverted,[14] low in extraversion (introverted) or somewhere between these two extremes. The FFM

---

[9] Schwartz et al., "Identity Development, Personality, and Well-Being in Adolescence and Emerging Adulthood," 2012; "Personality," *American Psychological Association Dictionary* (2019).

[10] Gordon Allport, *Personality: A Psychological Interpretation* (New York: Holt, Rinehart, and Winston, 1937).

[11] David Matsumoto and Linda Juang, *Culture and Psychology*, 4th ed. (Belmont, CA: Wadsworth Cengage Learning, 2008), 264.

[12] Robert R. McCrae and J. Allik, eds., *The Five-Factor Model of Personality across Cultures,* International and Cultural Psychology Series (New York: Kluwer Academic / Plenum Publishers, 2002). In this book thirty-five contributors discuss the replicability, validity, and applicability of the Five-Factor Model (FFM) in some forty cultures.

[13] See P. T. Costa Jr. and R. R. McCrae, *The NEO-PI/NEO-FFI Manual Supplement* (Odessa, FL: Psychological Assessment Resources, 1989)

[14] *Extraversion* is the technical term used by psychologists, while *extroversion* is the common spelling for the same idea.

comes out of early personality research's focus on trait theory, which is the idea that a person's temperament and behavior can be understood in terms of individual traits (e.g. self-confidence, friendliness, or melancholy). The FFM's five dimensions are openness, conscientiousness, extraversion, agreeableness, and neuroticism, easily remembered using the acronym OCEAN.

Cross-cultural research in the past decade or two has supported the validity of the FFM in different countries and cultures and has continued to support claims of universality. One of the most widely used trait theories, it takes a lexical approach to personality, which assumes that traits can be described using single adjectives or descriptive phrases. If enough people regularly exhibit a form of behavior and no term exists in a given language to describe it, then according to the lexical hypothesis, a term will be created so that the trait may be considered and discussed with others.

We now look briefly at these five personality factors and draw implications for benefits to priesthood and religious life in areas such as screening, assessment formation, and leadership implications.

Openness to Experience

The *openness to experience* dimension of personality is characterized by a willingness to try new activities. People with higher levels of openness are amenable to unconventional ideas and beliefs, including those that challenge their existing assumptions. They enjoy artistic and cultural experiences, visiting art galleries, museums, and theaters, listening to music, and traveling to new destinations. They are more open to unfamiliar cultures and customs. People with low levels of openness—those who are closed to experience—are wary of uncertainty and the unknown. They are more suspicious of beliefs and ideas that challenge their status quo. They feel uncomfortable in unfamiliar situations and prefer familiar environments. Less-open individuals value the safety of predictability and like to adhere to well-known traditions and routines. Openness to experience is often associated with intelligence when measuring personality factors. Individuals who score highly on verbal/crystallized intelligence measures also report being more open to experience, which may be important to consider within religious-life circles.

Conscientiousness

People who are *conscientious* are more aware of their actions and the consequences of their behavior than people who are unconscientious. They feel a sense of responsibility toward others and are generally careful to carry out the duties assigned to them. Conscientious individuals like to keep a tidy environment and are well organized. They are eager to maintain good timekeeping. People who are highly conscientious also exhibit more goal-oriented behavior. They set ambitious goals and are motivated to achieve them. Undeterred by hard work, they are driven to succeed in every aspect of their lives, including academic achievements and in furthering their careers. Low levels of conscientiousness are reflected in less motivated behavior. Such individuals are less concerned by tidiness and punctuality. This may result in them arriving late to appointments and meetings and being more relaxed in setting life goals. Unconscientious people tend to engage in more impulsive behavior. They will act on a last-minute whim rather than considering the consequences of their choices. Research suggests that both environmental factors and heritability may influence conscientiousness.

Extraversion

Extraversion is characterized by outgoing, socially confident behavior. Extraverts are sociable, talkative, and often forward in social situations. They enjoy being the center of a group and will often seek the attention of others. Extraverts enjoy meeting new people and are happy to introduce themselves to strangers, thriving in the company of others. This personality trait is measured on an introversion-extraversion continuum. Individuals who fit in the middle of the two traits are described as ambiverts.

People with low levels of extraversion (introverts) display contrasting behavior. They are quieter and often feel shy around other people. They may feel intimidated being in large groups, such as parties, and will often try to avoid demanding social gatherings. Introverts enjoy being a part of smaller social groups, preferably with familiar people. Introverts thus tend to enjoy smaller social networks, maintaining a close group of trusted friends.

Agreeableness

Individuals who score highly on *agreeableness* measures are friendly and cooperative. Often considered likable by their peers and colleagues, agreeable people are trusting of others and are altruistic, willing to help others during times of need. Their ability to work with others means that they often work well as members of a team. Agreeable people dislike being involved in arguments, conflict with others, and other forms of confrontation. They seek to pacify and appease others, acting as the mediating "peacemaker" of their group. Individuals who are disagreeable score lower on this dimension of personality. They are less concerned with pleasing other people and making friends. Disagreeable individuals are more suspicious of other people's intentions and are less charitable. Instead, they are motivated to act in accordance with their self-interest, showing less regard for the needs of others. As a result, they are perceived by others as being more selfish than agreeable personalities. While disagreeable individuals find it easier to promote their own interests, those who are more agreeable tend to enjoy better relationships with others. From an early age, this can be beneficial. It has been found that children with higher levels of agreeableness were less likely to be subjected to bullying at school.[15]

Neuroticism

This personality dimension is measured on a continuum ranging from emotional stability to emotional instability, or neuroticism. People with high *neuroticism* scores are often persistent worriers. They are more fearful and often feel anxious, overthinking their problems and exaggerating their significance. Rather than seeing the positive in a situation, they may dwell on its negative aspects. Neuroticism can result in a person coping less successfully with common stressors in their daily lives. Instead, they will often become frustrated with others and may feel angry if events do

---

[15] See L. A. Jensen-Campbell et al., "Agreeableness, Extraversion, and Peer Relations in Early Adolescence: Winning Friends and Deflecting Aggression," *Journal of Research in Personality* 363 (2002): 224–51.

not occur as they wish. People with low neuroticism scores are less preoccupied by these negative concerns. They are able to remain calmer in response to stressful situations and to view problems in proportion to their importance. As a result, they tend to worry about such problems to a lesser extent. Neuroticism can have repercussions in terms of a person's relationship with others. A study found that people in relationships were less happy than other couples if their partner scored high on neuroticism.[16]

INTERACTION OF PERSONALITY, CULTURE, AND OTHER FACTORS

Despite the presence of FFM across a multitude of cultures, it is important to keep in mind that the five personality traits are still developed within a particular sociocultural context, which shapes the ways in which these traits are expressed in different cultures and countries. Different cultures place different values on the specific traits. For instance, extraversion will likely have more value in American culture than in a rural Chinese culture. Similarly, characteristics of openness may have little value in traditional cultures where there are limited options for life choices.[17]

In addition to the personal and cultural aspects of our identity and our personality traits, the story one constructs about one's life, known as a personal life narrative, provides a sense of purpose and meaning to one's identity. "Narrative identity gives individual lives their unique and culturally anchored meanings."[18] Narration of one's life is particularly important for helping others understand how one's life story has shaped one's ways of relating to the world

---

[16] A long-running German panel survey shows that personal and economic choices, not just genes, matter for happiness. See B. Headey, R. Muffels, and G. G. Wagner, *Proceedings of the National Academy of Sciences of the United States of America* 107, no. 4242 (2010): 17922–26.

[17] Robert R. McCrae, "Cross-Cultural Research on the Five-Factor Model of Personality," *Online Readings in Psychology and Culture* 4, no. 4 (2002).

[18] D. P. McAdams and J. L. Pals, "A New Big Five: Fundamental Principles for an Integrative Science of Personality," *American Psychologist* 61, no. 3 (2006): 210.

and others. Furthermore, personal narratives can give voice to additional aspects of one's cultural experience and identity that may be difficult to articulate in other ways, such as experiences of privilege, oppression, immigration, and assimilation and acculturation. Such experiences also shape one's personality development.

Let us take a closer look at the cultural experiences listed above. *Privilege* can be understood as "unearned advantages that are conferred on individuals based on membership in a dominant group or assumed membership."[19] Many of us carry privilege in some area (educational level, vocation, income, and so on), and it is important to recognize when our privilege might make it difficult for us to understand the perspective of someone who is different from us and does not share our same areas of privilege. *Oppression* can be considered the state of being burdened spiritually or mentally, suppressed or crushed by an abuse of power. Individuals' experience with oppression and oppressive systems affects their worldview, often making them more aware of and sensitive to issues of oppression, and significantly influences their identity. *Immigration* is the international movement of people into a destination country of which they are not natives or where they do not possess citizenship. It involves separation from their country of origin, family members, and familiar customs, and it requires navigation of unfamiliar cultural contexts. *Assimilation* can be understood as a process of adapting to a new culture where the minority group or minority member is absorbed into the dominant culture. Individuals who assimilate lose aspects of their culture, which can result in a loss of self-identity. *Acculturation* also involves the process of adapting to a new culture; however, with acculturation there is a transfer of values and customs from one group to another and, unlike with assimilation, the minority members retain aspects of their own cultural identity while learning aspects of the main culture.[20]

---

[19] Society of Counseling Psychology, American Psychological Association Division 17, "Exploring Privilege," div17.org.

[20] See P. A. Hays, *Addressing Cultural Complexities in Practice: Assessment, Diagnosis, and Therapy*, 3rd ed. (Washington, DC: American Psychological Association, 2016); Schwartz et al., "Identity Development, Personality, and Well-Being in Adolescence and Emerging Adulthood," 2012.

The filter through which we experience and perceive interactions with others occurs at the intersection of the multiple aspects of our identity and theirs. When we attempt to separate culture and personality, we are experiencing ourselves and others as fragmented parts instead of as an integrated whole. An integrated perspective is needed to understand who the person is and what contributes to the expression of the person's self. By asking if something is due to personality or to culture, we dismiss or minimize important details and complexities of the individual that can help us empathically connect and foster healthy relationships.

SOME PRACTICAL APPLICATIONS FOR RELIGIOUS LIFE AND PRIESTHOOD

Understanding and supporting the whole person require holding a space that shows empathy for difference. This starts by understanding how deeply embedded identity factors are and being curious and open to learning about the varying aspects of one's identity, including personality and cultural factors that are central to the individual. It is also important that all persons in a cross-cultural exchange are aware of their own identity and the ways in which their areas of privilege, oppression, and other cultural experiences have developed areas of bias that may make it difficult to empathize with a different perspective. In addition, it is important to not expect individuals to assimilate to majority cultural norms that would encourage individuals to give up important parts of their identity. Instead, communities and dioceses should be encouraging acculturation, where bi-directional cultural learning can occur between the individual acculturating and those in the majority culture. Scheduling opportunities for cross-cultural sharing, where individuals of different backgrounds can share their personal narratives and voice important aspects of their identity, can assist with coming to a better understanding of what shapes the behaviors and interactions witnessed in cross-cultural exchanges.

In addition, the FFM is being used around the world in practical applications. The universality of this approach means that we need not "start from scratch" in each culture. Rather, we can compare and contrast both individual traits and grouping of traits across cultures and draw practical implications for candidate screenings, formation, and ministry. For example, persons with open and mature spirituality seem to be higher in emotional stability. Not surprisingly, religious fundamentalism is associated with low openness.[21]

Knowledge of this information, in conjunction with the utilization of measures that assess the FFM, can assist communities and dioceses in the screening and formation of candidates, or the assessment of current members, in order to gather a better understanding of an individual's personality traits and how they may manifest as strengths or areas for development in formation and ministry. Information from formal personality measures should be combined with information about individuals' cultural backgrounds and other information relevant for understanding where they are in the development of different aspects of their identity (gender identity, sexual identity, and so forth). The more aware we are of the ways in which multiple and intersecting aspects of one's cultural identity influence personality development and behavior, the more effective we can be in our intercultural relationships and in our understanding, screening, and formation of religious, priests, and seminarians.

---

[21] Vassilis Saroglo, "Religion and the Five Factors of Personality: A Meta-Analytic Review," *Personality and Individual Differences* 32 (November 2002): 21.

13

Ensuring New Wineskins for New Wine

Leadership in Intercultural Communities

Antonio M. Pernia, SVD

If we employ the imagery of new wine in new wineskins, and if we grant that interculturality is the new wine that is fermenting in consecrated life today, then the need is to ensure that religious communities become the new wineskins that can hold this new wine. The imagery implies that old wineskins are those that have lost their elasticity, so that when the new wine ferments and expands the wineskin, the old wineskin bursts and the wine is wasted.[1] Leadership in intercultural communities is fundamentally the task of ensuring that the religious community maintains its elasticity or flexibility so as to hold the new wine of interculturality as it ferments, and continues to ferment until it becomes old wine for, as the Gospel of Luke puts it, "the old is good" (Luke 5:39). The document *New Wine in New Wineskins* says: *"New wine*

---

[1] See Patricia Murray, IBVM, "Leadership for Transformation in Today's Intercultural World (Part I)," Recollection Conference given to the XVIII SVD General Chapter, Centro Ad Gentes, Nemi (Rome), Italy (June 29, 2018).

must be left to ferment, almost breathe, inside the wineskin so that it can age properly and eventually be savored and shared."[2]

A PARADIGM SHIFT

Interculturality, therefore, requires a shift of paradigms in leadership in religious communities—basically, a shift from leadership as maintaining order and stability to leadership as allowing, if not provoking, some "disorder" and restlessness in religious communities; from leadership as instilling structures of discipline and regularity to leadership as creating conditions for flexibility and irregularity.

> One evening at our SVD Generalate in Rome, the community had an hour of adoration before the Blessed Sacrament. After a few prayers and songs, there was a longer time of silence for personal prayer and reflection. The lights were dimmed and there was complete silence. After some minutes of solemn silence, suddenly, a confrere from Africa began singing "Amazing Grace." Everyone turned around to look at him. The solemn silence was disturbed, their adoration was disrupted. This was not usual. This was most unusual. The superior, instead of standing up and going to the confrere to stop his disturbance of the silence, started singing along with the confrere. Eventually, although reluctantly in the beginning, the whole community joined in the singing. In the end, everyone felt his prayer and adoration were enriched by that disturbance of the order in the chapel.[3]

This shift of paradigms, I think, is concretely expressed in the shift from leadership as individual or personal leadership to

---

[2] Congregation for Institutes of Consecrated Life and Societies of Apostolic Life (CICLSAL), *New Wine in New Wineskins: The Consecrated Life and Its Ongoing Challenges since Vatican II* (Città del Vaticano: Libreria Editrice Vaticana, 2017), 2.

[3] Adapted from a story shared by Father Andrew Recepcion, spiritual director at the Pontificio Collegio Filippino in Rome.

leadership as team leadership. On the one hand, individual leadership usually relies on the unique personality of the leader, on his or her strength of character, broadness of vision, competence in administration, depth of faith, and genuineness of spirituality. The lines of authority are clear and are usually vertical or hierarchical. The individual leader usually embodies order and stability. On the other hand, team leadership represents diversity and flexibility. It relies on the collaboration of the team, its unity of vision, spirit of co-responsibility, multiplicity of perspectives, diversity of experiences, and representativeness of the community. The lines of authority may not be very clear and could be horizontal and fraternal. As *New Wine in New Wineskins* puts it:

> In the broader view of consecrated life since the Council, we have passed from the centrality of the role of authority to the centrality of the dynamic of fraternity. For this reason, authority must be at the service of communion: a true ministry to accompany brothers and sisters towards conscious and responsible fidelity. (no. 41)

Indeed, team leadership is indispensable in intercultural communities. It is unrealistic and unfair to expect a single individual adequately to represent, serve, and lead a religious community with a membership that is culturally diverse and most likely also engaged in a diversity of ministries. Even secular organizations that are not explicitly intercultural rely more and more on team leadership. The complexities of modern life are simply such that no single individual can effectively exercise the function of leadership.

Obviously, team leadership in intercultural communities needs to be intercultural itself, that is, the team must comprise members coming from different cultures or nationalities. For this reason there will be greater need for efforts at team building, not just at the start of the leadership team's term of office but also regularly throughout its term of service—exactly the same efforts that team leadership needs to foster the culturally diverse membership of the community. In other words, the leadership team will need to mirror for the community what it means to be truly intercultural. Thus, team leadership will be leading by example. I believe this is what is meant by the statement of *New Wine in New Wineskins*

192 Antonio M. Pernia, SVD

regarding the move "from the centrality of the role of authority to the centrality of the dynamic of fraternity" (no. 41).

In fact, team leadership has a revered parallel in the church in the principle of collegiality. The idea of a college or a council assisting a superior is a venerable tradition in the church. Thus, we have expressions like "Peter and the college of the apostles" or "the pope and the college of bishops." In religious congregations the practice of having local, provincial, and general councils is enshrined in most rules and constitutions. Indeed, I believe it can be said that team leadership originated in the church, and within the church, in religious congregations. This should not come as a surprise for, after all, the gospel idea of authority is service and the model of leadership is Jesus and his disciples. Although not cultur- ally diverse, the disciples were a group of diverse personalities—a tax-collector, a zealot, a skeptic, some fishermen, two "sons of thunder" (Mark 3:17). In a certain sense the community of Jesus and his disciples can be considered a model for an intercultural leadership team.

Incidentally, *New Wine in New Wineskins* also stresses the importance of team leadership over individual leadership (nos. 19–21). It insists that superiors respect decisions of chapters and invite the collaboration of the council. It calls for the implemen- tation of the principles of subsidiarity and co-responsibility and warns against the dangers of too vertical an exercise of authority, which is open to the manipulation of the freedom and dignity of community members. This, the document says, is often one of the reasons for abandonment of the religious life. Two quotations from the document serve to illustrate this:

> The government [of religious communities] may not be centralized in the hands of only one person, thereby cir- cumventing canonical bans. (no. 19)

> No authority figure, not even a founder, must think to be the exclusive interpreter of the charism or to be excluded from the norms of the universal law of the Church. (no. 20)

Team leadership, however, is more than just a council assisting a superior to do his or her job. It entails the council sharing in the responsibility of leadership and assuming some of the duties of the superior by delegation.

Some time after I took office as superior general I was often asked by confreres and friends how I was doing in the job. My spontaneous answer was that I was happy that I had a good council to bear the responsibility with me. In the beginning this was simply a perfunctory response to a question that was difficult to answer. However, over time I truly experienced how important it was to share leadership with a team. It not only lightened the burden (by sharing responsibility), but it also ensured that the task of leadership was done well (since matters could be studied more thoroughly, decisions could be based on a wide variety of experiences and perspectives, and the views of the confreres from below could be better expressed and represented).

Building teamwork often requires not just holding official meetings with one's team members but also coming together unofficially to get to know one another better. Often it also demands that the team come together for moments of prayer and reflection.

BASIC TASKS OF LEADERSHIP IN INTERCULTURAL COMMUNITIES

Let me now move on to what I think are the three fundamental tasks of leadership in an intercultural community: (1) promoting diversity, (2) mediating differences or conflicts, and (3) guarding unity.[4] A word on each of these tasks.

Promotion of Diversity

The first task is the promotion of diversity. I mention diversity first because the usual tendency is to begin with unity. Indeed, our initial tendency is to avoid or ignore difference because very often we do not know what to do with it and therefore are

---

[4] These tasks are based on Henry Barlage, SVD, "Leadership in the SVD," talk given at the workshop for the SVD provincial superiors of the European Zone, held at the Centro Ad Gentes, Nemi (Rome), Italy (1995).

uncomfortable with it. Thus, the initial tendency is to ignore minority cultures and recognize only the one dominant or prevailing culture of the members of the community. The unconscious expectation is that everyone in the community learns or adapts to the dominant culture.

But if we are convinced that interculturality is not just a situation to be tolerated but a goal to aim at, then our starting point should be our diversity and differences. We should start from the fact that we are different from one another. To achieve this, the leadership needs to be attentive to the minority cultures in the community. The leadership needs to create an atmosphere that allows the minority cultures to be visible in the community. In the concrete, this means allowing, or even promoting, the use of elements of the minority cultures in community activities such as worship and prayer, meals and recreation, meetings, and days of reflection.

However, doing so will create, apropos to what was said in the beginning, a certain amount of "disorder" in the community. Consider, for instance, the community dining room. Where there used to be only bread and pasta and wine, rice and fish and all kinds of spicy condiments begin to appear because of the presence of Asians or Africans. Or the liturgy. No longer only solemn organ music, but also "noisy" guitars and drums and percussion instruments. Or clothes. No longer just black and gray and white but colorful shirts from Africa and multicolored batik from Indonesia.

In the task of promoting diversity, leadership is called not just to protect diversity where it is actually present, but also to foster it where it is not yet a reality. When I was still in Rome, there was a provincial superior who wrote to our Generalate every year asking that young confreres from "other cultures" be assigned to his province. Today, that province is now composed of confreres coming from about twenty different nationalities. This forms part of the task of leadership in an intercultural community, that is, the active promotion of cultural diversity in the community or province. This requires making the province or community conducive to diversity or attractive to the coming of young confreres from other cultures or countries.

This first task coincides with one of the essential attitudes for interculturality, namely, recognition of other cultures—in other words, the recognition and acceptance of diversity, the recognition and acceptance of differences. This implies ensuring that those of the minority cultures feel they belong to the community or province. This entails making them feel that they are welcomed, acknowledged, and appreciated, not just tolerated. While this task will need to involve the whole community, the leadership will nevertheless have a special role to play in it.

Mediation of Differences and Conflicts

A second task is the mediation of differences and, at times, of conflicts. If we allow diversity and differences in the community, then we should be ready for tensions and conflicts. It is important, however, to be clear about the source or the nature of the conflicts and tensions, that is, whether they are due to personal differences or to cultural diversity. Of course, in the concrete, it is often difficult to distinguish between the sources of conflicts. Often personal and cultural differences converge or combine to create tensions and conflicts. Sometimes, too, members intentionally disguise the nature of the conflict by presenting personal conflicts as cultural conflicts and vice versa. Nevertheless I believe that, as far as possible, an effort should be made to try to distinguish between personal and cultural conflicts.

In any case, even before tensions and conflicts arise, it would be good for the leadership to foster among the members of the community a conviction about two elements of interculturality:

First, that everyone in the community should develop a genuine respect for cultural difference. Respect goes beyond simply recognizing or acknowledging cultural difference. Respect for cultural difference means coming to terms with these facts: (1) diversity is not going to go away, but that it is here to stay; (2) diversity is not a temporary situation, but that it is a permanent feature of our reality; and (3) diversity is not just a cause of problems and conflicts but also a source of enrichment and growth.

Second, that everyone in the community should realize that genuine interculturality will have an impact on community structures, religious lifestyle, ways of worship, methods of work, and systems of government. New wine needs new wineskins. If our membership becomes international but our surroundings do not change at all, then something is wrong. Everyone should expect changes to occur in the community because of our cultural diversity. And so it follows that, because we expect our community structures and lifestyles to change, the community must come together often to talk about these changes as part of ongoing formation. Mediating differences and conflicts will often demand that the leadership team act impartially. However, trying to be objective and neutral does not have to mean that leaders act as if they were "culture-less" or as if they were not influenced by their own particular culture. Here, it is important that the leadership team members acknowledge their own cultural limitation and from there try to mediate between conflicting individuals or groups in the community. Because of its members' own cultural limitations, the leadership team will need to make the effort to try to understand all sides of the conflict. In this way its members need not only to promote dialogue among the conflicting individuals or groups, but also to be themselves part of the dialogue.

Protection of Unity

The third task is the preservation of unity in the community. Unity is, obviously, the ultimate aim of genuine community living. The two other tasks—the promotion of diversity and the mediation of differences or conflicts—are ultimately to be directed toward the third, which is the attainment and preservation of unity. Here, of course, unity should not be understood as uniformity or as the dominant culture subsuming the minority cultures in the community. Rather, unity should be understood in terms of "unity in diversity" or a unity that is the fruit of the true interaction of the different cultures of the members. Thus, a genuine interculturality.

This task coincides with another essential attitude for interculturality, that is, the promotion of healthy interaction among cultures, which entails the creation of a climate whereby each culture allows itself to be transformed or enriched by the others. In this way each individual member, as well as the entire community, is enriched by the interaction of the different cultures. In a certain sense, then, the unity that we want to achieve in intercultural communities is not a static but a dynamic kind of unity; not some preconceived idea of unity to which everyone needs to conform, but a reality that is constantly in the process of being built through the interaction of different cultures.

The word *healthy,* in the expression *healthy interaction,* needs to be emphasized, because in many cases the interaction among cultures is unhealthy, that is, marked by suspicion, racism, discrimination, and conflict. Healthy interaction is based on confidence about the value of one's own culture, and a sense of security that is not threatened by an encounter with difference. Its hallmark is the openness and willingness to be changed by the other and to incorporate aspects of that otherness into one's own culture.

In this context unity is achieved not when differences are erased or eliminated, so that everyone begins to be or to look like each other. Rather, unity is achieved when differences are respected and are made into a source of mutual enrichment and growth. Unity is realized not when everyone learns to do things in exactly the same way, but when the community manages to attain its goal despite the fact—or because of the fact—that everyone does things differently but authentically.

Thus, leadership in an intercultural community needs to foster the mentality among the members that each one is a gift to the others, despite—or precisely because of—their differences. Leadership needs to promote the conviction that there is something to receive from everyone, and that everyone has a gift to offer. But this vision of everyone being a gift to the others flourishes only in the context of friendship and love. In the end, then, the third task of leadership as guardian of unity is really the task of fostering love and friendship among the members of the community.

CONCLUSION

In the Society of the Divine Word, we declared the year 2003 as our Year of Grace. This was the year when our founder, Arnold Janssen, and our first missionary, Joseph Freinademetz, were canonized in Rome. The theme chosen for our Year of Grace was "One Heart, Many Faces." This theme was meant to express an essential characteristic of our congregation, namely, the cultural diversity of our members. Today, our congregation comprises members belonging to about seventy nationalities, working in about eighty countries, in all five continents of the world. And so, "One Heart, Many Faces" was a particularly appropriate theme. Indeed, as the Prologue to the Society of the Divine Word Constitutions states: "As a community of brothers from different nations and languages, we become a living symbol of the unity and diversity of the Church." We also had a special prayer for that year. One line of that prayer said: "Teach us to rejoice in the abundant diversity of peoples and give us a loving heart ready to embrace all peoples of our one world."

And so, leadership in intercultural communities is precisely the challenge of promoting the "many faces" without endangering or jeopardizing the "oneness of heart," or vice versa, of fostering the "one heart" without eliminating or downplaying the "many faces." The challenge, in other words, is one of knowing how to promote a genuine unity in diversity—a unity that protects diversity and a diversity that preserves unity. For, as French philosopher Blaise Pascal once said: "Diversity without unity is chaos; unity without diversity is tyranny."[5]

---

[5] The exact quotation is: "The multitude which is not brought to act as a unity, is confusion. That unity which has not its origin in the multitude is tyranny" (Blaise Pascal, *Pensées*, #77 [1670], Eng. trans. O. W. Wight, *Thoughts, Letters, and Opuscules of Blaise Pascal* [New York: H. W. Derby, 1861], 382).

14

Interculturality and Formation

JUDETTE GALLARES, RC

I would like to begin with an adage that is an appropriate description of what we are about to engage in here: *Awareness of the other starts at the encounter of difference.* This is more discernible today, when diversity makes up the very fabric of societies and religious communities.

If interculturality "exists as an itinerary, as a process or a journey that seeks to foster a new level of relation with others without prejudices," then it seeks to unite the two essential aspects of intercultural relations: encounter and diversity.[1] Just as dialogue cannot be imposed but must remain open to the other, interculturality calls for an open heart and an open mind in order to encounter the other. In interculturality, both identity and diversity are affirmed, leading to open exchange and enrichment of one another. Thus, interculturality and formation are intertwined but, as a process, interculturality must be introduced from the very start in the formation of consecrated persons.

---

[1] Peixoto J. Oscar, "Formation and Mission: The International Houses of Formation," *International Mission Congress OFM Conv*, Cochin, Kerala, India, January 12–22, 2006.

BEGINNING WITH SELF-AWARENESS

As in dialogue, interculturality always begins with self-awareness, especially of how one is formed in and influenced by one's culture. There are several problems that can be encountered during the process of interculturality, especially in the area of consecrated life.

First, the present practice of the vows in the church as experienced by non-Westerners is influenced by trappings from the West. Often Western spiritual practices are presented as a better or more superior way of growing in the spiritual life. This does not mean that the traditional, Western-oriented spiritual practices that are part of the institute's charism are no longer important. It just means that there is a greater challenge for the institute, as part of the process of interculturation, to allow the spirituality and spiritual practices coming from another culture to enrich its charism.

Second, there are concrete difficulties a culture may encounter in the practice of the vows. For instance, strong family ties in the Asian context and a sense of "familial self" may appear to the individual self in the West to have trappings of dependency or may be seen by Western-oriented formators as emotional immaturity.

Third, formative processes tend to be patterned after Western paradigms of understanding the self.

Fourth, there can be challenges to the vows coming from cultures. Since no culture is perfect, it needs to be evangelized by the Gospel, while at the same time, consecrated life can also be enriched by culture itself. For example, certain forms of prayer are enriched by Asian culture. Furthermore, the special context of our changing times may be equally challenging to the way religious women and men understand and practice their vows.

These are not problems of interculturality alone but are issues of *deculturation*, that is, the process by which aspects of one culture are lost after contact with another culture, especially a dominant one such as the Western culture that became the vessel of Christianity, bringing it to the world. We need to detach what is essential from that which is peripheral. *Transculturation* challenges the vows and forces the culture to change. *Incultura-tion* allows the culture to enrich the practice of the vows and the living of our consecrated vocation. *Interculturality* enriches our relationship within our religious communities, inviting us to encounter others who are different from us and to enter into communion with one another.

DRAWING MY CULTURE

The process of interculturality is not a logical one. This is because culture in itself is like the eyes through which we look at reality. We do not see the very eyes through which we see and look at others and the world. Therefore, we do not see things the way *they* are, but the way *we* are. Our "seeing" is always biased and subjective. And since it is not a logical process, we need to have an awareness of the culture that formed us first as a person and the biases that can block the process of interculturality.

We will use a reflective exercise entitled "Drawing My Culture"[2] to become aware of the cultural influences that formed our identity and our sense of self.

Remember that culture is like our eyes. What has influenced the way we see things? How has our culture formed us as we are? What are the various cultural influences in our lives that have formed our *personal culture*?

In the following illustration we can see the major cultural influences that normally shape a person from birth to adulthood. Cultural psychologists agree that where a child grows up and who his or her parents are will influence the cultural wisdom—or emphasis of certain values and skills—that are passed to the child. In early childhood these cultural differences become increasingly significant in our identity formation and can be reinforced by meaningful persons and events in our life.

In the process of formation it is important that candidates be helped to reflect on how these cultural influences, especially those coming from childhood, have influenced their moral and spiritual values as well as their behavior and attitudes in life. For instance, one of the main characteristics cultural scientists observe in analyzing cultures is in the area of morality, especially behavior and attitudes toward human sexuality. Morality or moral values

---

[2] Gert Jan Hofstede, Paul Pedersen, and Geert Hofstede, *Exploring Culture: Exercises, Stories, and Synthetic Cultures* (Yarmouth, ME: Intercultural Press, 2002), 210.

and behavior tend to come from the family more than from the school and classroom. For example, Asian children, who come from a culture that teaches modesty and whose family and significant persons avoid discussing openly anything related to human sexuality, might seem to be the polar opposites of Western children, who come from a culture that reveres self-esteem and self-expression. All other cultural influences, such as the school or church, merely reinforce earlier learnings. It is often during adolescence that young people, through peer pressure, begin to experiment with challenging the culture that influenced them from childhood. This is an important stage in identity formation and in establishing their autonomy beyond the family.

Figure 14–1 shows the various cultural influences that affect one's development from birth. These are often referred to as the key formative settings.

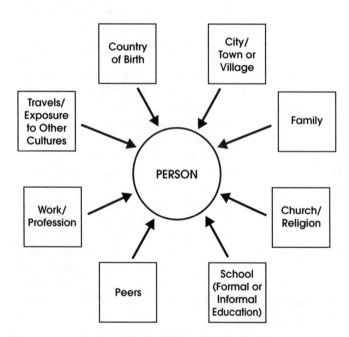

Figure 14–1. Key Formative Settings

The following reflective exercise helps us become aware that the cultural dimension of our identity contains nonverbal, nonrational, and symbolic elements that are difficult to express in words.

Use this exercise as a way of loosening up the atmosphere for open sharing and as a tool for getting information about the ways by which the other perceives his or her sociocultural and religious environments and influences.

1. Reflection

- Draw or select symbols meaningful to your culture or any combination of designs, doodles, or lines that have meaning to you in terms of your culture. *(Do not write or use words yet. Instead, engage the right side of your brain, which is more intuitive, holistic, synthesizing, and subjective.)*
- After your drawing is complete, use words to write conclusions and insights you have gained as a result of this exercise about your culture and the cultural influences that have contributed to the development (or lack of development) of your sense of identity and selfhood.

2. Share your insights with another person

3. Share learnings in the big group

(Note: In using this exercise with an individual or a group, you can suggest the use of crayons, colored pencils, and other art materials. You can also provide longer periods for reflection. There are multiple ways of sharing: in dyads, triads, or small groups of four or five persons. A spiritual companion or formator can also adapt this reflective exercise as a way of preparing a directee or candidate at the beginning of a spiritual accompaniment relationship.)

From this self-awareness, which is a necessary first step, we can move on to consciousness raising from the two sides of culture and the vows. The process of interculturality will only happen when we begin to live the vows creatively in the culture.

CULTURE AND THE VOWS

It is a challenge for formators to live their consecrated vocation as authentic witnesses to the practice of interculturality. Doing so requires critical thinking and discernment in appropriating cultural values that are congruent with the gospel and in purifying those that are incongruent to consecrated life. This task must be done by those who belong to the culture where the formation house is located. They are the ones who will evangelize their culture and show their newer members, through their attitudes and behavior, the transformative process of consecrated life. As formators living in their own culture, they are called to give witness to the power of the gospel to evangelize culture. If the formators are foreigners, they must create the space and a sense of freedom to allow the newer members or local religious to find ways by which culture can enrich the vows and vice versa. Providing an open space for dialogue and learning from one another can be part of the intercultural program in the community.

REFLECTION ON VALUES AND CULTURAL PRACTICES

We begin by reflecting critically on the values and cultural practices that have affected our understanding and living of the vows. There are two important elements that facilitate the process of interculturality: (1) open vision and (2) concrete action.

We sometimes get trapped in the concrete situations we live in. When that happens, we need to broaden our own vision.

A great danger in the church today is to be trapped in paradigms of formation that are no longer relevant to the changing times. We can give in to our tendency to stifle the Holy Spirit by reducing the practice of the vows to a common denomination. The pressure is toward some sort of uniformity to bring the religious to a common mold. But consecrated persons are not supposed to live the vows in the same way in every age and culture, simply complying with external structures dictated by cultural practices that may have worked in the past but are no longer transformative in the present. The evangelical counsels call us to a transformation of the human heart as we engage in constant dialogue with the culture(s) that have formed our self-understanding and identity.

Consecrated persons are challenged to inculturate the vows in different ways and should not accept confinement to antiquated structures or juridical law.

An open vision allows us to think critically of how culture forms the person. In this vision we ask critical questions: What cultural characteristics or practices have formed my identity and self-concept within my culture? What cultural value system influenced or formed me? How is that value system congruent or incongruent to gospel values or values of consecrated life? How is it congruent or incongruent to the particular charism of my institute that incarnates the gospel? Based on the answers to these questions, we need to ask further: What formative process or processes will facilitate my growth as a person? What concrete action or actions am I challenged to take?

(The worksheet, Figure 14–2, can be prepared ahead of time as a response sheet for the reflection exercise. Depending on the length of time for personal reflection given to the participants, more rows can be added to the table.)

TOWARD INTERCULTURALITY IN FORMATION

Theological studies have shown that interculturality is a reciprocal movement, as people of different cultures enrich one another in striving to overcome any prejudice in the transmission of knowledge or an imposition of practice. Interculturality fosters respect for our own culture and the culture of the other. The mind is fixed on the point of view of others as well as our own: their life history, their origin, their stories, and their world of fantasies. This, in the area of affectivity, implies empathy.[3]

As a theological process, interculturality must become an integral part of the formation of consecrated persons, especially as our world today is becoming more multicultural. How do we move multiculturality toward interculturality? It must first be introduced as a journey, an itinerary that begins with self-awareness

---

[3] Stephen B. Bevans and Roger Schroeder, *Constants in Context: A Theology of Mission for Today* (Maryknoll, NY: Orbis Books, 2004), 384.

CULTURAL CHARACTERISTICS/PRACTICES	FORMATION: IDENTITY/SELF-CONCEPT WITHIN YOUR CULTURE	FORMATION: VALUE SYSTEM WITHIN YOUR CULTURE	HOW IS YOUR CULTURAL VALUE SYSTEM CONGRUENT/INCONGRUENT W/GOSPEL VALUES	NAME FORMATIVE PROCESSES THAT WILL HELP YOU GROW IN INTERCULTURALITY
Example:	Example:	Example:	Example:	Example:
Man-woman relationship: no touching.	A good unmarried woman must not be seen touching a man in public.	Sexuality is shameful—actions connected to it should not be seen in public; it should also not be discussed in public.	Incongruent: sexuality is sacred and God's gift—Jesus related freely with the opposite sex and allowed himself to be touched by a woman in public.	1) Spiritual direction; 2) Attend seminar-workshop on human sexuality and the vows; 3) Group-sharing among peers about the topic.

Figure 14–2. Reflective Experience

and develops a capacity for critical thinking and discernment along a way that fosters a new level of relationship with others without prejudices. We follow the example of Jesus in his various encounters with those coming from different religious and cultural backgrounds.

This is concretely demonstrated in Jesus's encounter with the Syrophoenician woman in Mark 7:24–30. There, we see the humanity of Jesus. Being human means being implanted in a culture. It means growing up with a certain worldview—inheriting religious traditions, language, and biases that can be insensitive to those who do not share the same religion and culture. In this gospel story Jesus illustrates the Jewish people's bias against the Gentiles, whom they exclude them from the community of faith and those deserving compassion. The Syrophoenician woman's audacity in engaging Jesus in dialogue brought the relationship beyond the confines of culture into the deeper realm of faith.

The process of interculturality allows us to critique the structures of society and the culture or cultures that formed us. It challenges us to be formed by the gospel values, as Jesus shows us. The reality of love should be a message to the world in giving witness to our intercultural relationships.

When we think of the vows, we become entrapped in concrete and limited actuations with the nonessentials and forget that the very heart of the evangelical counsels is to love without prejudice. We need a sense of the vision of Christ, to look at how we have been enriched by our culture and, at the same time, to look at what needs to be redeemed in our culture so that our love for one another will not be blocked by prejudice.

We allow the vows to challenge the cultural trappings that may not be close enough to what God wants of us and who God wants us to be.

15

Intercultural Living in the Spirituality and Experience of the Focolare Movement

BIRGIT OBERHOFER, FOCOLARE

The world seems to shrink as we become increasingly interconnected. Even in areas that in the past have manifested a clear cultural and ethnic identity, people are becoming accustomed to welcoming new immigrants from different parts of the world. While living side by side with people from a variety of backgrounds can be an enrichment, it can also be a challenge.

Communities of consecrated men and women have also been affected by growing diversity within their communities. While such diversity can be a gift for the community, cultural differences can also create obstacles for day-to-day community living, including subtle internal isolation and even open conflicts. In order to embrace the situation, those living in community need to expand their intercultural knowledge and skills. In doing so, they also need to find a *spiritual* approach to the integration of cultural diversity.

This chapter explores how the Focolare Movement's spirituality of unity supports intercultural living within its communities of consecrated men and women, and how a communitarian spirituality can not only enhance the life within the community but also become a strong witness of unity in diversity for others.

The first section gives a brief overview of the history, goal, and structure of the Focolare Movement. The second section describes three key points of its spirituality that nourish and enhance community life. The third section offers a description of the personal, relational, and communal dispositions that can help to further and support intercultural living in communities. The chapter concludes with a brief reflection on the church as communion serving as witness to the world.

WHAT IS THE
FOCOLARE MOVEMENT?

History

In recent decades religious organizations that promote and develop a spirituality that is focused on the aspect of communion have flourished within the church, especially among various lay movements. One example is the spirituality of the Focolare Movement, often referred to as the spirituality of unity. The Focolare Movement, an ecclesial movement officially known as the Work of Mary, was founded by Chiara Lubich in Trent, Italy, in 1943. It was first approved by the Catholic Church in 1962.[1] From its origins in the midst of the destruction of World War II, the experience of communion has been at the center of Focolare spirituality. Twenty years before the Second Vatican Council the Holy Spirit inspired the first members of the growing movement to go beyond the individual search for holiness to go toward God together. In the midst of the terrors of frequent bombings, they were drawn to the practical application of the words of the Gospel, especially the new commandment to love one another (John 13:34). They understood that their mutual love had to reach the point of experiencing the unity that Jesus had prayed for: "that they may all be one" (John 17:21).

---

[1] The Pontifical Council for the Laity approved the updated General Statutes of the Focolare Movement in 1992.

Goal

Over the years the Focolare Movement has spread to 182 nations across five continents. Today more than two million people share closely in its spirituality and activities. Its goal is to bring the life of unity and universal brotherhood to all people and to further a vision of a world in which diversity is valued and respected. To achieve this goal, members engage in various activities that help to build dialogue and fraternal relationships among individuals, between cultural groups, and in every area of society. Its different branches and groups include young people, families, priests, religious, and even members of different denominations and religions. The Focolare website describes the movement in this way: "At the heart of the movement are small communities of consecrated lay people. They take vows of poverty, chastity and obedience, according to the evangelical counsels, and live in households called 'focolares,' from the Italian word for 'hearth.'" Married people living with their families are also an essential part of these communities: "They too make the same radical choice of the gospel and offer their lives to bring unity in the world."

Community Life

Focolare houses are usually made up of four to seven single men or women and, when possible, they are formed with an intentional effort to reflect a variety of different cultural backgrounds. Often there is also diversity in age, education, and personal experience. Community members are assigned to the different households by the regional co-directors in agreement with the international headquarters, located in Italy, and the individual member.

The spirituality that sustains the life of these communities can be considered a communitarian spirituality, because it provides tools and practices for its members to journey toward God together. In a communitarian spirituality love of God and love of neighbor are closely related: Love for our neighbors increases our personal union with God; at the same time, deepening our union with God increases our love for our neighbors. We journey toward God together, as a community: "We will reach sanctity if we march towards God in unity."[2]

While the spirituality of the Focolare Movement does not address intercultural living in an explicit way, its main aspects provide helpful spiritual tools and practices to build up communities in which relationships are based on the dynamic tension of unity and diversity, modeled on the interpersonal relationships of the life of the Holy Trinity, where the three persons are one and distinct at the same time.

KEY ASPECTS OF THE FOCOLARE SPIRITUALITY FOR COMMUNITY LIFE

The spirituality of the Focolare Movement is based on twelve pillars, known as the key points of the spirituality.[3] While most of these points are present in other expressions of Christian spirituality, the unique characteristic of a communitarian spirituality is to make mutual love and unity the center of the spiritual life: "Building relationships of love and unity constitutes the heart, soul, and driving energy of every Focolare community, project, or activity."[4]

The following aspects of the Focolare spirituality play an important role in community life and support the daily effort to build relationships of mutual love among its members.

Going to God Together

From the very beginning Chiara Lubich and the first group of *focolarini* recognized that love of neighbor is not only a commandment and a consequence of loving God, "but the indispensable path to loving God. Love for God *inevitably* leads to love of neighbor, and loving one's neighbor in turn leads to union with

---

[2] Chiara Lubich, *A New Way: The Spirituality of Unity* (Hyde Park, NY: New City Press, 2006), 35.

[3] For a complete list, see Thomas Masters and Amy Uelmen, *Focolare: Living a Spirituality of Unity in the United States* (Hyde Park, NY: New City Press, 2011), 42.

[4] Ibid., 40.

God."[5] Chiara Lubich wrote in 1946: "Jesus our model taught us two things alone, and which are one: to be children of only one Father, and to be brothers and sisters to each other."[6] Communities place a strong emphasis on the quality of relationships within the household to the point that each person aims to be interested in his or her neighbor's spiritual growth as much as in his or her own. In that way, community members not only follow their personal call to holiness but support and accompany one another on their journey toward God.

In the Image and Likeness of the Trinity

The theological foundation of community life lies in Lubich's intuition that "if the Trinity is in me and in you, then the Trinity is among us, we are in a Trinitarian relationship. . . . Therefore our relationship is in the image of the Trinity; indeed, it is the Trinity that lives this relationship in us."[7] Modeling interpersonal relationships on the Holy Trinity has significant impact on ministry and community life. It presupposes a personal attitude that follows the example of Jesus's self-emptying love. As Christian theologians like Ed Hahnenberg have pointed out: "In healthy and life-giving relationships with others, we come closer and closer to what God most fundamentally is: self-emptying love."[8] Within the Focolare communities all members try to make a concrete effort to welcome other persons as they are, so that the relationships can always be renewed with the attempt to live in constant mutual love.

Instruments of a Communitarian Spirituality

This personal disposition toward a self-emptying love for the other and the focus on building relationships modeled on the life of the Holy Trinity are the spiritual roots of community life. Therefore,

---

[5] Ibid., 39.

[6] Chiara Lubich and Michel Vandeleene, *Essential Writings: Spirituality, Dialogue, Culture* (Hyde Park, NY: New City Press, 2007), 18.

[7] Lubich, *A New Way*, 20.

[8] Edward P. Hahnenberg, *Ministries: A Relational Approach* (New York: Crossroad, 2003), 88.

besides the moments of personal prayer, Focolare members also practice a set of tools that support and develop community life called the instruments of a communitarian spirituality. These tools serve the goal of accompanying one another on the journey toward God and are made up of a set of five distinct practices: the pact of mutual love, communion of soul, sharing of experiences, the hour of truth, and private talks. The instruments are usually practiced on a regular basis—for example, during weekly community meetings and monthly retreats—and require a certain amount of trust.

The *pact of mutual love* is at the basis of our community life and consists of a "solemn declaration of readiness to live out the new commandment, even to the point of laying down one's life,"[9] based on Jesus's invitation: "Love one another as I love you. No one has greater love than this, to lay down one's life for one's friends" (John 15:12–13). By declaring the pact, members of the community assure one another of the disposition to let go of their preconceived ideas, judgments, and stereotypes, and to welcome all persons as they are.

Through the *communion of soul* individuals share with the others the spiritual gifts they have received and how they see God working in their lives. This could be insights from personal moments of prayer, challenging situations, or simply little signs of God's presence in day-to-day life. These spiritual experiences are communicated as a gift to the others and to help all grow in holiness.

Another practice is the *sharing of experiences* of living the gospel. Since the beginning of the Focolare Movement it has been the custom to put into practice a specific phrase from the Gospels each month and then share life experiences. "In this form of sharing, members acknowledge the Word as the real actor in a particular situation, and contemplate the Word's transforming power."[10] The sharing of experiences makes love grow among all and it helps all members to see more clearly God's working in their lives through the power of God's word.

The practice of the *hour of truth* is probably the most challenging tool in a communitarian spirituality. It is based on the tradition

---

[9] Masters and Uelmen, *Focolare*, 46.
[10] Ibid., 47.

of fraternal correction within the early Christian communities (see, for example, Matt 18:15–17). In the hour of truth, members tell one another where improvement is needed and point out the positive steps and signs of growth that they see in another's spiritual journey. The practice requires a moderator who can confirm or correct what is being said. Before anything else, all those who are present renew the pact of mutual love, so that everything may be carried out in an attitude of charity and mutual support. "When done in the fullness of charity, the moment of truth generates the joy and freedom to travel together with greater speed and ease."[11]

Regular practice of having a *private talk* with another community member functions as a kind of spiritual "checkup." The practice does not require a spiritual director per se but can be simply a mature member of the community. Private talks can be helpful for personal discernment, when difficulties in relationships arise, or when an individual passes a personal crisis.

Going to God together, building relationships modeled on the life of the Trinity, and practicing a communitarian spirituality are important elements of community life. While the intercultural dimension is not expressed explicitly, all of these elements contain very profound and helpful tools for fostering mutually enriching and challenging intercultural living in a community. It is important to note that their practice requires a strong personal, relational, and communitarian disposition, as illustrated in the section below with examples from Focolare members who currently live in the United States.

SPIRITUAL FOUNDATIONS OF INTERCULTURAL COMMUNITY LIFE

Personal Disposition: Self-Emptying Love for the Other

Gesuina is a consecrated Focolare member who is originally from Hong Kong. She moved to the United States in 1995 after living in various Focolare communities in Japan for over twenty years. When she first arrived in the United States, she faced the challenge of opening herself to a completely different culture and way of

---

[11] Ibid., 48.

life. She explains that in Japanese culture, people learn how to foresee the needs of others and help them without saying anything: "For example, in Japan we try to help others avoid mistakes and therefore we explain things with many details. This is usually received with appreciation." She continues:

> Coming to the United States, I was used to loving others in this way, but soon I realized that my way of doing things was not always received well. I realized that in the United States people like to be self-sufficient and don't appreciate being told what to do. In fact, one of the women in my Focolare, who was from the United States, let me know that my way of explaining things felt imposing and arrogant, because she thought I was trying to teach her.

Gesuina remembers a specific moment of conflict:

> One day I tried to explain to her how to operate the washing machine, because I knew from previous experience that it worked best if loaded in a certain way. My friend was annoyed that I was giving her all these details. She told me that she had grown up with washing machines all her life and didn't need to be lectured how to run the machine. I tried to explain that I was doing it out of love and wanted to help her avoid a bad experience. I saw that she understood my explanation, and she apologized for her reaction.

Reflecting on this experience, Gesuina realized that there was more to this conflict than just the washing machine. She explains:

> It was more that we had such different ways of seeing the world, and even how to help each other. It took me some time to learn how to do things in a different way. It is not always easy, because it feels like I am going against everything I had learned. Sometimes it feels like I am not really helping the others. But I understood that my love needed to leave the other person free, even if that means letting them learn from their own mistakes.

Constantly renewing the effort to live in mutual love in order to build relationships on the model of the Holy Trinity requires a profound personal and ascetical practice. Making room for the other means experiencing a certain "emptiness" within oneself so that there is space to welcome the other and the gifts each person brings. Chiara Lubich describes this dynamic: "Jesus shows us that I am myself not when I close myself off from the other, but rather when I give myself, when out of love I lose myself in the other."[12] Because we are created in the image and likeness of God, who is Trinity, we experience true fulfillment precisely by living those relationships of total openness, gift, and love. When we make space for the other—for the other's specific personality, cultural background, and life experience—we often notice that cultural differences are no longer an obstacle in our relationship. In the self-emptying love of Jesus on the cross, we can find the necessary strength to overcome the tensions and conflicts that our differences may provoke in order to experience the gift of unity.

Relational Disposition: Making Ourselves One with the Other

Eduardo, a *focolarino* from Spain, currently lives in a community in Corpus Christi, Texas, together with Bob from Chicago and Darryl from India. He shares:

> Darryl loves to watch British comedy shows. It relaxes him and makes him laugh. Being from Spain, my sense of humor is quite different from his and I usually don't watch comedy shows. One evening I saw Darryl watching one of his favorite shows by himself and to keep him company, I decided to join him even though I didn't feel particularly attracted to it. After a while I realized that I was getting more and more into it, and I started to have fun too. After the show ended, we continued to talk about it and this led

---

[12] Lubich and Vandeleene, *Essential Writings*, 211.

to a deeper conversation about our lives in general. Letting go of my own preferences and trying to understand the other more deeply, putting myself into his shoes, allowed us to share this moment of fun and relaxation, and also to strengthen the relationship among us.

The personal disposition toward self-emptying love and the desire to make room for the other allows us to go deeper in our relationships and understand the other person in a more complete way. It enables us to treat others as "another me" and to understand their needs and desires, their joys and their sufferings. It allows us to love everyone without distinction, like our heavenly Father who "makes his sun rise on the evil and on the good, and sends rain on the righteous and the unrighteous" (Matt 5:45). We can begin to love the other as ourselves, knowing that, as Gandhi is often credited with saying: "You and me. We are one. I can't hurt you without hurting myself." We can make ourselves "one" with the other, that is, we can make our own the other's burden, thoughts, sufferings, and joys.

Community Disposition: Finding Unity in Diversity

The instruments of a communitarian spirituality described above can be helpful tools for learning how to understand one another more deeply. The diverse Focolare community in Los Angeles includes several married women of Korean background. I remember an occasion when we practiced the hour of truth during a retreat. I am originally from Germany, and in my culture authenticity and honesty are highly valued. During our sharing I noticed that the Korean women did not address the other Koreans in the second person when commenting on the positive and negative aspects they had noticed; instead, they used the third person, thus avoiding addressing the others directly. This seemed strange to me, but I did not say anything because I did not want to interrupt an important and delicate moment. After the retreat, while driving home with one of the married *focolarinas* from Korea, I shared with her my observation, and I asked her if the choice of language in addressing the older women in the third person was somehow rooted in Korean culture and their respect for the elders in the community. As soon as I had asked the question, I could tell she was uncomfortable with the conversation; she told me that she had not noticed it and didn't know how to answer my question. I tried to explain that I was just asking out of curiosity and to learn about her culture, but I soon realized it was better to let it go.

During our next retreat I was the one receiving the hour of truth, and the same person brought up the conversation in the car. She suggested that I should try to be more attentive to other people's sensitivity and less direct with my questions. She explained that in her culture it was embarrassing to be asked a question in such a direct manner and that she had felt uncomfortable. I was glad that she was able to express her uneasiness, and it helped me to learn that my way of communicating may not always be understood according to my intention. I also felt that she was right in saying that I needed to grow in my sensitivity toward other people's feelings and perceptions, and I was glad we were able to talk about it openly. Even though we did not resolve the issue that day, she helped me to understand her point of view better and how to love more. It is not always easy to live together and welcome and respect our differences. It is often uncomfortable and we are not always able to resolve situations of conflict. But opening our hearts to others, with a sincere desire to love them as they are, allows us to discover little by little that unity is possible despite our differences.

Unity is not something we can create, but rather a gift we receive. It is the gift Jesus prayed for when he asked the Father "that they may all be one" (John 17:21). This unity is not uniformity but rather a unity in diversity, modeled on the life of the Holy Trinity itself. This unity requires that we learn to bear our differences and experience the tension they create. Only if we commit and recommit to the effort of living mutual love in our relationships can the differences in cultural backgrounds, age, and personalities become a gift and make each person shine also in his or her individuality.

THE CHURCH AS COMMUNION:
A WITNESS TO THE WORLD

Living together with people of different cultures, generations, and backgrounds is a challenge. We need a strong spiritual foundation if we want to overcome our tendency to categorize and stereotype in order to feel more comfortable. The experience of living a communitarian spirituality within the Focolare Movement has shown that intercultural living in communities requires a *personal spiritual disposition* (the willingness to open ourselves in a self-emptying love that is able to fully welcome the other); a *relational disposition* (the practice of concrete love of neighbor that treats the other as "another me" and knows how to make its own the other person's joys and sufferings); and the generation of a *community life* that gives witness to unity in diversity, capable of sharing our differences as mutual gifts and as an enrichment for the entire community.

In today's world intercultural living is not only a necessity but a calling. In a world as divided as ours is today, we have a responsibility to give witness of a community life characterized by mutual love and respect, despite and *as a result of* our differences. The world around us needs to see places where differences are not perceived as threats, but become gifts that enrich the community and each person.

Unity cannot be achieved without a solid spiritual approach to intercultural living. This is not a new issue. In his 2001 letter *Novo Millennio Ineunte*, Saint John Paul II stated the need to promote a *spirituality of communion* "if we wish to be faithful to God's plan and respond to the world's deepest yearnings." Along the same lines, in his November 21, 2014, letter on the occasion of the Year of Consecrated Life, Pope Francis invited all consecrated men and women to become "experts in communion" and "witnesses and architects of the 'plan for unity.'" He writes:

> In a polarized society, where different cultures experience difficulty in living alongside one another, where the powerless encounter oppression, where inequality abounds, we are called to offer a concrete model of community which, by acknowledging the dignity of each person and sharing our respective gifts, makes it possible to live as brothers and

sisters. So, be men and women of communion! Have the courage to be present in the midst of conflict and tension, as a credible sign of the presence of the Spirit who inspires in human hearts a passion for all to be one (cf. Jn 17:21).

Our church and our society need communities of consecrated men and women who are able to model a life of communion and of unity in diversity, and who can show this life to the world. Implementing a spirituality of communion in our communities can be a powerful tool to face the current challenges and divisions and bring the gift of unity to a fractured world. This was Chiara Lubich's dream. To conclude, let us be inspired and encouraged by her invitation to bring the life of unity wherever we see it lacking: "Let's make unity among us, which gives us the fullness of joy, peace, and strength, the springboard for rushing to . . . wherever there is no unity and to bring it there."[13]

---

[13] Lubich, *A New Way*, 55.

16

Intercultural, Decolonial Pilgrimage Journeys

Joanne Doi, MM,
and Michel Andraos, PhD

Decolonial pilgrimage to shadowed ground and contested histories reveals sacred traces of suffering and hope, and fosters reconnection with ancestors, land, mystery, and the depth of life. Land holds memory. We remember in specific places in order to heal, to mourn, to decolonize ourselves, and to recover memory. Pilgrimage is a collective experience, a practice of remembering as resistance and reparations through memory. This can promote entry into an intercultural process of reconciliation toward social transformation and systemic change as well as compassionate actions of solidarity.

The first section of this chapter, by Joanne Doi, revisits the impact of the annual Manzanar Pilgrimage and Days of Remembrance on the movement for redress and ongoing healing of the intergenerational Japanese American community with a deepening intercultural commitment to life in solidarity with those suffering from similar constraints today.

The second section, by Michel Andraos, is a reflection on his three-week, collective canoe pilgrimage for reconciliation that took place in the summer of 2017 on Indigenous lands and waterways in Canada. He provides some historical background to situate this pilgrimage and shares some of the highlights of his learning and transformative experience from an intercultural, decolonial perspective.

REVISITING MANZANAR
WAR RELOCATION CENTER

During my pastoral ministry in Peru as a Maryknoll Sister from 1983 to 1994, the resonance and affinities I experienced with the unknown world of the Aymara people challenged and encouraged me to enter into my own unknown world as a third-generation (Sansei) Japanese American woman, to enter into our "underside of history."[1] It was an experience of deep intercultural mutuality and friendship. Revealing other ways of knowing, popular religious practice among the Aymara relates profoundly with the earth. This undoubtedly strengthened their resistance and resilience during centuries of colonization as the memories of the earth and ancestors returned them to their transcendent integrity and cosmovision. At present, many find it necessary to migrate to the urban centers for work. However, annually they return to their *fiesta principal* to reconnect to their people and *tierra* (earth). The earth holds memory, embedded with spiritual resonance through regular pilgrimage, prayer, and rituals.

During this time, even at great geographic distance and before the digital age of Facebook and YouTube, I was greatly affected by the Japanese American collective process of remembrance of the World War II internment[2] period at the Manzanar War Relocation Center in California. During graduate studies beginning

---

[1] Gustavo Gutiérrez, "Theology from the Underside of History," in *The Power of the Poor in History*, trans. Robert Barr (Maryknoll, NY: Orbis Books, 1983), 212.

[2] Roger Daniels, "Words Do Matter: A Note on Inappropriate Terminology and the Incarceration of the Japanese Americans," in *Nikkei in the Pacific Northwest: Japanese Americans and Japanese Canadians in the Twentieth Century*, ed. Louis Fiset and Gail Nomura (Seattle: University of Washington Press, 2005), 183–207.

in 1994, I learned that from the Manzanar Pilgrimage in 1969[3] and the Day of Remembrance in 1978—which brought over two thousand people to Puyallup, Washington—the redress movement had gained momentum with the catharsis of emotional release and commitment. The Commission on Wartime Relocation and Internment of Civilians, created in 1980 by President Carter, had as its purpose to review Executive Order 9066 of February 19, 1942, signed by President Roosevelt, which set in motion the "evacuation" and detention of 120,000 Japanese and Japanese Americans living on the West Coast to ten "relocation centers" in remote areas. Two-thirds of those detained were US citizens, and more than half were children.[4] Ten public hearings of the Commission on Wartime Relocation and Internment of Civilians were held across the nation and 750 witnesses testified. In 1983, the commission concluded that the exclusion, expulsion, and incarceration were not justified by military necessity, and that the decision was based on racial prejudice, war hysteria, and a failure of political leadership.[5] Its recommendations led to the passage of the Civil Liberties Act of 1988, signed by President Reagan. The provisions were for Congress to pass a joint resolution to recognize the grave injustice done and to offer the

---

[3] The Manzanar Pilgrimage has its roots in the compassion of two religious leaders, Rev. Sentoku Maeda, a Buddhist priest, and his friend, Rev. Shoichi Wakahiro, a Christian minister. Every year after Manzanar closed in November 1945, they returned to the Manzanar cemetery with a small group of Issei on Memorial Day to pray for the dead who were without family to do so. In 1969, the energies and struggles of the civil rights and redress movements converged with this practice of prayer and remembrance.

[4] Donna K. Nagata, "Intergenerational Effects of the Japanese American Internment," in *International Handbook of Multi-Generational Legacies of Trauma*, ed. Yael Danieli (New York: Plenum Press, 1998), 125.

[5] See *Personal Justice Denied: Report of the Commission on Wartime Relocation and Internment of Civilians* (Seattle: University of Washington Press, 1997; Washington, D.C.: The Civil Liberties Public Education Fund, 1997). Originally published by the US Government Printing Office in 1982 and 1983 (2 volumes).

nation's apologies and a one-time per capita symbolic compensation payment of $20,000 to each of the approximately eighty thousand persons surviving at that time.[6] It also provided for a public education fund and the authorization of the construction of a National Japanese American Memorial in Washington, D.C., inaugurated in 2000. The commission hearings and redress bill marked a significant moment in the process of healing the pain and suffering that had been shrouded in silence and shame for over forty years.[7]

The Days of Remembrance and Pilgrimages continue to this day in response to the continued spiritual need for the healing of wounds of both persons and communities. They open up the deeper layers where resilience and hope reside amid the suffering. And where only meaningless pain remained, these collective spaces began to break down isolation and offered the possibility to bear that pain together. These aspects of the ordeal affected

---

[6] On October 9, 1990, the first redress payments were made with the apology letter signed by President George H. W. Bush. The complete text of the apology reads as follows: "A monetary sum and words alone cannot restore lost years or erase painful memories; neither can they fully convey our Nation's resolve to rectify injustice and to uphold the rights of individuals. But we can take a clear stand for justice and recognize that serious injustices were done to Japanese Americans during World War II. In enacting a law calling for restitution and offering a sincere apology, your fellow Americans have, in a very real sense, renewed their traditional commitment to the ideals of freedom, equality and justice. You and your family have our best wishes for the future. Sincerely, George H. W. Bush (signed)." Roger Daniels, "Redress Achieved, 1983–1990," in *Japanese Americans: From Relocation to Redress,* ed. Roger Daniels, Sandra C. Taylor, and Harry H. L. Kitano (Seattle/London: University of Washington Press, 1986, 1991), 222.

[7] For further information on the complexities of the successful redress movement, see William Minoru Hohri, *Repairing America: An Account of the Movement for Japanese-American Redress* (Pullman: Washington State University Press, 1988); Mitchell T. Maki, Harry H. L. Kitano, and S. Megan Berthold, *Achieving the Impossible Dream: How Japanese Americans Obtained Redress* (Urbana: University of Illinois Press, 1999); Robert Sadamu Shimabukuro, *Born in Seattle: The Campaign for Japanese American Redress* (Seattle: University of Washington Press, 2001).

both the Issei (first) and Nisei (second) generations, who lived through the experience, and the Sansei (third), who inherited a legacy of painfulness and injustice that was left unexplained due to the silence of their parents and the US history books. Decades of struggle leading up to the civil rights and redress movements, and nearly two generations later, find us continually in need of a collective national and public process of facing the "shadows," remembering and mourning in order to comprehend their significance and lessons for the present and future.

This process involves recognizing the trauma and losses involved, which inevitably raises the need for appropriate emotional response, understanding, and the development of a political culture that promotes the conditions for emotional well-being. In other words, emotional well-being is not limited to positive feelings but also grows out of the energy for good that is released through negative or difficult emotions. We need to honor difficult emotions and give them a chance to teach us what it is we need to know. It is important to reframe mourning as an act of courage rather than humiliation. It is an act of resistance, rather than submission, to feel the full range of emotions. The capacity to enter into this process together provides an experience of related vulnerability that paradoxically results in a sense of shared strength as we experience a new or restored unity. Extraordinary predicaments of collective trauma require a different form of mourning process that includes victims, perpetrators, and all those in between, who are often the next generations—Yonsei (fourth), Gosei (fifth), and beyond.

Beginning in 1996, I began participating in the annual Pilgrimage to Manzanar, the "home" of my father, grandfather, and the Japanese Maryknoll faith community from Los Angeles, who were among the ten thousand detainees within a one-square-mile radius. The earth holds memory. It is a return to the center of pivotal events that have marked us and to narratives implanted in the land itself. The pilgrimage to return to our dangerous memory is a return to our *memoria passionis*, the memory of suffering. To walk our way of the cross is to be with our loss, to take death in as we recover our underside of history: the impact of the trauma of detention; incarceration; the harsh physical conditions; breakdown of the family unit; premature death caused by inadequate medical facilities; shootings and beatings; betrayal by one's own country; internal divisions and betrayals; and the chaos and threat of separation from family and community. The litany continues as layers and stories continue to emerge.

The pilgrim's journey seeks a restoration of wholeness by a recentering, a reentering, and a recovery *of* history and a recovering *from* history. It is a rediscovery that we are part of a living and vital collective memory. It is a listening to suffering, not to "wall yourself up in pain and memories as if in a prison," but to reconnect to its wisdom that "suffering must open us to others."[8] The act of remembrance is an act of mercy and grace. For our *memoria passionis* is also our *memoria resurrectionis*, as we experience our sadness and loss in the context of continuing life and depth of love, as we translate our loss into responsibility and restored relationality. The cemetery obelisk at Manzanar expresses this message: "This is the place of consolation for all of humanity." Manzanar is a bridge to compassion, not a barrier to forgiveness. We journey together, experiencing more together than we could alone. Stories also emerge of unexpected kindness, generosity, and solidarity that kindled hope and reasserted humanity in the darkest of times. The feeling of *kansha*, a profoundly soulful dimension encompassing appreciation, gratitude, and much more, focuses "not on bitterness or self-pity, but on what each of us can do today to prevent such injustice from happening ever again to any group."[9]

Since 2006, the Florin Chapter of the JACL-SV (Japanese American Citizens League–Sacramento Valley) and the CAIR-SV (Council on American Islamic Relations–Sacramento Valley)

---

[8] Rubem Alves, *Tomorrow's Child: Imagination, Creativity, and the Rebirth of Culture* (New York: Harper and Row, 1971), 111.

[9] Shizue Seigel, *In Good Conscience: Supporting Japanese Americans during the Internment* (San Mateo, CA: Asian American Curriculum Project, 2006), sponsored by the Kansha Project, a project of the Military Intelligence Service Association of Northern California. Regarding Maryknoll's solidarity during this period, see Stephen P. Judd, "The Maryknoll Journey: Coming Home by a Different Route," in *The Gift of Mission*, ed. James H. Kroeger, 3–5 (Maryknoll, NY: Orbis Books, 2013).

organizations have taken diverse groups of travelers on three-day pilgrimages to visit the Manzanar National Historic Site and converge with the annual Manzanar Pilgrimage. In 2018, with the theme "Silent No More: Liberty and Justice for All," the pilgrims included eight former detainees and persons from Jewish, Muslim, Buddhist, and Christian faith communities. Journeying south on the eastern spine of the Sierras, stops along the way included intergenerational discussion groups at the Tahoe Community Presbyterian Church and Mono Lake Interpretative Center.

The night before arriving at Manzanar, an evening of cultural exchange was shared with an Islamic Call to Prayer, the Native American Aka Mya Cultural Dance Group, Bakuhatso Taiko Dan, and Ondo Dance Group. It was a celebration and strengthening of friendship and solidarity as we live with the awareness that the mistakes of the past continue to happen today, as well as a disregard for the formal amends made to redress such mistakes. Some examples: Arab Americans in a post-9/11 world; undocumented immigrants and stigmatized refugees; family detention centers. As Omar Hashemyan of CAIR-SV reflected, "We must come together. If one group of people are being oppressed, stand up for them. That's how it is, how we create a unified community."

During its fiftieth anniversary year in 2017, the Diocese of Fresno in the Central Valley of California celebrated a series of commemorative masses throughout its jurisdiction. The Manzanar National Historic Site of the WWII incarceration camp in the Eastern Sierras was selected as one of these sites. Held in the reconstructed mess hall, a few survivors and their descendants were the invited delegation from the St. Francis Xavier Japanese Catholic Center (Maryknoll) in Los Angeles. The community was thrilled and moved, noted longtime parishioner Geoffrey Yamamoto, liturgical musician and, like myself, a descendant of survivors. The theme of the anniversary year was "*Siempre Adelante*—Keep Moving Forward." Organizers recognized that the past is very much a part of "re-embracing our mission, to go to those on the outskirts, those who are outcast, those who do not feel welcomed, to be who we are called to be." Our *memoria passionis* is also our *memoria resurrectionis* for our ongoing pilgrimage and struggle for life today.

REFLECTION ON A CANOE PILGRIMAGE
FOR RECONCILIATION WITH THE
INDIGENOUS PEOPLES OF CANADA

This is a personal reflection on my participation in the Canadian Canoe Pilgrimage (CCP) that was organized by the Jesuits of Canada in the summer of 2017 on the occasion of the country's 150th anniversary. The CCP was part of several other activities that were taking place in Canada that year, not only to celebrate an important anniversary year in the life of the young state, but also to respond to the Calls to Action of the Truth and Reconciliation Commission of Canada that calls on all Canadians to engage in reconciliation actions with the Indigenous peoples, who have been living on this land for much longer.[10] After a brief retreat and training, a group of about thirty people departed from the shrine of Sainte-Marie among the Huron in Midland, Ontario, also known as the shrine of the Jesuit martyrs, and site of one of the earliest Jesuit mission centers among the Indigenous peoples in North America, located at the lower end of the Georgian Bay. Traveling through multiple rivers and lakes, the final destination was St. Francis Xavier Mission in Kahnawake, a Mohawk reserve on the south shore of the St. Lawrence River in Quebec, across from the city of Montreal, where the remains of the recently canonized Mohawk Saint Kateri Tekakwitha are buried. This church is now an important shrine visited by people from around the world. The total distance traveled by canoe was about five hundred miles.[11] The approximately one-month journey on Indigenous land and waterways, lakes and rivers, traced the route that early traders and also the Jesuit missionaries used to take, often guided by Indigenous peoples, who canoed these waterways for thousands of years before European colonization.

---

[10] The Truth and Reconciliation Commission of Canada, *Canada's Residential Schools: Reconciliation: The Final Report of the Truth and Reconciliation Commission of Canada*, vol. 6 (Montreal: McGill-Queen's University Press, 2015).

[11] For work reasons, I only spent the first twenty-one days of the trip with the group and then joined for the closing ceremony at Kahnawake. Not all participants stayed for the whole trip. A good number, however, stayed from beginning to end. Approximately seventy-five people participated in the pilgrimage.

Not all participants had the same vision, expectations, or hopes for the pilgrimage. In addition, they had different personal experiences and levels of connections to the theme, history of the land, and its peoples, and were at different places in their personal commitment to the issue. However, Erik Sorensen, project manager of the CCP, articulated the overall scope in the following words:

> We are retracing this historic route on the 150th anniversary of Canada as a nation, but more importantly we are trying to work for reconciliation. . . . As a member of the Jesuits, a group that had a residential school that played an integral role in colonization efforts by early Europeans, there is a collective healing that I am participating in. And we are changing the way we do things.[12]

The CCP was not a traditional pilgrimage to a specific site that has religious significance in order to fulfill a religious duty or ask for favors or healing from a saint. Rather, it was intended to be an intercultural and interreligious journey of learning, dialogue, and reconciliation, primarily with the Indigenous peoples of Canada. The paddlers included Jesuits from English and French Canada, Indigenous peoples from different parts of the country, and friends of both.[13] The participants were not all Christian. Not all did

---

[12] Jesuits, English Canada Province, "Paddling towards Reconciliation with Canada's Indigenous Peoples," GlobeNewswire (April 20, 2017); see also "Canadian Canoe Pilgrimage," YouTube (November 19, 2016).

[13] For a broader discussion of the historical context and references, see my previous works on the topic: "Christianities and Indigenous Peoples: The Urgency for 'New Paths,'" *Critical Theology* 1, no. 2 (Winter 2019): 3–9; "Christianity and Indigenous Peoples: Another Christianity Is Necessary," in *Decoloniality and Justice: Theological Perspectives*, ed. Jean-François Roussel, 25–34 (San Leopoldo, Brazil: Oikos, 2018); "Doing Theology after the TRC," *Toronto Journal of Theology* 33, no. 2 (Fall 2017): 295–301; "Les Églises, la théologie et les autochtones: de la réconciliation à la décolonisation," in *Théologique* 23, no. 2 (2015): 59–73; *The Church and Indigenous Peoples in the Americas,* vol. 7, *In Between Reconciliation and Decolonization,* Studies in World Catholicism (Eugene, OR: Cascade Books, 2019); and "Long-Term Theological and Pastoral Challenges for Decolonizing the Relation with Indigenous Peoples: A Reflection from Canada," *Concilium* 4 (October 1, 2019).

the pilgrimage from a specifically religious perspective, and we had different motivations. Nevertheless, I believe the pilgrimage was a profoundly spiritual and transformative experience for all participants.

Historical Context

A new awareness of the colonial history and relationship in Canada of the state and churches with the Indigenous peoples has been unfolding over the past few decades. What have you done to your Indigenous sisters and brothers of the land? This question today haunts the conscience of the churches. The statistics about poverty, land dispossession, social exclusion, unemployment, racism, and other social problems caused by the long colonial relationship are well known, and the role of the Christian churches in this history is also well documented. All this happened in the name of "evangelizing and civilizing the Indians." Today, and particularly in the aftermath of the Truth and Reconciliation Commission of Canada, the mainline Christian churches of Canada are radically rethinking the future of their relationships with Indigenous peoples and their future existence in light of this relationship. This kind of radical rethinking is also happening globally. The Synod of Bishops for Amazonia, October 6–27, 2019, is a clear indication of how the Catholic Church worldwide is still trying to come to grips with its role in colonization and is searching for "new paths" in its relations with Indigenous peoples.[14] Many Indigenous Christians are themselves also rethinking their relationships with and within their churches and are looking for ways to transform the colonial Christian legacy and affirm their Indigenous spiritual experiences within their respective Christian traditions.

While the Canadian state, mainline churches, and many religious orders, including the Jesuits, have apologized for their role in the colonization of Indigenous peoples, and many good initiatives of reconciliation have been taking place over the past few years, the colonial wound is still open and deep, and the impact

---

[14] *Amazonia: New Paths for the Church and for an Integral Ecology (Instrumentum Laboris)*, working document for the synod (June 17, 2019).

of colonization continues to be devastating to many Indigenous peoples today.[15] This is the broader context of the CCP.

Highlights and Main Learning

A main highlight of this pilgrimage for me was gaining a deeper appreciation of the sacredness and power of the water. Several Indigenous leaders who led the group during certain parts of the journey made us particularly aware of these aspects and communicated this experience and learning to us in their own heuristic ways as we paddled upstream and moved around strong rapids. Instead of a pilgrimage to a particular sacred site, the whole canoe journey became for me a direct connection with the sacredness of the water in the vast rivers and lakes we crossed. This sacredness has been an integral part of Indigenous peoples' relationship with the water and Mother Earth in general and is a key theme in Indigenous spiritualities and rituals around the world, especially at this time of ecological devastation, water pollution, and commodification of drinking water. Reconciliation with the Water, the Spirit of the Water, and with Mother Earth is an essential part of the broader reconciliation we were seeking during this pilgrimage.[16] The fact that we were doing this trip in canoes, which is an Indigenous invention and was their main means for travel, doing trade, and communication with other peoples, was an added dimension to the depth of this spiritual experience and connection. Traveling such a long distance by canoe has a certain mystique. One is sitting on the surface of the water, carried by its power, between heaven and earth. Of course, canoeing in such waters, which were very rough at times because of high winds,

---

[15] For a more in-depth article that addresses this topic's theological dimension, see Brian McDonough, "The Truth and Reconciliation Commission of Canada," in Andraos, *The Church and Indigenous Peoples in the Americas*, 56–77.

[16] Canadian Indigenous scholar John Borrows discusses this concept at length in "Earth-Bound: Indigenous Resurgence and Environmental Reconciliation," in *Resurgence and Reconciliation: Indigenous-Settler Relations and Earth Teachings*, ed. Michael Asch, John Borrows, and James Tully, 49–81 (Toronto: University of Toronto Press, 2018).

rapids, canoeing upstream, and weather conditions, required a lot of physical effort and strength, and at times involved risks. However, there is a certain wisdom one learns from experienced Indigenous leaders about respecting and befriending the power of the water and learning one's limits in this relationship. This helped me establish a deeper spiritual connection with the power of the water, which was a new experience and learning during this trip, even though I had been canoeing and kayaking for many years. What I had been hearing for many years at meetings and ceremonies with Indigenous peoples about "Water is Life" took a much deeper meaning during this pilgrimage.[17] I believe the continuous connection with the water over a period of few weeks deepened this relationship and learning. Through this new experience with the sacredness of the water, the intercultural and interreligious dialogue, which was an important component of the pilgrimage, expanded to include dialogue with the Spirit of the Water and Mother Earth, which for me became a deeply transformative sacred experience that I am still unpacking.

Colonizing peoples and their lands, and the long-term impact of colonization, as we clearly see among Indigenous peoples around the world, is a great evil and injustice. Our pilgrimage took place on colonized land among many Indigenous communities that live on reserves by the lakes and rivers we traveled, and that are still experiencing today the full effects of colonization. On our journey we were welcomed by some of these Indigenous communities and were invited to camp on their grounds. They generously offered us hospitality and food. Among the participants in the pilgrimage there were also Indigenous peoples from some of these communities. We had several presentations and discussions along the way on the history and impact of colonization by both Indigenous and non-Indigenous teachers. An important goal of the pilgrimage for me was to learn and feel a deeper understanding of colonization from both the people we met and heard, and

---

[17] On the significance, sacredness, and protection of the water for Indigenous Nishnaabeg people, see Renée Elizabeth Mzinegiizhigo-kwe Bédard, "Keepers of the Water: Nishnaabe-Kwewag Speaking for the Water," in *Lighting the Eighth Fire: The Liberation, Resurgence, and Protection of Indigenous Nations*, ed. Leanne Betasamosake Simpson, 89–109 (Winnipeg: Arbeiter Ring Publishing, 2018).

from the colonized land. This learning, too, was for me another sacred and transformative experience and a space for imagining a decolonized relationship with the people of the land, the water, and with Mother Earth, who are all interconnected.

As you can tell from the list of references above, I have been thinking seriously over the past few years from my position in theological education and research on the colonial role of the different Christianities, churches, missions, and theology in these lands and among their Indigenous peoples. Some of the key theological questions that guide my research in this process are the following: What would a decolonized relationship between the churches and Indigenous peoples look like? What would a decolonial theology and ministry look like? How do we understand the sustained Christian religious violence against these peoples for many long centuries without realizing the destructive impact on their way of life, cultures, and whole being as individuals and peoples? Doing this trip in reverse, that is, from Sainte-Marie among the Huron back to Montreal, was symbolically significant for my reflection and thinking on reversing my understanding of the colonizing Christian mission theology, ministry, and the relation of the churches with Indigenous peoples.

These are only some of the many highlights of this intercultural, decolonial pilgrimage, and I could say a lot more on each of these points. As I said earlier, my reflection on this journey, which is connected to my broader life experience over the past couple decades, particularly as an immigrant living in a settler colonial state and benefiting from its colonization of the land and its Aboriginal peoples, is still in process and unfolding. I live in Quebec on an unceded territory of the Mohawk nation. The Canadian Jesuits who organized and supported this trip are also continuing their reflection on what it means to decolonize the Jesuits and their relations with Indigenous peoples. Imagining a decolonial way of living into the future continues to be an important unfinished task and hard work for the churches, as well as for the Canadian state and all its citizens. Could intercultural, decolonial theology play a role and make a contribution to decolonization? This question, too, is part of my ongoing research for which I still have not reached a satisfactory answer. Such decolonial pilgrimages and spiritual experiences do not undo colonization. However, they are spaces and moments for deep learning, transformation, and for imagining the future differently. From a theological perspective I believe they energize and stimulate our theological imagination and help us transform our still-colonial mission theologies and pastoral practices. This is what this canoe pilgrimage was for me.

Contributors

Michel Andraos, PhD, of Lebanon, has been teaching at Catholic Theological Union since 2000. The focus of his current research is reconciliation of the church with the Indigenous peoples of the Americas and the developments among the Christian communities of the Middle East in the late-modern European colonial period.

Maria Cimperman, RSCJ, associate professor of theological ethics and the director of the Center for the Study of Consecrated Life at Catholic Theological Union, presents nationally and internationally on contemporary religious life topics. Her work is at the intersection of moral theology, social ethics, and spirituality, and her publications include *Social Analysis for the 21st Century: How Faith Becomes Action.*

Joanne Doi, MM, served among the Aymara people in Peru for eleven years and is now very involved in the spiritual practice of reconciliation in the pilgrimage journeys to former WWII Japanese American detention camps. She currently teaches at Catholic Theological Union in the Intercultural Studies and Ministry Department.

Judette Gallares, RC, of the Philippines, is the director of Cenacle China mission in Macau, China, and is involved in the ministry of retreats and formation. She is professor of theology of consecrated life at the Institute for Consecrated Life in Asia and a visiting professor of theology at the University of St. Joseph in Macau.

Anthony J. Gittins, CSSp, professor emeritus of theology and culture at Catholic Theological Union, focuses on the interface between the social sciences and theological disciplines. His publications include *Living Mission Interculturally: Faith, Culture, and the Renewal of Praxis* and *The Way of Discipleship: Women, Men, and the Call to Mission.*

Teresa Maya, CCVI, who holds a PhD from El Colegio de Mexico in Mexico City, has a passion for the formation of ministers for Hispanics/Latinos in the United States. She currently serves as congregational leader for her congregation and is a former president of the Leadership Conference of Women Religious.

Kevin P. McClone, PsyD, a licensed clinical psychologist, is an adjunct faculty member for Catholic Theological Union and director of the Institute for Sexuality Studies. He serves as a consultant to religious communities of men and woman on topics such as healthy formation, intercultural dynamics, and addiction recovery.

Adriana Carla Milmanda, SSpS, was director of the Center for the Empowerment of Women in Vulnerable Situations in her native Argentina before her recent election as provincial. She continues to serve as a coordinator and resource person for interculturality programs on an international level for religious congregations.

LaReine-Marie Mosely, SND, is associate professor and chair of the religious studies department at Notre Dame of Maryland University in Baltimore. She is under contract with Fortress Press to write a book with the working title of *Toward a Womanist Ethic of Sheltering.*

Maria Hong Nguyen, OSB, of Mount Saint Scholastica at Atchison, Kansas, serves as a social worker at Fresenius Medical Care for Dialysis and Kidney Transplant in Kansas City, Missouri, and as a chaplain of the Vietnamese Eucharistic Youth Movement. She is a consultant for many religious communities on interculturality issues.

Tim Norton, SVD, a trained physiotherapist, did pastoral ministry in Mexico and formation and leadership ministry in his native country of Australia. Currently, he is director of courses at Centro Ad Gentes Conference and Retreat Center in Nemi, Italy, and serves as a resource person in interculturality for many religious congregations.

Birgit Oberhofer, of Germany, a member of Focolare, holds a master's degree in education science from Ludwigs-Maximilian-University in Munich. She currently serves as spiritual formation coordinator at the Newman Catholic Student Center at Texas A&M University–Corpus Christi.

Jung Eun Sophia Park, SNJM, is associate professor of religious studies at Holy Names University, California. Her publications include *Border Crossing Spirituality: Transformation in Borderland*. Her interest is in biblical and cross-cultural spirituality and in religious life from postcolonial and global feminist perspectives.

Antonio M. Pernia, SVD, of the Philippines, holds a doctoral degree in systematic theology and served in several leadership capacities, including as SVD superior general in Rome (2000–2012). Currently, he is the dean of studies at the Divine Word Institute of Mission Studies in Tagaytay City in the Philippines.

Robert J. Schreiter, CPPS, is professor of systematic theology and the Vatican Council II Professor of Theology at Catholic Theological Union. His many publications include *Reconciliation: Mission and Ministry in a Changing Social Order* and *The Ministry of Reconciliation: Spirituality and Strategies.*

Roger P. Schroeder, SVD, is professor of intercultural studies and ministry and the Louis J. Luzbetak, SVD, Professor of Mission and Culture at Catholic Theological Union. His publications include *What Is the Mission of the Church? A Guide for Catholics* and (with Stephen Bevans) *Constants in Context: A Theology of Mission for Today.*

Crystal Taylor-Dietz, PsyD, is a licensed psychologist and the director of Caritas Counseling Center, the outpatient department of Saint Luke Institute in Silver Spring, Maryland. She is also an assistant clinical professor of clinical psychology in the George Washington University Professional Psychology Program.

Sia Nyasari Temu, MM, of Tanzania, lives in an intentional intercultural community in Nairobi, Kenya, where she is a member of the Maryknoll Sisters peacebuilding team. She has been a facilitator of the Conversations for Social Change Program in different parts of Kenya that were experiencing conflict.

Index